THE OTHER PARIS

Stories by MAVIS GALLANT

The Luck of
Ginger Coffey

a novel by **BRIAN MOORE**

author of
THE LONELY PASSION OF JUDITH HEARNE

A CHOICE OF ENEMIES
Mordecai Richler

THE APPRENTICESHIP
OF DUDDY KRAVITZ

The Feast of
Lupercal
Brian Moore

MORDECAI RICHLER

WHY
ROCK
THE
BOAT

WILLIAM WEINTRAUB

Getting Started

ALSO BY WILLIAM WEINTRAUB

NOVELS
Why Rock the Boat?
The Underdogs

NON-FICTION
City Unique: Montreal Days and Nights in the 1940s and '50s

PLAY
The Underdogs

Getting Started

A Memoir of the 1950s

with letters from
Mordecai Richler, Mavis Gallant and Brian Moore

William Weintraub

National Library of Canada Cataloguing in Publication Data

Weintraub, William, 1926-
Getting started: a memoir of the 1950s

ISBN 0-7710-8914-7

1. Weintraub, William, 1926- 2. Authors, Canadian (English) –
20th century – Correspondence. 3. Authors, Canadian (English) –
France – Paris – History – 20th century. 4. Authors, Canadian (English) –
20th century – Biography. I. Title.

PS8545.E43Z53 2001   C818'.5409   C2001-900946-1
PR9199.3.W399Z469 2001

We acknowledge the financial support of the Government of Canada
through the Book Publishing Industry Development Program for our
publishing activities. We further acknowledge the support of the
Canada Council for the Arts and the Ontario Arts Council
for our publishing program.

Typeset in Goudy by M&S, Toronto
Printed and bound in Canada

McClelland & Stewart Ltd.
The Canadian Publishers
481 University Avenue
Toronto, Ontario
M5G 2E9
www.mcclelland.com

1   2   3   4   5   05   04   03   02   01

For Magda

I

In those days, journalism in Montreal was awash in alcohol. Most of us young reporters could only afford beer, but on that fateful night in 1950, the night that led to my downfall, there were several bottles of rye whisky on the table. Mind you, it was the cheapest rye available – Corby's Little Touch, aged in the cask for at least forty minutes before being bottled. That Little Touch was highly corrosive stuff, but by mixing it with ginger ale we managed to get it down in heroic quantities.

I think of it as the night that sealed my fate, but actually the pivotal event took place in the morning, at about two o'clock. I'd been there, at a party in the apartment of one of the senior reporters, since eleven o'clock, having hurried uptown from the office immediately after handing in my last story of the day, a supremely tedious obituary. As the night progressed, other *Gazette* reporters kept arriving, brushing snowflakes from the shoulders of their overcoats, and by 2:00 a.m. the hubbub was at its height.

We were all there, having a wonderful time, Joe and Larry and Brian and Betty and Frank and Gwen and all the others. The air was thick with scurrilous anecdote and cigarette smoke from our Sweet Caporals and Winchesters. The booze flowed. Bruce and Ronny were sprawled out in sleep, undisturbed by the baritone of Pete MacRitchie, who was singing "Loch Lomond" at the top of his voice, accompanied by Tiger Gilliece, who was howling his imitation of the bagpipes. Across the room, three Irish vocalists were waiting impatiently to torment us with "Danny Boy." But eventually there was a lull in the noise, as our host brought out the cheese and crackers. With this relative silence, I knew that my moment had come.

I walked, or perhaps lurched, across the room to the mantelpiece, where I had noticed a large china piggy bank, the repository of a child's savings. It was a glistening pink piggy, a really big one. I carefully lifted it into the air, to display it to the assembled company. "I guess we all know who this is," I said. During the evening Bruce and Eddie and Frankie and others had voiced many a brilliant witticism, but now, amid their uproarious laughter, my colleagues conceded that my remark – "I guess we all know who this is" – was the most brilliant aperçu of the year, if not the decade. I blushed as they slapped me on the back in congratulation. With these few words, my reputation was made. And my fate was sealed.

The next day, H. J. Larkin, managing editor of the *Gazette*, called me into his office. "I hear you called me a pig last night," he said.

"Well, uh, sir," I said, "I didn't mention any names."

"I'm going to give you this opportunity to resign," said Larkin.

"I don't suppose I have a choice, do I?"

"No, you have no choice."

I went back to the newsroom, to my desk, where I packed a few belongings into a brown paper bag. I said my goodbyes to Rusty and Harold and Vince, went down in the elevator and through the *Gazette*'s portals for the last time. I was twenty-three years old and it looked as though my budding career in journalism had come to an abrupt end.

With my collar turned up against yet another Montreal snowstorm, I trudged along St. Antoine Street, crossed Windsor Street and went into the warmth of Windsor Station – a shortcut to uptown. As I walked through the great marble cavern, with locomotives snorting at the gates, I realized that the Canadian Pacific Railway might loom large in my future. I ought to get out of town, if I wanted a job. That witticism of mine – "I guess we all know who this is" – would soon become known to every newspaper executive in Montreal, and thus I could never hope for a job with the *Star* or the *Herald*. No, my future lay far away, probably in the bush leagues. After I got the train fare and a bit of a grubstake together, I'd be knocking at the door of the editor of some country bladder like the *North Bay Nugget*. I would be clutching my scrapbook, ready to show him my byline feature of last August, a standout in an era when Montreal newspapers loved colourful language in their stories about summer heat waves.

"Addulced and salved," I had written, "by assuagingly lenitive cool air which came from the north to put an end to the tropical calidity of a week which had been sweating, sweltering, basking, smoking, stewing, seething, moiling, burning, singeing, scorching, scalding, grilling, broiling, blazing, smouldering. . . ." And so on, for many more such words. For a moment my spirits lifted. A newspaperman who could write a sentence like that, and write it under pressure, couldn't be kept down. A stint on the *Medicine Hat Bugle* would be the beginning of my long climb back, job by job, toward civilization.

But now, as I emerged from the north end of Windsor Station, the despair settled back in. The wind was howling down from the mountain and across Dominion Square, bearing cruel lashings of snow that bit into one's eyes, enough to elicit tears. The tears were appropriate to my grief at the prospect of having to say goodbye to Montreal for a job on the *Assiniboine Advocate*, or whatever. The thought of leaving this city, hub of the universe, for Outer Canada was profoundly depressing. Outer Canada – where, we were told, you had to have a doctor's prescription before they'd let you have a beer in some dingy cellar they called a beer parlour. As I fought my way into the wind and up Windsor Street, spitting snow out of my mouth, I tried not to think of what I'd be leaving behind. Never again would I know the warm, dark glow of the Alberta Lounge, just behind me across the street, where we used to sit for hours listening to Oscar Peterson's magic piano. And there across the square was Drury's, that great old English chophouse, where they served world-class roast beef with Yorkshire pudding. I had never eaten there, but I had always aspired to it – as soon as my income got somewhat bigger.

But even now, I was not a stranger to Montreal's culinary delights. Only the previous week I had devoured a gorgeous New York sirloin, with all the trimmings, at the Samovar, the Russian nightclub just up the street. At the Samovar I'd been the guest of Harold Whitehead, the *Gazette*'s portly, erudite nightclub critic. In those days, the paper carried lots of night-club ads on its entertainment pages, and when a new floor show opened at a club, Harold would write a review of it. He could bring a guest to share the free booze and grub on opening night, at places like the Samovar, the El Morocco, the Café de l'Est, Rockhead's Paradise and all the others. But now there would be no more of that. And there would certainly be nothing like those places in Minnedosa, Manitoba.

Gone too would be the special perks to be enjoyed on a big-city newspaper, like Stag Night at the *Gazette*. We'd had one of those only three weeks before my dismissal. After midnight, once the paper had been put to bed, the two female reporters still in the office had been sent home and cases of quart bottles of beer were brought in. A movie projector was wheeled in and, with the lights dimmed, we sat back to enjoy pornographic films. In those days, highly illegal movies of this sort were hard to come by, but we were always able to borrow ours from officers of the Quebec Provincial Police, who were diligent in seizing them whenever they could. In return for these loans, we obliged the QPP by keeping certain stories that might embarrass them out of the paper.

The films provided by the cops were primitive – silent, scratchy black-and-white efforts, a far cry from the elaborate, panting sexual extravaganzas you can now rent at your corner video store. Those 1950s flicks seemed to have been made furtively and hastily, and as we drank our beer and watched the undulations of the naked actors we noted that although the ladies were always undressed from top to toe, the gentlemen servicing them usually kept their socks on, presumably because the filming had been done in the cold climate of Sweden. But if these ancient pornos lacked sophistication, they were still forbidden fruit, and watching them gave us that feeling that journalists always cherish, the feeling of being insiders, privy to experience denied to mere mortals.

But now there would be no more porno for me, no more other assorted perks like free passes on the Saturday-morning CPR ski train to the Laurentians. Now, as I continued up Windsor Street, the soft, warm salve of self-pity was somehow mitigating the punishment of the January blizzard. And, as I reflected on the details of my firing, my spirits gradually lifted. I could look back on the scene in H. J. Larkin's office with considerable satisfaction, thanks to the brevity and surgical neatness of my execution. There had been no whimpering on my part, no shouting by Larkin, no histrionics at all.

Yes, mine had been a much less humiliating firing than that of Mad Mac Murchison, the proofreader, who had been chopped a few weeks earlier for allowing a disturbing typographical error, actually the most unprintable of obscenities, to slip through onto the Women's Page. When the composing room foreman had informed Mad Mac that he was being dismissed, Mad Mac had burst into Larkin's office to plead for a reprieve.

"You can't do this to me, Harry," the distraught proofreader had cried. "I have a wife and kids to feed."

"I'm sorry," said Larkin, "but we can't have that word in the paper. And for all I know, you little bugger, you did it on purpose."

"If you do this to me, Harry, it's all over for me!" Mad Mac shouted. "I'll jump out that window!"

Whereupon H. J. Larkin, a heavy-set man with an air of suppressed violence about him, went over to the window, opened it and, gesturing down to the street four storeys below, said, "Be my guest." Mad Mac stared at the open window for a long moment, then turned and went back to the composing room to gather his things, exit the building and head for the Taverne des Sports.

Now, in the wake of my own ordeal, I was heading not for the rowdy, sour-smelling tavern, but for the more refined solace of the Press Club, in the basement of the Laurentien Hotel. Here, Eric the bartender would comfort me with Black Horse Ale and there would be fellow journalists to sympathize with me. I hoped my Irish friend Brian Moore might be there, to see if he thought the real reason for my being fired might have been my involvement in efforts to set up a Montreal local of the American Newspaper Guild. The thought that newsmen might ever be unionized enraged Montreal publishers, and over at the *Herald* Ed Bantey had recently been fired for union activity. But which of our colleagues had been Larkin's spy at those clandestine union meetings, and at last night's party? Brian Moore, being a worldly-wise European, understood things like the mechanics of espionage, and he might have valuable ideas.

Brian had emigrated to Canada two years earlier and had found a job at the *Gazette*, first as a proofreader and then as a reporter. Before long he was recognized as the best and most versatile reporter we had. Politics, economics, dreary Kiwanis Club meetings – nothing fazed him. He was enterprising, accurate and – above all – fast. He'd come into the office at high speed and seem to start typing while still in the process of sitting down at his desk. He'd have his story finished while the rest of us were staring blankly at our typewriters and adding more sugar to our coffee. We all admired his succinct, lucid news-story prose, but there was no hint that one day Brian Moore would be the author of nineteen novels, winner of international literary awards and three-time nominee for the Booker Prize.

Despite our very different backgrounds, Brian and I soon became friends, thanks to a common liking for books and a common dislike of certain of our colleagues. But that afternoon, the day I was fired, he wasn't at the Press Club to hear my lament. There was nobody there, in fact, except for a few sportswriters. They were friendly fellows, but I didn't join them as I could never understand their jargon. And so I sat by myself, at the far end of the bar, nursing my Black Horse and pondering the implications of unemployment. In my gloom, I could never imagine that little more than a year hence I would be living fairly high off the hog, travelling in Europe and tormenting Brian Moore with postcards from Paris, Zurich and Cortina d'Ampezzo. One of these cards elicited this response from Brian, who, in his letters, usually addressed me with some fanciful cognomen.

February 6, 1951

Dear Vincent Sheehan,

I am writing this not from Rapallo or Viareggio but from an interesting little nook called the Gazette Police Desk (graveyard shift 6:00 p.m. to 2:30 a.m., 40 minutes for lunch. Signed H. J. Larkin). In case you think I am in disfavour, let me hasten to tell you that this is only a three-day assignment. . . .

We have secured a simple apartment with two bedrooms, living room, bath and kitchen, all very self-contained (whatever that means) at 1710 Dorchester West. Owner of said apartment is Maxie Shapiro [a major operator of illegal gambling dens]. Rent of said apartment is $90 per month. Date of moving in is February 15. We will give a party for you in said apartment when you return – or do you intend to rot your days out on that rotten continent full of weak and puling foreigners. . . . Remember what Fitz [a *Gazette* editor recently back from a holiday in Europe] said: "All those countries make me thank God I was born in Canada."

And in the immortal words of Harry Larkin: "Nothing good ever came out of Ireland. Live like pigs over there. You never had it so good, Moore, since you came over here. Wonderful opportunities for advancement here. Stick with this company and you'll get along." I treasure those words. I pass them along to you in the hope that you will stop your wanderings and come home to us all.

Yours,
Larry Conroy

If I, sipping Cinzano in the Swiss Alps, was Vincent Sheehan, the dashing foreign correspondent, Brian Moore, stuck in Montreal, was signing himself Larry Conroy, borrowing the name of a tired veteran police reporter. But wherever we were, our ominous managing editor was never far from our thoughts. And when he died, twenty-four years later, in 1975, the *Gazette's* obituary of Harry Joseph Larkin noted that he believed, with some pride, that he had served as the model for the managing editor in not one but two novels – the irascible MacGregor of the fictional Montreal *Tribune* in Brian Moore's *The Luck of Ginger Coffey*, published in 1960, and the tyrannical, penny-pinching Philip L. Butcher of the fictional *Montreal Daily Witness* in my own *Why Rock the Boat?*, published the following year. Both books eventually became movies, showing a new generation what journalism was like in the good old, bad old days – before computers, before newsrooms were carpeted in broadloom, before reporters drank Evian rather than Corby's Little Touch.

2

Dear Bill:
I got your highly unintellectual letter yesterday (Can't you
think of anything important to say? Don't you know we live in
highly explosive times?) and it confirmed my suspicions that
you slipped a chair under your arse in the Deux Magots as soon
as you arrived in Paris and probably haven't moved since. And
so the sad parade of life passes you by, son. . . .

The letter, dated June 27, 1951, was from Mordecai Richler,
who was sojourning in Spain. I was in Paris, preparing to
return to Montreal. My financial resources were evaporating and
there were no more freelance assignments in the offing. I had
been in Europe for eight months and couldn't stretch it out any
longer. In those days, so many of us wanted to be in Europe for
as long as possible, and possibly forever. But I personally lacked
the dedication of some of my young contemporaries who were
willing to scrape by in abject poverty, living on borrowed pit-
tances, sleeping on someone's floor and desperately waiting for
that cheque from home. No, I was too corrupt for that, too fond
of comfort and regular meals, preferably with a few glasses of
Beaujolais. Besides, unlike Mordecai and others I'd met in Paris,
I didn't aspire, at all costs, to literary heights; I simply wanted to
earn my living as a journalist and live an interesting – perhaps a
very interesting – life.

Fortunately there was a job waiting for me back home. It seems I was no longer in total journalistic disgrace; at least one editor seemed ready to overlook the fact that I was the cheeky young upstart who had insulted the boss. Now I would just be another one of those ink-stained hacks who bounced from one paper to another, fired here and hired there. In those days, there were three English dailies in Montreal, plus the *Standard* on Saturdays, and there was said to be at least one elderly reporter who sometimes couldn't quite remember which paper he was working for that week.

I had written to Mordecai that I was going to be hired again – a full-time job, not just more freelancing – and his response, in that June 27 letter, was typically encouraging:

> O how you must miss the roar of the presses and the urgency of life as a devil-may-care, carefree, swashbuckling newspaperman – those deadlines! – knowing that the innocent public (with bated breath) awaits daily your jolly little articles that do so much to cheer up the office girl – the little people, you and me – on her way to work.

Actually, my new job was to be with a magazine, not with a newspaper. That Saturday *Standard* was about to transform itself into *Weekend Picture Magazine*, a slick supplement that would be included in the Saturday edition of several daily papers across Canada. *Weekend*'s first edition was to appear in September and I would be part of the crew getting it out.

After being fired by the *Gazette*, I had become, perforce, a freelancer. I wrote articles for the travel section of the *New York Times*, broadcast talks on the CBC's shortwave service and was assigned by the *Standard* to cover things like the need in Montreal for air-raid shelters that would withstand the hydrogen bomb. I also covered a visiting flea circus, whose owner trained his little critters to pull tiny wagons. These chores, plus various other writing and editing tasks around town, allowed me to save up enough money to contemplate, toward the end of the year, a trip to Europe, where I would try to continue freelancing.

I persuaded the British Overseas Airways Corporation to give me a free ticket to London, promising to write something nice about their new airplane, the Stratocruiser, which had a spiral staircase down to the lower deck, where there was a bar, with red-leather bar stools, presided over by a jolly bartender. It was my first transatlantic flight, and late into the night the bartender enlivened it for me by leaning across the bar and whispering, "The captain just phoned down to tell me that we've lost Engine Number Three. He's trying to decide whether to turn back or try to make it to Ireland. I thought you'd like to know, sir, but let's not tell the other passengers. No point in disturbing them, is there?" Here was another instance of how, as a journalist, I was privy to information denied to mere mortals. The bartender, having taken me into his confidence, gave me a cognac on the house, to help steady my nerves.

We made it to Ireland, on three propellers, changed planes, and before long I was in London. During my few weeks in England I researched several stories that I would later write. My first inspiration came while I was having my shoes shined on the street in Piccadilly Circus. The bootblack, sixty years old, told me he spoke five languages, had been a pilot in the Royal Flying Corps, a soldier in the Mexican army, an adviser to the Paraguayan air force and an agent of the British Secret Service. But he found contentment only when he decided, late in life, to become a shoeshine boy. His name was Vivian de Gurr St. George and he was a local celebrity. As he finished buffing my black brogues, I decided that this man personified the dignified decline of the British Empire. The story I eventually wrote carried the heading, "This Bootblack Dines with Ambassadors."

While I was in London I went to Lillywhite's to buy a very heavy Shetland wool sweater. I was going to need it in Paris. Before leaving Montreal, I'd had a letter from Mavis Gallant, who by now was well established in Paris, and she warned me what to expect:

October 31, [1950]

Dear Billy:

All our problems seem to be very basic in this city – how to keep warm, where to get the most to eat for the least money, and how to get rid of a cold. I think I mind the cold more than anything. My room is enormous and the radiator very small indeed. Around three o'clock in the afternoon it seems to reach its lowest temperature and if I am working my hands get numb and I have to soak them in warm water. I can now understand why the French never sleep alone. They aren't any sexier than any other race, but it's the only way of keeping warm. . . . Actually I like Paris and if I find I can provide myself with some sort of income, I shall try to find an apartment and stay for a bit. . . .

Are you coming over this winter, and if so when? I can show you all the places where one can eat under 300 francs [less than a dollar] – I've become an expert. . . . Much love,

Mavis

I'd known Mavis in Montreal, where she had been the leading feature writer for the *Standard*'s magazine section. A few months earlier, even before she sold her first short story to the *New Yorker*, she had astonished us all by quitting her staff job and heading to Europe to write fiction – a reckless act, many of us thought.

Soon after I arrived in Paris, late in December 1950, we had dinner together in the Romanian restaurant on Rue Monsieur-le-Prince, where the polenta, the mititei and the tuica were unexcelled. After we gossiped about all the wretched wage slaves we'd left behind in Montreal, Mavis asked me if I knew Mordecai Richler. No, I didn't. He was from Montreal, Mavis told me, and he had recently arrived in Paris. He was nineteen years old and very determined to become a serious writer.

The next day Mavis introduced me to Mordecai, whom she called Mordy. And during the next few weeks the three of us, plus my Montreal friend Alex Cherney, visited many of the bars, bistros and boîtes of Saint Germain des Prés, the Latin Quarter and Montparnasse. We listened to the music of Francis Lemarque in the Bar Vert and the songs of the incomparable Cora Vaucaire in l'Échelle de Jacob. At midnight we went to the Rose-Rouge to hear Les Frères Jacques and, although we couldn't afford it, we ventured into the Club Saint Germain-des-Prés to mingle with the snobs from Passy and marvel at *"un nouveau style de jazz: le Be-Bop."* It was wonderful how much music you could listen to for the price of a single drink.

We were all writing, or pretending to write, but at the cocktail hour some of us would gather, for Pernods or *fines à l'eau*, with a growing tribe of expatriates. On prosperous days it would be the Deux Magots, on thin days it would be the Mabillon. If a cheque arrived in the mail, there was the possibility of dinner at the Brasserie Lipp or in the ancient rooms of the Procope, where Voltaire used to dine. Other times it was in the dim little student restaurants. It was the golden age of the Left Bank and in its watering holes we were on the alert to catch sight of Jean-Paul Sartre, Jacques Prévert, Albert Camus, Juliette Greco.

The glory of it all was that it was cheap. Brian Moore, back in Montreal, wanted details, and I supplied them. (In those days, I not only kept letters from friends, but I also made carbon copies of the letters I sent to them. These, I told myself, would constitute my diary, something I could read in my old age to help me recall exactly how I had wasted my youth.) To guide Brian, who was contemplating a trip to Europe, I wrote:

Hotel Acropolis,
31 rue de Buci, Paris 6

January 15, 1951

Dear James Joyce,
I share a hotel room with your friend Alex Cherney – a room that is good and clean and true, with bath (a comparatively rare item in Paris), bidet, sink but no john, which costs us

$2.75 a day. If you want to forego the bath it's much cheaper. You have to spend at least a dollar for a good meal, but that includes wine, and you can imagine how much better this is than it is in Montreal. Theatre and concerts are very cheap – a third of what we pay in Montreal. You can see ballet for less than a buck. A bottle of cognac costs $2. Drinks at bars vary widely, from 15-cent brandy upwards.

We frequent the Royal St. Germain, the Old Navy and other gin mills of note, meeting the unbarbered, the unemployed and the uninhibited. Half the world's poetic misfits are huddled together in Saint Germain des Prés and the language is American. Some of them live in a-buck-a-day flops and some of the gals (average age 16 to 21) commute from bed to bed in order to pay nothing.

However the atmosphere is no longer quite Henry Millerish and most flies are kept buttoned in public and I suppose some people are managing to get some work done. Among the more interesting types met were the editors of New Story, a revival of Story magazine. They are David Burnett, son of Whit Burnett and Martha Foley, who ran the old Story; one Sylvia Something and somebody else called Protter. The mag looks good and will be on sale soon in the U.S. as well as in Paris.

I hear your nuptials are fast approaching. I'd like to know the exact hour and date, so that, wherever I am, I can pause in silent tribute and drink a solitary toast. Please don't get hitched after 7:00 p.m. EDT because that's 1:00 a.m. here and I'm in bed early these days [a statement that was not exactly true]. And are you coming to Europe for your honeymoon? If so, please let me know and I'll give you detailed information on how to make two dollars do the work of one, and other little tricks.

> Yours truly,
> Scott Fitzgerald

Brian was indeed about to get married, to the recently divorced Jacqueline Sirois (née Scully), a friend of Mavis and, like her, a

staff feature writer at the *Standard*. But the possibility of their
making it over to Europe seemed slim, as Brian explained in a
letter telling me about his wedding plans:

Montreal, January 20, 1951

Dear Boulevardier,
Sanctified by the nuptial rites of Unus Sanctum Fidum
Catholicum, Rev. M. J. O'Brien officiating, Jacobina Scully,
spinster, and Irlandicus Brian Moore will unite in unholy
matrimony, joined in a sacrilegious state of sin and with many
perjuries and malfeasances, in St. Anthony's – or is it St.
Patrick's? – Church, St. Antoine Street, Montreal, February 28.
Rites to be consummated with disapproval of bride's parents,
modicum of fuss and maximum desire to get said act over as
quickly as possible.

    This to be followed by a trip to Europe via B.O.A.C. or Air
France, or, in the most likely event that they will not take us
[with complementary tickets], a trip to Chicago, Texas,
Missouri, New Orleans and New York. See America first, boy.
It's GOD'S OWN COUNTRY.

    If to Europe, I will advise you. But chances look grim.
Since I have become entangled in the myriad arrangements
necessary for what I considered to be a simple, unassuming
ceremony, I have had little time to pursue my art. In fact I
have had no time for same. Which depresses my balance with
MY BANK.

    Carl, Chiefie, Petie, Charlie and Brucie send their very best
and hope you are finding your feet.

Yours,
Harry Larkin

    By "my art," Brian was referring to the moonlighting he was
doing during the years he was on the *Gazette* staff, writing commercial magazine stories and paperback thrillers in his spare time.

It was all to accumulate enough money to allow him, eventually, to leave the paper and devote himself to writing serious fiction.

∼

I left Paris on January 16, heading south by train to ski in the Alps. That long-cherished ambition, to slide down those sublime slopes, was perhaps my main reason for having come to Europe. Besides the skiing, there was the prospect of après-ski, also known as *le ski de chalet*, sipping spicy mulled wine with lovely ladies in charming mountain hotels. But, above all, there was work to be done, and money to be earned. I would visit seven great ski resorts in Austria, Italy, France and Switzerland, and this would provide me with material for seven radio broadcasts for the *Black Horse Skicast*, to be heard on Thursday nights on CJAD Montreal. That blessed Black Horse brewery, makers of my favourite ale, had given me an advance of two hundred dollars for the great work I was going to do for them. That, of course, would not be nearly enough to pay for the luxury I was contemplating. To augment the limited cash that I had in my wallet, I was armed with free tickets for many railways, plus invitations to stay at fine hotels, either gratis or at greatly reduced rates. All this I had obtained by conducting diligent correspondence with various government tourist departments, promising them that my broadcasts and magazine articles would send hordes of free-spending skiers from Canada to their various Alps. My corruption was complete.

And so, on that January night, I got on the train at the Gare de l'Est, carrying my Smith Corona portable typewriter, while a porter followed with my skis, my rucksack and my heavy suitcase. I was bound for St. Anton am Arlberg, in Austria, the historic cradle of modern skiing and birthplace of the Arlberg technique, with its snowplow turns and stem Christies. I had timed my arrival in St. Anton to be able to witness the big international downhill race, for the Hannes Schneider Cup, only to find that the race was cancelled. There was simply too much snow and too great a danger of avalanches. It had been snowing steadily, twenty-four hours a day, for almost a week. As I said in my radio broadcast:

> Toward the end of the week, the avalanches started and in Switzerland, to the west, more than thirty people were killed in snowslides, in remote areas. Roads were blocked and villages were cut off. People in St. Anton told me they hadn't seen this much snow in twenty years. Only the hardiest skiers – and I was not one of them – braved the blizzards to take to the hills.
>
> But for those of us sheltering in the valley, the scene was certainly picturesque. The narrow, winding streets of this ancient town had become slim corridors between shoulder-high snowbanks and all day long you saw people shovelling snow off the roofs of their houses, making the snowbanks higher.
>
> In the evening, after an avalanche would hit a power line somewhere, the lights would go off all over town, including my hotel, and you can imagine how the candlelight in the bar – to say nothing of the zither music – added to the charm of old St. Anton.

Here again was proof that in the Alps, nature at its most ferocious could only intensify the joys of après-ski. But doing my broadcast was considerably less joyful. Those were the days long before satellite transmission, or even reliable transatlantic telephone service, and what I had to do, for every broadcast, was to make my way to the nearest city – for St. Anton it was Innsbruck – search out a radio station and persuade them to make a recording of my talk – usually on a big 78 rpm disc, 16 inches in diameter. Then I had to get the disc shipped to Montreal by air express. The arrangements for this, and the paperwork, often in a foreign language that I didn't speak, took infinitely more inventiveness than writing the scripts for the broadcasts themselves.

Innsbruck
Austria

Jan. 23, 1951

Dear Mavis,

So there I was at midnight Thursday, prone with exhaustion
and fast asleep, when the phone here in the hotel room rang.
"Entschuldigen sie bitte, it is Montreal, Canada, U.S.A. calling."
My maternal parent, in fact. It seems that some blockhead
back home, short of tripe one evening for his radio blather,
announced that Wm. Wntrb. was missing in an Austrian
avalanche. Whereupon the phone in my parents' home started
ringing with queries, condolences, congratulations. Half the
family fortune was immediately expended on cables. Then, on
Thursday, Bell Telephone finally caught up with me here. And
so, with the St. Bernard dogs yapping in the background and
the brandy sloshing about in the little casks around their
necks, we draw a curtain on this painful scene. . . .

    Trust you are well and flourishing. . . . Love,

Bill

Paris, February 1

Cher Billy:

I knew you would be safe. As Alex pointed out, you would be
in the bar, and the bar is usually in the basement. I had a letter
from Montreal about your demise: "His family was in a dither
about him, thinking he was buried under an avalanche or
something." It all seems to be rather a source of amusement.
Perhaps you should show up with just a little wound to justify
all this – a frozen foot, or something.

    The news from the NYorker was heartbreaking. I had a letter
saying they couldn't take one story because the theme was like

others they had run and it was too bad I had "innocently stumbled" on the same idea, although it was "wonderful." Fine words butter no croissants. They went on to say they liked the other one fine and were doing a preliminary editing and would let me know soon. I was sure that meant yes (this is the heartbreaking part) and then had another letter saying it was like part of a novel and wouldn't work as a story although it was "funny and delightful." They said "although at the end one is finished with the story one isn't finished with the people." This isn't sour grapes, but I don't consider that valid. The point of a short story is just that: that you should be quite through with the story, but the people should have continuity. It's had rather a bad effect on me. Everything I'm now doing looks horrible. . . . Love,

Mavis

∾

As the train plowed south from Innsbruck, through the heavy Tyrolean snows, I realized that I was deep in Hemingway country. Had anybody ever written more eloquently about the joys and terrors of skiing in the Alps? I had with me, to read during my travels, a collection of Hemingway's short stories, and every line struck me as being perfect, like his description of how George, hurtling down the mountain, suddenly hit a patch of soft snow and took a spill: "and he went over and over in a clashing of skis, feeling like a shot rabbit, then stuck, his legs crossed, his skis sticking straight up and his nose and ears jammed full of snow. . . ."

O noble Hemingway, majestic Hemingway! What an honour for me to ski in your tracks, to capsize like your shot rabbit, to swallow a mouthful of snow! Reading this stuff on the train, from Austria to Italy, made me so drunk with his muscular prose that it influenced the letter I was writing to Brian Moore and his wife-to-be:

On the train, Southward

Jan. 25

Dear Brian and Jackie:

Move over, little rabbit, and I will tell you about the bridge.
Right now we are passing a place called Colle Isarco, which the
Austrians called Gossensass before we took it away from them.
Those things up there are called mountains and they are good
and clean and true. When the leprosy I picked up with General
Prato doesn't bother me, I ski the mountains, good and clean
and true. This wine we are drinking is called Meleto and it is a
good kind of Chianti and it comes from Baron Ricasoli's place
in Firenze and it is good and clean and cheap. And we have
just come through the Brenner Pass, which I negotiated
without running into anybody we know.

Anyway, this is being written in a second class carriage and
not third (thought I'd put on the dog today) going south from
Innsbruck toward Rome. But I, fool that I am, will change at
Fortezza, in the Italian Tyrol, and go east to Cortina D'Ampezzo
(where Ernie broke his leg and where I will research my next
broadcast). The train, of course, is filled with the usual
complement of international spies and smugglers. Hope they
don't find my industrial diamonds, hidden you know where. But
I've just been successfully customed and immigrated, the
gendarme looking suspiciously at this little typewriter, which
sits quite well on the little table gadget near the window.

I find that I speak fluent Italian, which I never realized
before. I also find that I have, in minuscule amounts, eight
different kinds of currency on my person: U.S. dollars, a
ten-bob note, about 80 Austrian schillings, some French francs,
14,000 lire (worth 20 bucks), 50 German pfennigs that
somebody passed off on me in Basel, a few Swiss francs,
and an Irish half-crown that I accepted in change from some
wretched bartender at Shannon Airport, when we made our
heroic landing there. That half-crown, as you know, has a

picture of a horse on it and can't be spent anywhere in the civilized world.

At the Brenner Pass buffet (where Hitler and Mussolini used to meet) I brought some lunch to eat on the train – a piece of cheese, two salami sandwiches, one orange, one sausage made of sawdust and nitric acid, and a litre of Meleto. The whole works cost me less that 90 cents. Now, between the lurching of the train and the Meleto, I occasionally hit the right key on this typewriter. . . .

Yr. Obt. Servt.,
Guillermo

In Cortina d'Ampezzo, Signor Otto Menardi of the Aziènda Autonoma Soggiorno Turismo got me set up, as the Aziènda's guest, in the best hotel in town, a five-star palazzo called the Miramonti Majestic. In the dining room, as I surveyed the starchy white napery and the glittering crystal, I realized that I had transformed the grubby business of journalistic freeloading into a fine and elegant art. After the waiter carefully poured the Risserva Ducale into my glass, I drank a silent toast to Signor Menardi, to Herr Schiller of the Kur-und Verkehrsverein in Zermatt, to Monsieur Curchod of the Syndicat d'Initiative de Val d'Isère and to all the other chamber-of-commerce officials who knew that their domains would soon be inundated with Canadian tourist dollars, thanks to my broadcasts.

In the parking area behind the Miramonti Majestic, Ferraris and Maseratis glistened in the moonlight. Inside the hotel, after dinner, *il fior fiori* of Italian ski society undulated to the strains of the dance band. The ladies wore gorgeous après-ski creations from the couturiers of Milan, with the gentlemen in equally gorgeous attire from the tailors of Rome. In contrast to these sleek, silky garments, I presented a somewhat rustic British appearance, in the hairy tweed hacking jacket I had bought in London and the plaid waistcoat they'd sold me at the Scotch House, across the street from Harrods.

For my broadcast, I thought I should tell my listeners that this was not the Italy of their imagination, of sauce bolognese on the balmy shores of the Mediterranean. These were the frosty Dolomite Mountains, draped in snow, where they might serve you a fricassee of wild boar as you gazed out the window at pinnacles like Tofana di Mezzo, rising to 10,500 feet, or the Marmolada Glacier, 300 feet higher. Here the village square, at an altitude of 4,000 feet, meant that you started your skiing from a base higher than the top of our revered Mont Tremblant back home. From this base, the cable car whisked you up to a little restaurant at almost 7,000 feet, where you could have a calzone before plunging down the mountain.

Cortina had been chosen as the site of the 1956 Winter Olympics, and the week I was there, the Settimana Internazionale dello Sci was something of a preview of the Olympics. All the big boys were on hand for the downhill race – Nogler of Austria, Mulei of Yugoslavia, Nillson of Sweden, Perrin of Switzerland and many others. Standing at the finish line, I took notes for my broadcast. I would wax rhapsodic about the surprise victory of Eugenio Monti, a young Italian outsider who was two-tenths of a second faster than the favourite, James Couttet. Always striving for the sportswriterly flourish, I would refer to the humiliated Couttet as the tardy cannonball from France.

After watching the women race in the Discesa Femminile, I reluctantly packed my bags in the Miramonti Majestic and caught the train for Milan, where I would record my broadcast. As we chugged through the Alto Adige – more Hemingway country – I set up my typewriter on the little table under the bronze plaque containing my two favourite bits of Italian railway advice and regulation: *Non sputare nella carrozza* (Do not spit inside the carriage) and *È pericoloso sporgersi* (It is dangerous to lean out the window). Could there be any mundane injunction that was not melodious in that wonderful language?

≈

During my one night in Milan, after recording my broadcast, I had to decide whether to go to La Scala to see Gian Carlo Menotti's *The Consul* or go to the Ice Palace to watch the Lethbridge Maple Leafs, who were touring Europe, play an Italian team. Neglecting my journalistic duty, I chose the opera, but when that was over I went across the street to the Marino Hotel, where the Canadians were staying, to see how they'd made out in their game. I found them very cheerful over their beers in the bar, having spanked the Red and Black Devils of Milan 10-3. A few nights before they had beaten an American team from Maine 11-1. The lads from Lethbridge had been winning games all over Europe.

"You can tell the folks back home," said Dick Gray, the team's manager, "that we're going to win the world championships in Paris next month. No doubt about it."

"People here think we're NHL champions," said Shorty Malacko, one of the players. "When we tell them there are hundreds of teams in Canada that could beat us, their mouths hang open." I took notes of my conversation with Shorty, Hector, Bert, Whitey and the others and sold the notes to Andy O'Brien, the *Standard*'s sports editor, for twenty dollars, which paid for my ticket to the opera three times over.

From Milan the train took me north to Switzerland, through the scary gloom of the Simplon Tunnel, twelve miles long. After spending the night in Sion, I piled my skis, rucksack, suitcase and typewriter onto the mountain tramway, which would take me across another border, into France. Labouring uphill and down, the tram took three hours to travel the thirty miles from Sion to Chamonix.

I arrived in Chamonix in time for more international competition, including illuminated ski jumping at night, with the dim mass of Mont Blanc, highest peak in the Alps, rising in the background behind the brilliantly lit jump tower. As expected, the Finns and Norwegians led the field with stylish leaps of more than two hundred feet. But it was the downhill race that was the highlight of the week, with all the European national champions out for revenge after the drubbing they'd received from the upstart Eugenio Monti in Cortina. But again it was the young Italian who won, with a wildly reckless run down a course that dropped four thousand feet in less than a mile and a half.

~

Chamonix, Feb. 9

Dear Mavis,
I hope you haven't allowed the news from the NYorker to depress you unduly. I can't say that their editorial acumen, as you quote it, impresses me very much. Perhaps you've rallied by now and sent the stories off somewhere else, which would be the wise thing to do – if I may offer unsolicited advice. And I'm not just trying to be a cheery old uncle when I say that the story-in-progress you showed me in Paris looked sure-fire to me, really excellent, even though I was beset with a hangover and other distractions when I read it. . . . Much love,

Bill

From Chamonix I headed south again, this time to the Mediterranean, to the Riviera, where I would do a magazine piece about the Mardi Gras carnival in Nice. On the train I opened the mail that had been handed to me, grudgingly, by the clerk at the post office in Chamonix. I suspect that he disapproved, Frenchily, of the way I pronounced Poste Restante. Perhaps I didn't make Restant-uh sound feminine enough. His grimace was irritating; I had not yet gotten used to waiters and hotel clerks correcting my grammar, always anxious to protect the purity of the French language. "Mais c'est *la* soupe, monsieur, pas *le* soupe."

The mail was disappointing. From Bob Sabloff in Montreal came a clipping from the *Herald*, an ad proclaiming that Sally

Rand was taking her clothes off and doing her fan-dance at the Gayety, and that Bozo Snyder, the nonpareil clown, was also on the bill, probably brandishing a large rubber salami and chasing shrieking chorus girls across the stage with it. Bob occasionally sent me items like that ad to remind me what I was missing in Montreal. But what I was looking for in the mail was not there – not a dollar, not a franc, not a quid. From the British Broadcasting Corporation, London, there was a cute note saying, "Dear Sir, We are seeking Bank of England permission to remit to you the sum of seven guineas, etc., etc." Christ, I'd made the damn broadcast for them way back on December 21, and the bloody foreign exchange regulations were still holding up my measly reward. It was at times like this, when my exchequer was plummeting, that I wished I wasn't a writer, part of that threadbare clan of writers, where almost all conversation, and much thought, revolves around money. How much healthier it would be to have an ordinary job with a salary, say in a bank, or an insurance company, where you weren't always obsessed by money and could dwell on loftier subjects, like art and literature.

The letter I most wanted, from the *Standard*, was definitely not in the scrawny little sheaf from Poste Restante. Dammit, they owed me one hundred dollars for the story I sent them from London, about the football pools. Where was the money? Was there anything wrong with the story? As the train chugged past another alp, Mount Something or Other, I rummaged through my papers, found my carbon copy, and started reading it.

One evening not long ago a representative of one of Britain's big football pools rang the doorbell of a humble Bristol household. "Congratulations," he said to the housewife who answered. "You've won and I have a cheque for you."

The woman – one of Britain's 16,000,000 regular football gamblers – had invested a shilling. She had won $200,000. "Thank you very much," she said as she accepted the cheque. "Sorry I can't ask you in, but we're having dinner."

Other football pool winners take the news less calmly; many
faint and some fall down and get hurt. . . .

And so on, for six more zippy pages. Now was there anything
wrong with that? I could just see the dimwits at the *Standard*
saying that the "Canadian angle" should come in earlier than
page two, how lotteries and pools were strictly illegal in Canada,
etc., etc. I groaned at the thought that before they paid me my
hundred dollars they might want a pissy little rewrite, which
would delay things for a few more hungry weeks, what with the
mail going back and forth across the Atlantic.

The trip from the mountains to the sea, across France, took a
wearisome eighteen hours, with several changes of trains. At one
point I was sharing a compartment with two priests, who seemed
disturbed by the clacking of my typewriter. When darkness
descended, and it was time for dinner, they were even more dis-
approving as they watched me reach into my rucksack and pull
out yet another can of sardines. As I started opening the can
carefully, determined not to spill oil on my hacking jacket, I
noticed that the clergymen were also tucking into their dinner,
which they had produced from a black, ecclesiastical-looking
bag – golden brioches, slices of ham (probably costly jambon de
Bayonne), important-looking paté, Roquefort cheese.

~

In Nice, on the Riviera, I worked with Al Taylor, photographer,
on a magazine photostory about the Mardi Gras carnival. I took
notes for the captions I would write to go with Al's photos:

 - A group of murderers amuses the crowd and frightens the
   children with their long knives.
 - Rabbits on horseback are popular.
 - This float shows the Goose that Laid the Golden Egg,
   except that in France the goose is a chicken.

— Policemen are the favourite target for boys throwing pellets.
They wear goggles to protect their eyes and don't interfere
in brawls.

These photos and many others were taken during the parade
that was circling Place Massena, climax of the most spectacular
and exuberant of Europe's pre-Lenten carnivals. As I wrote in
my story,

> This year the floats in the four parades attained pre-war
> lavishness, depicting in bright colors such stories as the Wolf
> Who Became a Shepherd, the Miser and His Son, the City
> Mouse and the Country Mouse. Among the floats, harlequins
> and columbines danced and huge figures with plaster heads
> wobbled through the crowd. Brilliantly dressed horsemen and
> zany cyclists added to the animation.
>
> Besides parades, fireworks, banquets and masquerade balls,
> there was the traditional Battle of the Flowers on the seaside
> Promenade des Anglais. Here society women and pretty girls,
> riding in flower-bedecked carriages, showered the crowd with
> mimosa, lilacs and violets. Later in the day came the Battle of
> the Plaster, a more humane version of the violent scuffles that
> marked many old-time carnivals. For a few cents, people buy
> bags of plaster pellets, about the size of peas, and hurl them at
> each other by the handful. The pellets sting and vendors
> circulate through the crowd selling mesh masks to protect eyes
> and face. By five o'clock Place Massena is white with plaster and
> everybody goes home to wash up before turning out again in
> the evening to see the effigy of King Carnival go up in flames.

After the Carnival, Mademoiselle Antonietti of the local
Syndicat d'Initiative drove Al and me up through the mountains
above Nice to have a look at the chapel at Vence that Matisse
was decorating, and to visit an inn called the Colombe d'Or. At
the chapel, the nuns wouldn't let us in unless we had permission

from Matisse. We phoned Matisse but were told that he was
asleep and couldn't be disturbed. So we had to satisfy our religious fervour with an examination of the model of the chapel
that was on display. Fortunately access to the Colombe d'Or, at
nearby St. Paul, was much easier, and I told Brian Moore about it
in my next letter to him:

> This little hotel is much closer to Paradise than Matisse's
> chapel. It's medieval, hangs on a cliff, has 35 rooms. The
> chickens are roasted on a spit in the foyer and you eat
> them on a terrace shaded by orange trees. Matisse, Braque
> and Picasso are all over the walls. Alpes Maritimes in the
> background, doves all over the roof. Le patron says he gets ten
> dollars a day for room and three meals, but is willing to accept
> considerably less from bonafide writers and painters, whom he
> likes to have around. I thereupon took a vow to either become
> a writer or a painter, or knock off a bank immediately when I
> get back to Paris, so I can spend the rest of my days at the
> Colombe d'Or.

Now I headed north again, with my skis, to Val d'Isère, *la belle
station sportive française de haute altitude.* Here there were thirty
peaks that could be climbed on skis, ranging from 9,000 to
12,000 feet. Climb six of them and they'd give you a bronze
badge, climb twelve and you'd get your silver, climb eighteen and
you'd get the gold. But, with typically French distrustfulness,
they wouldn't take your word for your achievements. At the
summit of each mountain there was a little stone cairn with an
aluminum box in it. If and when you reached the top, you'd open
the aluminum box and find a notebook in it. You'd write your
name and date on a page, tear it off and put it in a little slot in
the box. You would keep a carbon copy for yourself and present
this to the committee, which would note your particulars. But
they still didn't trust you, and in the spring a team of verifiers
would climb all the peaks and check the contents of all the

mountain mailboxes. Only then would they tote up the final results and hand out the badges.

On my first day in Val d'Isère, having decided that trying for a badge didn't offer sufficient challenge, I went skiing instead. And it was in the cable car, going up the mountain they called La Solaise, that I met Nicole, the lovely but lonely Nicole. She was a better skier than I was, but we skied together all afternoon. On our second trip up in the cable car she told me that she was from Lyon and that her husband was off in Algeria, doing something or other to further the glory and grandeur of France.

Nicole was beautiful to watch on skis, having mastered the new French parallel technique, with its side-slipping *dérapage*, its *appel et rotation* leading into a *Christiania pur*. My own Christie was much less pure, being part of the old Arlberg technique, the more stolid, Teutonic method that I'd been brought up on back home. But Nicole, at the end of a long, svelte swoop, would wait patiently for me at the bottom of the hill as I came down with more caution than style.

At the end of the afternoon, much exhausted by our exertions, we propped up our skis outside the Hotel Grand Paradis, where we both happened to be staying, and went in to revive ourselves with cocktails. For dinner there was a wonderful *gigot d'agneau* and for dancing there was a trio in the bar. We danced for a while – a few slow, close numbers – and then we went up to her room, where I was only too happy to help her get her revenge for some scurvy misdemeanour of her husband.

Four days and four nights with the delightful Nicole made Val d'Isère paramount for me among all the mountains of Europe. But now she had to go back to Lyon. Philippe was coming home from Sidi bel Abbès, or wherever, and I had to be on my way to Geneva, to record my next broadcast. We said goodbye, sadly, as she drove off in her little Renault, her skis strapped to the roof.

≈

Paris, February 16

Cher Billy,

Alex was packed off yesterday, tearful and owing everyone
money, including me. At the station he discovered he had only
2,000 francs [about six dollars] to see him to New York, so I
gave him another 1,000, at which he promptly dashed off and
bought a book on how to play the guitar. . . .

We had a wonderful farewell party in his room with the
concierge threatening to call the cops every ten minutes, and a
noisy and oddly-assorted crew dispersed over the bed and bidet.
Alex had spent a week inviting everyone but had made no
provision until the last minute, when, accompanied by a
Serbian bee-stung beauty called Danya (whose hair covered her
flashing piggy black eyes) he bought a dozen glasses and hardly
any booze. Fortunately a number of people came armed with
wonderful things and there was much left over as we were all
put out around midnight.

Everyone, by the end of the evening (much later), was moist
and promising eternal friendship. Harrie Stalinof (remember
the tall Dutch chap in the Bar Vert?) was also leaving the next
day, for Amsterdam, but instead of crying he was kissing all the
girls. Well, now he's gone and I miss him, although we quarrelled
all the time. I mean *all* the time.

Joan is married but her husband (a photographer) bought
himself a wide-angle lens instead of getting her a ring. Martha is
having a baby. She told Alex it was because one night in London
she and Sam didn't have a shilling for the gas meter, or
something like that. Jackie got married in the arms of the
church. Everyone who writes about it is very amused. The
Duffys' child is called Catherine Johanna. . . . I may go to
Marseille in a sailboat on my way to Spain, but this is uncertain
because the man who owns the boat is a negative mystic (this
means he just looks knowing but says nothing) and I think a
month on the Rhone with a negative mystic would be a bit
thick. Also his wife is pregnant.

I saw Steve last night and have finally come to the firm belief that he bores me. He's 25 now and so youth is no excuse. He's become a Socialist and has a French girlfriend. Whatever next? . . . Isn't Liliane AWFUL? She had a terrible fight with Kleber in the Royal. . . . Your trip sounds wonderful. I have no money so I can't go anywhere unless something happens. With love,

Mavis

At the railway station in Geneva, I was given the envelope that had been promised to me by the Swiss tourist office, with train tickets for my route – Geneva to Visp to Zermatt to Brig to Spiez to Interlaken to Wengen to Interlaken to Bern to Zurich to Landquart to Davos to Zurich to Basel. The Swiss trains looked new and shiny, with carriages that were spotlessly clean, in contrast with the grubby, shopworn trains of France and Italy. It was another reminder that prosperous Switzerland had been neutral during the long, terrible years of war, which had ended less than six years ago.

To make sense of the tickets that had been given to me, I bought a thick booklet that contained all Swiss railway timetables, with curious addenda like postal-delivery routes in very obscure mountain regions that were served by letter carriers on horseback. Even these alpine postmen operated on strict timetables, on horses that presumably were regulated, like the trains, by precision Swiss chronometers.

During my travels in Switzerland, this railway guide became compulsive reading for me. I couldn't put it down, trying to figure out things like how long it would take me, theoretically, to go from the town of Murg to the town of Chur. That was a particularly slow train, wasting time by stopping at Flums, Mels and Zizers. Was there another country in the world with such wonderful place names? In my timetable I visited Mumpf, Frick, Turg and Zuoz. I pictured Bumplitz as a welcoming place, as opposed to the forbidding Belp and Eigg. And what about Bex, Au (yes, Au) and Ruti? There was so much to explore in these massive hills.

Zermatt was my first stop on this hegira. I had come, of course, to gaze on the Matterhorn. And to describe it to my radio listeners I took them with me on the narrow-gauge cog railway from Zermatt up to the Gornergrat station, where the altitude is 10,289 feet:

> Many people consider the panorama from Gornergrat to be the world's greatest mountain view. It's all blue and white and grey – ice and snow and rock as far as the eye can see. There's a parade of peaks that all seem to be competing for your attention. And between the peaks, the glaciers stretch downwards. Occasionally, on the unbroken white of a glacier, you can see a few black dots – a line of ski mountaineers slowly making an ascent. Face south and you see Monte Rosa, the second highest mountain in Europe. To the right, the Twins – Castor and Pollux – both well over 13,000 feet. Then the Breithorn and the Theodule Pass, where Roman armies once marched northward. And finally the spire of the most famous of mountains, the Matterhorn.
>
> The natives of Zermatt call it the Horn, and the Italians, on their side of the mountain, call it La Becca. Its beauty and mystery have challenged men for centuries and it has killed more than a hundred people who have sought its summit, 14,780 feet up.
>
> This huge stone pyramid dominates life in Zermatt and there are still arguments in the village as to exactly what happened that day in July 1865, when the Englishman Edward Whymper became the first man to reach the summit – and when his three companions plunged to their death on the way down. But the Matterhorn has been tamed since then, and now about a thousand people climb it every year, with the aid of fixed rope lines. And last August something happened that caused almost as much sensation as Whymper's ascent: a cat followed a party of

climbers right up to the peak of the Matterhorn and then calmly made its way down into Italy, on the south side of the mountain.

~

From Zermatt I went on to Davos, deciding to skip Wengen and Mürren, having been told that these were British outposts where, after skiing, you were expected to change into a dinner jacket for the evening's snobbery. On the train to Davos I put aside my railway timetable to read a letter from Brian Moore. As always, he was bringing me up-to-date on office politics at the *Gazette*:

Montreal, Feb. 28

Dear Gillis,

Mr. Christopherson, a crisp young man, is subbing for Myer on the City Desk and working generally as understudy. I am beginning to look at Myer with that tenderness of feeling I got for Harold when we felt he was having his throat slowly cut.

I am sitting opposite a big-titted new staffer called Maureen. Ever since you quit this office your seat has been occupied by succulent arses. Long may it continue.

Jacqueline Sirois now gets $100 per week [at the *Standard*] and will write you all the dirt. . . . Two new people are needed, says Stanley [a *Standard* editor], and one of them must be Walter Winchelltraub.

Mr. Moore, author, will be interviewed on CJAD Monday on the subject of his writings. His book sold 44 percent of its total in Montreal in the first ten days. 700 copies of 5,020 remain in warehouses. Mr. Moore plans to take his profits, if any, and fly to Europe one day.

Jackie's mother sees no reason why I should have put all that disgusting sex into the book. Jackie's stepfather says, "In certain questionable French novels I have read about men

tearing women's clothes off. Now where would Brian have read
a thing like that?" . . .

Regards,
Al (Mr. Montreal) Palmer

The book Brian was referring to was *Wreath for a Redhead*, the
first of seven thrillers that he would write between 1950 and
1957, to earn money that would buy him time to work on serious
novels. This first book and the next one, *The Executioners*, were
"by Brian Moore," but the next five would carry suitably Irish
pseudonyms like Bernard Mara and Michael Bryan.

Wreath for a Redhead was a paperback "pocket book" with a
lurid cover that depicted a beautiful, terrified woman in a low-
cut dress about to be strangled by two male hands. The blurb on
the back cover said:

> John Riordan thought his stay in Montreal would be just a
> dull wait for another ship. But when he met the luscious
> redhead he was plunged into a deadly maelstrom of lust,
> intrigue – and murder. . . . His search for the missing girl led
> him to a mysterious black notebook and a frightened group of
> people – a sex-starved debutante, a degenerate photographer, a
> soldier of fortune and a cunning cripple. . . . In his desperate
> pursuit of the titian temptress who had betrayed him, Riordan
> found himself the quarry, hunted by the police and by a gigantic,
> illegal combine whose tentacles stretched across Canada.

The first two thrillers were published by Canada's Harlequin
Books, but the others, like *French for Murder* and *A Bullet for My
Lady*, found publishers in New York and London. Brian always
regarded these works as being strictly commercial potboilers.
Unlike Graham Greene, who never disowned his "entertain-
ments," Brian refused to talk about his thrillers and in his later
years he vainly hoped that nobody would unearth these
ephemeral works and decipher the pseudonyms. I personally

could never understand this. From the very beginning it was obvious that he had completely mastered the genre. The books were immensely readable and his genius for atmosphere, dialogue and plot was everywhere evident, but when I said that to Brian it only irritated him.

Perhaps because he tried to disown them, these thrillers of Brian's were destined to become collectors' items. In 2001, one Canadian rare books dealer was asking $1,300 for *Wreath for a Redhead*. When it was originally published, fifty years earlier, this little pocket book sold for twenty-five cents.

~

The next and last stop on my winter itinerary was Davos, in a broad, sunny valley in southeastern Switzerland. In my final broadcast I reported that every well-travelled skier I spoke to agreed that Davos offered the best skiing anywhere on the planet. And in my report I couldn't refrain from bragging about my last downhill run of the season:

> In twenty minutes the little red cable railway takes you up to your starting point – Weissfluhjoch, 8,737 feet above sea level. Here there's a restaurant with a sunny terrace and a ski shop where you can get your skis waxed. There's a big map on the wall showing you the thirty different downhill runs you can choose from. If you want to run down to the village of Kublis, as I did, you press a button at the bottom of the map and your itinerary lights up.
>
> It was Trail No. 17 that I chose – almost eight miles of downhill running, which, needless to say, I planned to do in sections. No. 17 starts with a steep pitch that levels into three long, easy schusses. Then you go though open country, with slopes of varying steepness. You're way above the treeline and you ski down through huge snowfields, down through passes and gullies and along ledges. The landscape is ever-changing, with a constant array of towering peaks to the left and right.

You stop now and then to consult your pocket map and identify the peaks. And, of course, to rest your legs.

Eventually you're down at the treeline and you slither over a very bumpy stretch of clearings and meadows. You know you're about halfway down when you come to a place called Schwendi, where there's a chalet with a terrace for sunbathing. You stop here for a real rest, with a cup of coffee and a piece of linzer torte. Then you push off again, heading down through steep, terraced meadows, along paths, over a bridge and through forests and farmers' backyards. When you get to Kublis you will have dropped 6,000 feet and you're ready to shed your skis and take the train back to Davos and a hot bath in your hotel.

3

In Switzerland, the sun was providing the first hint of spring. Back in Paris, after I'd recorded my last broadcast, the surest sign of spring, they told me, was that little priest walking up and down Boulevard St. Germain again with his big placard saying LA VIE EST DEVENUE UNE COMEDIE, UNE GRANDE COMEDIE. It was quite warm now, and one could sip one's aperitif outdoors, on the terrace of the Mabillon. The more fashionable bars and terraces were out of the question, as I was again painfully short of cash. The *Standard* owed me money for two articles and some expense accounts, but despite my urgent letters to Montreal no money was forthcoming. "Be patient, laddie," my editor wrote to me. "You'll get it by and by. It's just that those geniuses down in the business office are a bit slow."

In those days in Paris we were forever borrowing from each other or lending each other small sums, but that spring there seemed to be nobody to borrow from. Everybody I knew, Mavis included, was on short rations. Now, as I ordered the Mabillon's budget-priced *croque monsieur* for dinner, I wondered whether I would be able to pay my weekly bill at the budget-priced Acropolis Hotel, just across Rue de Buci. But one day, late on a sunny afternoon, I did find myself on the more costly terrace of the Deux Magots, sipping Pernods. They were being bought for me by an acquaintance who had just arrived in town, a man with money, lots of money.

He was Douglas W. Connor, a pilot who had flown with the
Royal Canadian Air Force during the war and who was entitled
to wear the Distinguished Flying Cross. He was from Vancouver,
but he now lived in Geneva, where, as he liked to say, he was in
the second-hand business – buying and selling used airplanes,
big ones like DC-4s. I'd met him two years earlier, while I was
still a *Gazette* reporter. I'd been sent out to Dorval Airport to
look into a story about an airplane that had been "arrested" by
the authorities and couldn't take off for Africa. With Connor
and his partner, Red O'Meara, another soldier of fortune, at the
controls, the plane had put down in Montreal for refuelling, on
its way to Nigeria, where it had been chartered to pick up some
pilgrims and fly them to Mecca. But no sooner had it landed at
Dorval than it was besieged by lawyers and bailiffs. In the story
I wrote about the brouhaha at the airport, I tried my best to
explain an extremely complex situation whereby Connor claimed
he had legitimately rented the plane in Kansas, but a company
purporting to be its owners was claiming that the renters were
themselves renters and not entitled to do any subletting. The
big, silvery airplane, the lawyers were saying, was in essence
stolen. It would not be the last time that I would hear of Connor
being involved in opaque international transactions.

Now, two years later, sitting at the Deux Magots, he was
telling me that he was just stopping in Paris for a day or two and
would then be driving up to Brussels to look at a promising airplane that was for sale. But after Brussels, he said, it would be
time for him to take a holiday. Would I like to drive down to
Spain with him? He knew interesting people in Barcelona and I
could get material for great stories about life under the Franco
dictatorship. When I said I'd love to go but didn't have any
money, he said he'd lend me whatever was necessary.

Connor was telling me about his friends in Barcelona, who
were very rich but were secret Republicans, when we were distracted by the scene at the next table. A young woman had just
arrived and was ordering an Orangina. Then, from a portfolio,
she produced a sketch pad and started sketching the ancient St.

German des Prés Church across the street. With her long blonde hair she was, without doubt, the most beautiful woman I'd yet seen in Europe.

After a minute or two, Connor was on his feet and looking over her shoulder. "Excuse me, miss," he said, presuming that she spoke English. "Can I look? I'm very interested in art." Believe it or not, that idiotic remark seemed to be sufficient and, after the briefest of pauses to think it over, she accepted Connor's invitation to join us at our table. After all, Connor was a tall, handsome man who, as he managed to let her know before long, was a championship bobsled racer at St. Moritz.

Her name was Christina and she was a nurse, from Stockholm. What she really wanted was to be an artist, and she was on her way to Villefranche, on the Côte d'Azur, to spend her vacation painting. After the long grey gloom of the Swedish winter, she needed the hot colours of the Mediterranean to inspire her. She'd been in Paris for two days and tonight she'd be catching the train south.

"Villefranche!" Connor exclaimed. "What a coincidence! I happen to be driving down to Antibes tonight, right next door to Villefranche. I've got to look at an airplane down there. Why don't you drive down with me? It'd be much nicer than the train."

She seemed to be giving the matter some thought, as Connor ordered champagne cocktails, and I refrained from pointing out that a minute ago he had been going north to Brussels, not south to Antibes.

"That is very generous of you," Christina finally said, "but I cannot accept. After all, I don't really know you, do I?'

"It's a long drive," Connor said. "We'd have lots of time to get to know each other." By this time I was starting to feel superfluous and I said that I'd be running along. But Connor persuaded me to stay, perhaps feeling that my presence provided some aura of innocence to his scheme. After another champagne cocktail, he announced that we were all going to have dinner at the renowned and hideously expensive Tour d'Argent, on a quai on the Seine, with a superb view of Notre Dame.

Leaving the Deux Magots, the three of us went around the corner to where Connor's car was parked. There were very few American cars in Europe in 1951, and I could see how Christina was taken aback when she saw this *bagnole*, this enormous, brand-new, powder blue Lincoln Continental. There probably wasn't another one like it in all of France. Over dinner, Connor elaborated on the advantages of driving instead of taking the train. They could stop in Grenoble, where he knew of a three-star restaurant that would make this Tour d'Argent (incredibly lavish and delicious, I thought) look like a soup kitchen. Christina seemed to waver for a moment, but finally she was adamant. No, thank you very much, but it would have to be the train, and so after picking up her luggage at her hotel we drove her to the Gare de Lyon and there we said goodbye to her. As we left the station, Connor said to me, "Do you mind taking a taxi home? I've to get going, right away."

"Get going? Where?"

"To Villefranche, of course. I want to see if I can get there in time to meet the train."

"Jesus, Doug, it's five hundred miles."

"Piece of cake, as we used to say in the Air Force."

A week later I got a postcard from Villefranche, showing the famous trick cyclist who used to cavort on the pier. "Having a wonderful time," the postcard said, and it was signed "Christina and Doug."

So I wouldn't be driving down to Spain after all. I wouldn't be writing a penetrating article about the anti-Franco underground, the sort of solid political stuff that I wanted to write, as opposed to the lightweight "features" (bootblack in Piccadilly Circus, etc.) that they wanted from me in Montreal.

I was now devoid of any feature ideas, so I decided to make the rounds of Paris's major attractions to see if I couldn't get some material for a piece about American tourists blundering around in their garish shirts, their cameras at the ready. Not exactly an original idea, but perhaps I could come up with something witty or, better still, something convulsively funny. So I took the elevator all the way up to the third platform of the Eiffel Tower, gazed out on the city and observed two schoolmarms from Indiana who seemed more nervous than funny. They were of no use to me. At Napoleon's Tomb, I was disappointed to hear a group of Americans putting intelligent questions to their guide. Listening in, I heard him tell them that the emperor's body reposed in six coffins, each one contained inside the other – the iron coffin inside the mahogany coffin, the mahogany coffin inside the oak coffin, and so on. For my article, it would take some thinking to make that information funny.

I gleaned nothing on top of the Arc de Triomphe, where I was the only tourist on hand, and in the Jeu de Paume the group from Milwaukee was properly reverent as it studied the Monets, the Cézannes, the Gaugins. Next I went to the Conciergerie, one of my favourite museums, with its memories of the French Revolution. Here there were some rowdy children being silenced by a guard, but, disappointingly, they were not American. Still, I lingered a bit, communing with the spirit of Marie Antoinette in the cell where they kept her for a few months before taking her off to get sliced. Outside in the courtyard you could almost hear the swish of the guillotine during the Terror, especially in the little Côté des Douze in the corner, where the twelve men and women selected daily for execution could say their last goodbyes as they awaited their turn. There was nothing for me here either, but perhaps I could cheat a little and make up a few black humour gags that I could attribute to some fictional, heartless Americans.

My museum legs were by now more weary than they had ever been on the ski hills, but I forced myself to make one final foray – to the Louvre. And there, in the Grande Galerie, I struck gold. It came to me in a flash, and I rushed out to the nearest Métro station to catch a train back to the hotel, to get to the typewriter while the idea was still hot. My hands were trembling a bit as I fed a sheet of my best paper into that trusty old Smith Corona portable and slowly typed the first thirteen immortal words: "The frame was empty. The *Mona Lisa* had been stolen from the Louvre." Yes, this was not going to be another lightweight feature, this was going to be fiction, a short story!

The *Standard* was paying $250 for short stories. Brian Moore had sold them a few, so why couldn't I? Following some of Brian's advice on how to write fiction, I typed quickly. Don't start your story at the beginning, he had told me, start in the middle, or at some kind of climax or turning point. So I would hit them hard in the very first line, with the theft of this most famous painting in the world, and then I would flash back to show how the crooks had done it. I typed for hours, magnificently I thought, as I detailed the outrageous scheme whereby these gentlemen thieves were able to cut the picture out of its frame. And how they rolled the canvas up and got it out of the building and into the waiting black Citroën, the classic getaway car. But then, as they roared off toward Orléans, I – not they – hit a roadblock. Yes, I had a damn good beginning, but where was the rest of the story? What the *Standard* wanted most was short, snappy stories in the manner of O. Henry, with a quick epiphany – what Brian called a "come to realize" scene – and/or a surprise ending. We used to amuse ourselves over a beer by concocting great surprise endings, without necessarily having stories to lead up to them, the best clincher we came up with being "For, you see, he was blind."

But for my *Mona Lisa* caper, I so far had neither epiphany nor surprise. What happened to these guys after they got hold of the picture? After a good many hours in my room, I still had no inkling of an answer. So I left my old Acropolis Hotel and went for a long walk in the quartier, thinking hard and waiting for that flash. I wandered onto my favourite little streets in search of inspiration – Rue des Ciseaux, Rue du Chat-qui-Pèche, l'Impasse des Deux Anges. I had a drink in places that writers frequented, in the hope that their auras would kindle my flame – the Closerie des Lilas, where Hemingway imbibed, Jean-Paul Sartre's Café Flore. I walked the Rue des Canettes, where Balzac used to visit his mistress. But all to no avail. At the end of two days I still had no ending for my *Mona Lisa* story. I had to write *something*, so in disgust I sat down at the typewriter and composed yet another demand for the money that was owing to me, sending it not as a letter but as an angry cablegram to my editor at the *Standard*. And now, at last, I was finally successful. Two days later I got a cable in reply:

MONEY CABLED TO YOU CARE OF ROYAL BANK PARIS
BRANCH STOP FAIL TO UNDERSTAND CLAMOR STOP AFTER
ALL ITS ONLY MONEY
— STANLEY HANDMAN THE STANDARD

At last I was in the chips again. Now I would be able to properly entertain Brian and Jackie Moore, who had just arrived in Paris on a belated honeymoon. They were happy to join me on my standard tour for visiting firemen, including dinner at La Grenouille (The Frog), where *le patron* greeted all the ladies with a kiss, and lunch at Le Mouton de Panurge, where some of the rolls they served you were shaped like penises and some like female breasts or genitalia. It seemed strange, as we munched these exotic breadstuffs, to be gossiping about the mundane world of Montreal journalism.

With Brian and Jackie, I visited the usual Left Bank night spots, but we also tried a few new places. We took the bus up to Montmartre and visited a club called Le Ciel (Heaven). For Brian, as a lapsed Catholic, this place was particularly interesting, being a replica of a church, with stained-glass windows and plenty of crosses. We sat in pews and were served by waiters dressed like angels, replete with wings. The lady angels were hardly dressed at all. An archbishop wearing a tall mitre presided in the pulpit, making observations about the lady angels, telling jokes about the Virgin Mary and commenting on the clergy ("It was a small parish, only sixty-seven souls, and of course the priest and his housekeeper made sixty-nine"). All the while, a bearded old gentlemen claiming to be St. Peter wandered around, trying to pinch the women customers.

We visited the Bal Nègre on Rue Blomet, where, although we were among the few white people on hand, we were urged to join in the wild Senegalese dancing. At Le Monocle, in Montparnasse, we were also somewhat out of place, with almost all the patrons being women, many of them wearing tuxedos and dancing with each other. Up till then, in my 1951 innocence, I had never known about the existence of lesbians.

After twelve days in Paris, Brian and Jackie flew back to Montreal, exhausted by sightseeing and museums by day and pub-crawling by night. I accomplished very little by way of work during this period, although I did manage to spend a good deal of time trying to solve the *Mona Lisa* riddle – but still without success. Now, back at the typewriter, I procrastinated further by composing a letter to Alex Cherney, my former roommate in the Hotel Acropolis who was now back in Montreal:

Paris, March 25

Dear Alex,
On Friday night a party occurred here in our old Room 62, in honour of the visiting Moores, resulting in widespread drunkenness (vin blanc, Pernod, cognac). On hand: the Steinhouses, the Taylors, Mme. Gallant, Monsieur Dughi, Mlle. Calvert, unidentified Englishman, girl with red hair, Madeleine, invited by I'm not sure who, but cute. I am in deep trouble with Sourpuss down at the front desk as a result of a deep cigarette hole burned in the carpet. I will be assessed on Tuesday. You know how severe these French damage assessments can be, from which there is no appeal.

The Mabillon has never been more bizarre, the Royal more crowded, the Pergola more hateful. There are two new guitarists at the Bar Vert now and the lying owner says she is making more money without the music of our old pal Frank. Mischa still sings and nothing else seems to be happening around here. Had dinner with the Levinsons the other night and much political arguing. Mavis leaves for Italy soon. Connor is in Amsterdam, either buying an airplane or selling an airplane or renting an airplane, I'm not sure which. Second-hand reports are that Mordecai Richler is the happiest man in Spain, having trouble choosing between Conchita and Juanita. I am getting the wanderlust again and want to go to Spain or Scandinavia.

Roberte, our charming chambermaid, has a bouncing baby boy. She has a month's *congé*. Are you the father? Please write.

Wm. Wntrb.

~

If I was to travel again, Scandinavia would seem to be a choice destination. Was it true, as one heard, that free love – super free love – was rampant in Denmark? That if you met a girl at a dance she might invite you home afterwards and, in the morning, the two of you could have breakfast in bed, with her mother bringing in a nice tray of goodies? If true, this could be a really great magazine piece. It would not be just another lightweight feature, it would be a serious examination of the socio-economic implications of this sexual revolution. I would, of course, consult local sociologists. When writing semi-porn one always had to get the imprimatur of a sociologist. Also, I could inject the "I was there" flavour if I could personally experience the phenomenon with some young Ingrid or Astrid. And there could be a bit of humour, too, when Mother came in with the breakfast tray and I made some witticism about my fondness for Danish pastry.

After Copenhagen I might hop up to Stockholm, to see if the phenomenon was being experienced there too. The ravishing Christina was probably back in Stockholm, after her idyll on the Riviera with Connor. Perhaps she had a sister, or a friend, and between the two of them they could give me some insights. I was already writing the article in my head, in quite sprightly prose, as I lay on my bed in the Acropolis Hotel, a bed that by now had been too long chaste. But when I went to see the Paris public relations man for Scandinavian Airlines to see whether he would spring for complementary tickets to Copenhagen and Stockholm, I was met by a cold refusal. Perhaps I shouldn't have told him the

kind of story I wanted to write, but I would have thought the free
love angle would have caused his airline to have to put on extra
flights to accommodate the hordes of gentleman tourists.

Fortunately there were still possibilities for seeing more of
Europe, but to the south, not to the north. Here was a letter
dated April 1, from Mordecai Richler, who signed himself
Mordy. He was in Ibiza, one of the Balearic Islands off Spain's
Mediterranean coast. He had been trying, without success, to get
in touch with Mavis, to see whether she wanted to share a rented
house with him, something they had discussed in Paris.
Presumably she was travelling. If I were to see her when she got
back to town, would I pass on his invitation? Also, he was inviting me to come down. But first he wanted to fill me in "on the
state of my banking in Spain."

> DEAR BILL: i'm broke and i'm not broke, a rather curious
> position to be in – i have three hundred dollars in can.
> travellers checks still but they're not valid in spain – also a
> friend owes me $200 payable in sept. – but meanwhile, as long
> as i'm in spain i'm broke – (no, not quite: a hundred u.s. dollars
> is forthcoming from canada in may i think) – mavis said – god
> bless you – you might be able to lend me a few bucks until sept.
> – if so, fine – if not, i know your type! actually i don't think you
> can get money out of paris into spain but if you can and can
> spare $25 or $50 until sept. or oct. to say i would appreciate the
> whole thing would be putting it mildly – right now i owe small
> sums all over spain and i don't expect things to improve until
> may – o well enough about money – anyway i have this house
> which is an absolute delight – honestly the best thing going in
> san antonio – it has three bedrooms, a living room with
> fireplace, kitchen, BATH, etc. – the big advantage is the garden
> – each bedroom has an independent entrance extending onto a
> huge patio (in the summer shaded with palm leaves) – directly
> off the patio are two huge palm trees offering a whole bloody
> universe of shade – and then between the house and the road
> are fig, orange and almond trees – also grapevines, flowers –

there is also a small garden in the back with a shaded alcove
which i reserve to work in mornings in the summer
heat – tell Mavis the rent on this place (like every other house
here in the summer) is one thousand pesetas (about $20-25 per
month) and to be quite truthful i've taken it fully hoping mavis
would share the place with me and cut expenses that way –
while mavis and myself are alone here we could each have an
independent work room – and when you come bill (you must
come here bill – san antonio is a fantastic place in many ways
that are best not enlarged on thru the mails) there is a third
bedroom for you – now as soon IMMEDIATELY as mavis gets
back have her write to say 1. when she is coming. 2. if she is
willing to share the place. 3. if not, also write immediately –
i'm afraid if mavis for some reason cant come to share this
place with me (something which would be damn easy to do)
i'll have to make rapid arrangements to try to get someone else
to split expenses – possibly eric protter – drop me a line even if
you cant spare the money.

While I was pondering Mordecai's invitation, and checking
maps and timetables to figure out just where Ibiza was, I got a
letter from Brian Moore, now back home after his honeymoon in
Paris. He was reassuring me, seeing that I too would eventually
have to go home, that being a newspaper reporter in Montreal
was much more stimulating than anything Europe had to offer:

The Gazette, Montreal

April 5

Sir:
"I am delighted to have visited the Azores," Mr. Moore told
the Bystander yesterday, "but you cannot beat Montreal."
      Mr. Moore said his most delightful experience on getting
back was the privilege of covering a session of the Montreal
Advertising and Sales Executives Club in the Mount Royal

Hotel on the day after his return from Europe. The speaker was Chester E. Tucker, president of John Price Jones Ltd., New York, and his subject was "The Art of Raising Money." Mr. Tucker discussed philanthropy as "big business."

In an interview later with Mr. Bob Sabloff (currently working for the United Israel Appeal), Mr. Moore said: "You can keep that Mabillon crap. These talks are the stuff of existence."

H. J. Larkin, managing editor of the Gazette, Montreal, said: "How did you find the Old Country? Bloody awful, eh? I told you when you went away that the finest thing you would see over there was the plane home."

Mr. Moore seconded this vote.

Montrealer

∾

It was now, in Paris, the season for visiting firemen from Montreal, and there were far too many of them. Some, of course, I was happy to see, like Louis Jaques, one of Canada's best photo-journalists. And I definitely wanted to talk to Craig Ballantyne, the editor of the *Standard*. There were rumours that the *Standard* was going to be turned into a new kind of picture magazine and I wanted to know if there would be a job for me there. I was getting tired of scraping along as a freelancer. Yes, Craig told me, there was a good chance of that, but, like the other visiting firemen, he hadn't come to La Belle France to talk business. Unadulterated pleasure and stimulation was what these visitors wanted and, wearily, I had to take them on the rounds, guiding them to favourite haunts of mine, like the Bar Vert, on the Rue Jacob, as well as awful places on the Right Bank that they had read about, like the Crazy Horse Saloon and Harry's New York Bar. Around the corner from Harry's, I would take them to Brentano's English bookstore, on Avenue de l'Opéra, where they could have the thrill of buying forbidden books. The clerk at Brentano's would make a great show of it, looking around nervously and then reaching under the counter to produce the latest Henry Miller and other dirty stuff, like my own favourite, *Harriet Marwood, English Governess* by Anonymous. (It was not until years later that I learned that Anonymous was none other than a man who was to become a friend, the Montreal poet John Glassco.) After buying their naughty books, the visiting firemen would repair to the Café de la Paix up the street to leaf through the pages and discuss how these volumes could best be concealed from the eyes of Canada Customs at Dorval Airport.

~

Hotel Acropolis, Paris

April 10

Dear Mordy,

Yes, I definitely want to visit your little haven of luxuriance and lechery, but I can't be sure just when. For the moment I'm off to Brussels for a few days with a rich friend who drives a Lincoln Continental. It seems that Brussels is the only place in Europe where they know how to tune up a big, vulgar American car like this.

Meanwhile I would like to send you some money, but the exchequer has not been very weighty these days. Still, something may come to me soon and I'll be able to send you a slender portion to help you keep the flamencos happy.

Mavis didn't go to Italy after all, but she's out of town at the moment and I don't know when she'll be back. I saw her briefly last week (the town has been hell; we've all been wildly occupied with visiting firemen) and I showed her your letter. She shuddered appropriately at the apparition of Eric Protter and said something about writing you soon and possibly coming down in the summer.

Sorry I (like everybody else) can't be more concrete about my plans, but I hope in a week or two to let you know when I can come down. Meanwhile I hope you can hold the fort, or at least the patio.

Bill

I'd never had the slightest curiosity about Brussels, but my trip there, in the Lincoln Continental, had a purpose. My problem with the *Mona Lisa* project had become an obsession, and I hoped the answer would come to me on this trip. To start with, I'd decided that the gang that stole the *Mona Lisa* was headed by a mastermind who resembled my friend Douglas W. Connor, DFC. I had to study Connor a bit more, at close hand. Also, I thought airplanes should be involved, and from Connor I could learn things about airplanes that I needed to know. Tentatively I figured that Sir Basil Zaharoff, the villainous international arms dealer, had hired Connor to steal the picture, a caper that would bring him a million dollars if he could pull it off. Why did Zaharoff want *Mona*? To have her as part of the decor inside his enormous and sinfully luxurious private airplane.

Brussels, April 15

Dear Brian,
I felt slightly Scott Fitzgeraldish last night as the Lincoln Continental pulled up in front of the Palace Hotel ("It's a pretty good little brothel," says my friend Connor) and the lackeys leapt out for our luggage. The Palace turns out to be a palace, but Connor, who knows everybody, gets a rate here and so it's not too steep.

Yes, you're absolutely right, Montreal has it all over Europe, especially Brussels. You can imagine how shocked Connor and I have been to see how many ladies of easy virtue there are walking the streets here. The doorman at the hotel last night had the nerve to say to us, "Quelque chose de special, messieurs?" Some of the natives here speak a weird language called Flemish and I was agreeably surprised to learn that I fully understand it. Flemish man by the name of Tits has a shirt shop down the street. Big neon sign that says Tits.

What am I doing in Brussels? Well, I'm working on a project, but it's too embryonic for me to talk about. By the way, would you be good enough to look something up for me in the Gazette library? Sir Basil Zaharoff, the notorious international arms dealer. Is he still alive? Could you dig up a few basic facts about him? Thankee.

I'll be off to Spain soon after I get back to Paris. You can write me there: c/o Richler, Bar Escandell, San Antonio, Ibiza, Spain. He gets his mail at the local bar. Did I tell you about this Richler, who I met through Mavis and who invites me to visit him? He's from Montreal, has a peculiar first name – Mordecai – and wants to be a writer. Very young and rather cheeky, without proper deference when dealing with older citizens like myself. Still, he seems to be O.K., especially as he has rented a great-sounding house on an island paradise.

Willem

I arrived in Ibiza at eight o'clock in the morning, in the *Ciudad Mahon*, the overnight boat from Barcelona. Mordecai was on the dock to meet me, and we immediately went up to the Hotel España for breakfast, taking our coffee-with-cognac on the terrace overlooking the sea. We watched the fishermen bringing in their night's catch, strange-looking creatures that I later learned were cirviolas, bonitos, picados and huge meros with frighteningly red open mouths.

We were in Ibiza, the capital town of the island of the same name, an island about the size of the island of Montreal. It was an ancient town, with narrow streets climbing up a hillside that was crowned with a fortress built in the sixteenth century.

Whitewashed houses, gleaming in the sun, lined the streets, which were bustling with women on their morning errands. Most of the women were dressed in black, always in mourning, Mordecai told me, for someone recently deceased.

Leaving the hotel, we took a taxi across the width of the island, only about ten miles, to San Antonio Abad, where Mordecai had his house. On our way we passed farms and orchards, with small white farmhouses in brilliant contrast to the green of many pine trees. Driving through this serene country-side I could never have imagined that within my lifetime it would come to be disfigured by Miami-style tourist hotels and gigantic nightclubs. One of these would be a barn big enough to accommodate seven thousand young tourists dancing con-vulsively in "raves" that ended at dawn. With ear-splitting electronic music, Ibiza would, at the end of the century, become the rave capital of Europe. And if there were no indications, in 1951, that such things could ever come to pass, it would have been equally impossible for me to imagine that this young fellow, sitting beside me in the ramshackle taxi, who so far had pub-lished nothing more than three short "mood pieces" in an obscure little magazine, would someday become an acclaimed author, the winner of many literary prizes. Not only would there be ten novels bearing his name, plus several children's books and works of non-fiction, but the Toronto newspaper that ran his weekly column would emblazon the word "MORDECAI," in huge letters, on the side of buses going up Avenue Road.

Arriving in San Antonio, our taxi deposited us at Mordecai's house, which fully lived up to his enthusiastic description of it. Going in, I noticed on the doorstep a litre bottle of white wine, and my host explained that although there was no daily milk delivery here there was wine delivery every morning, and if I liked we could increase the daily ration to two litres of this very drinkable local product.

After I unpacked my bags, we walked down to the beach, three minutes away, a very wide expanse of white sand with only two or three bathers in sight. And beside the beach was the Bar

Escandell, the local fishermen's hangout, which was also Mordecai's
hangout and his mailbox. Here, to my surprise, I found a letter
waiting for me, from Brian Moore, who was now the *Gazette*'s
waterfront and shipping news reporter:

April 25

Dear Lincoln Continental:

As I take my pen in hand to pass you my greetings, Jean
Marchand and Thomas Earl [public relations officers] of
Canadian Pacific Steamships are busily debating the drinking
habits of certain Canadian scribes. I am passing a reposing day
at the Hotel Château Blanc, Pointe au Père, Quebec, waiting
for the cutter Citadelle to take me out to the 20,000-ton
white-hulled Empress of France when she arrives tomorrow
morning at 7 a.m. in the St. Lawrence Gulf. Aboard is Prince
Sayn-Wittgenstein, cousin of the Czar of All the Russias, who
will be interviewed by l'Evenément Journal, Le Soleil and
La Gazette.

Fitz tells me the best time he had in Paris was in Harry's
New York Bar. "Really tied a bun on there." Louis Jaques has
sworn off drink after his Paris venture. "I'm not so young as I
was, Brian. Shit, I can't take the stuff any more. I guess I'll just
lay around the house for a couple of weeks and read."

I notice that when I mention William (Freelance)
Weintraub in recounting my Paris adventures, my fellow
pressmen stop me.

"How's he doing, by the way?"

"Very well, etc. Looks prosperous."

Then they look very sad and surprised. Nothing succeeds
like envy. Wonderful country, Canada. Why don't you come
back where you came from?

Regards,
Patriot

San Antonio Abad, Ibiza

May 15

Dear Patriot:
You're going to hate me for this, but I feel impelled to tell you
that I have the typewriter out on the patio and the palm trees in
the garden are rustling. The figs and the lemons on the trees
aren't ripe yet, but occasionally one of the lemons will do for
tea. This is lotus-land. Just came back from a swim and, filled
with sudden energy, I decided to write to you instead of taking
the usual siesta.

Our cook is now preparing dinner. The rent for this hacienda,
with the abovementioned botanical accoutrements, comes to
about $30 a month, with the services of the cook thrown in. It's
cheaper in the off-season. Cognac in the fishermen's bar is two
and a half cents a shot, but who likes cognac? Or champagne at a
buck a quart? Or laundry at two cents a shirt?

Somebody had better come and get me out of here *fast*. As
my friend and host Mordecai Richler says, it's expensive here
not to drink.

Guillermo

Mordecai and I would spend the mornings at our typewriters,
he working on his first novel and I tapping away at that obsessive
Mona Lisa idea, which by now was becoming tiresome. But suddenly – eureka! – I realized that what I had here was not merely
a short story but a novel! Sir Basil Zaharoff's aircraft, with the
stolen painting in it, landed at his hideaway on an obscure
Mediterranean island and . . . Details to be worked out, of course,
with the French art police in hot pursuit. . . . It would be a
thriller, highly remunerative. If Moore could do it, so could I.

In the afternoons, after work and lunch, Mordecai and I would
go down to the Bar Escandell to play chess and sip a brandy.
Or sometimes we would venture, by taxi, to some of the other

villages on the island – San José, San Juan, Santa Eulalia del Rio. All of them had fishermen's bars that were worth exploring.

~

San Antonio Abad, Ibiza

May 19

Dear Mavis,
San Antonio is a gem – much better than I had expected. Mordy knows everybody on the island and is considered both a character and a respected citizen. The people are the friendliest I've ever met. We are rapidly becoming the leaders of social life here. Our reputation was established by the fiesta we held in the house the other night. Its success was assured by the two guitarists who out-Catalaned them all, by the solo flamencos of Pepe the Gypsy, by the unexpected animation of the English lady, by the inebriation of Vincente the mechanic, by the efforts of Pepe to make the French ladies, by the solemnity of Mariano the bus driver, by the rambunctiousness of Juliano the fish merchant. The evening ended in a near riot. Great fun.

But all good things must come to an end. I'll soon have to head back northwards and do some work, earn a few francs. Meanwhile, Mordy wonders when he'll hear from you, as a possible sharer of this house. Love,

Bill

Menton, May 27

Dear Billy,
Mordy must be furious. I was so vague about everything in March and April. But give my love to him and tell him he'll

see me yet. . . . The proofs from the New Yorker piece arrived this week, looking beautiful beyond words. I'm returning them with a new story, so as you see all is not lost. . . . Everybody writes from Paris that you are touring Europe with a Turkish girl. Whatever next? . . . Love,

Mavis

That rumour was wide of the mark. The Turkish girl was Suzy, Connor's girl, not mine. She was an aristocrat from Istanbul, whose mink coat was very appropriate in the Lincoln Continental. I had, of course, been seen with the two of them in Paris, and she had come up to join us in Brussels. But in Ibiza I was not without female companionship. While Mordecai was enjoying the company of a lively young woman called Helen, I was fortunate enough to meet Mercedes, on holiday from Barcelona. In an era when respectable Spanish girls did not associate with boys unless there was a chaperon present, Mercedes had managed to escape to the island on her own, and once there seemed eager to break all the other rules.

But these pleasures could not go on forever. Helen eventually departed for the Côte d'Azur and Mercedes, her vacation over, had to go back to Barcelona. And then the long-awaited letter arrived from Montreal, offering me a job on the staff of the new *Weekend Picture Magazine*, which was to be launched in a few months' time. I had to start thinking of going back home and so, after a round of boozy farewells in San Antonio, I took the boat to Barcelona and the plane to Paris, where I hoped to linger as long as possible.

~

Walking down the Boulevard St. Germain again, I felt I'd been away for ten years. Paris was celebrating its assertion that it was now two thousand years old and everything seemed to have been tarted up and varnished for the occasion. Even the Quinquina ads on the pissoirs were an unusually dazzling white, and there was dancing in the streets. I conveyed all this, plus some gossip about mutual friends, in a letter to Mordecai, asking him to bring me up-to-date on events on the island. He was back there now after a trip to Valencia, on the mainland. His response:

San Antonio

June 9

BILL, YOU SWEET SHIT: i know, i know, i promised to write the day i arrived but you know how it is. things are bumping along at a pleasant pace. i got back to work and my world shattering novel should be ready in about six to eight weeks. i'll write you down for a copy now if you like . . . that'll be $3.25 please . . . nothing from protter the bastard! i wrote him but will you pul-eeze look him up and find out what the fuck happened to my stories. if they've been rejected [by *New Story* magazine] i'd like to have them back as soon as humanly possible. shit, rené and his fascist outfit spread lots of rumours about me while I was away. . . .

1. i was arrested for disorderly conduct in palma.
2. i was arrested for anarchist activities in barcelona and was expelled from the country.
3. i eloped to paris.
4. i eloped to tangier.

no mail for you here. vincente and all the boys have been asking for you. last night i drove into ibiza on a motorcycle with juanito villian-gomez (the doctor, remember him?) we were at rosita's until four a.m. we had to retire early as he had to do operations the next day. keep well, love to joe dughi et al. drop me a line. i keep worrying about helen, and her monthlies, but i expect to hear from her shortly. have one for me in the bar vertes, i just had ten for you at the bar frites. arriba espana! ole! love,

Mordy

In my response, which was not very reassuring, I addressed him not as Mordecai or as Mordy, but with the name that had been bestowed on him by his Spanish cronies:

Welcome Hotel
66 Rue de Seine
Paris 6

June 21

Dear Mauricio:
I ran into Protter the other day and he promptly borrowed 300 francs from me to get home in a taxi. I have since retrieved 150 of it and the rest in trade – one issue of New Story and a cognac. I told him you were anxious to know about your story and he said it was still in the works. He said he's read it but the others hadn't. You should have a verdict soon, but I might as well tell you that he didn't sound optimistic. He says the magazine is doing well, that they're swimming in manuscripts and that a few types like Tennessee Williams and Sartre have kicked in a few hundred dollars each.

I came across René sitting in front of the Flore and he says the harmonica player's girl is a fine type and a good lay. Says he slept with her for a few weeks and it resulted in absolute solidification of his friendship with the harmonica player. Sometimes I wonder if René isn't full of crap.

Regards to Japps, Billie and John, Juanito, Cuba, Peron, Veterano and everybody. Kiss Lise when you see her.

Bill

San Antonio, June 26

BILL, OLD BOY: working very hard, running into many problems re book. also problems of another nature. I told you

about the rumours that preceded my return here, well the
secret police are investigating me now! they were up to see me,
friendly talk and all that shit, and i'm to drop into their office
in ibiza on thurs. for another "friendly" talk. i'd hate to be
thrown out of spain at this point as i'm broke and can't think
of anywhere to go. helen writes to say that the bull-fighting
posters are in the mail.

Mordy

Paris, July 5

Dear Mauricio,
What's happening? I've been anxiously waiting for a follow-up
from you elaborating on your troubles. I've been picturing you
in the clutches of jade-eyed Torquemadas, panting in the
hotbox, groaning on the rack and finally succumbing in the
Iron Virgin. Seriously, I hope everything is all right. Without
even a fig leaf, this is no time to get kicked out of the Garden
of Eden. After getting your letter I remembered a chat I had
with René here in the Montana bar in which he observed that
you were in some bad political repute around the island. I
didn't pay any attention to it, knowing René and knowing it
was probably some crap he picked up at a bridge game with the
Countess or our stormtrooper pal. But in any case, you should
be careful, said Papa.

I was on the bus the other day when I spotted Connor's
vulgar big car with Connor in it. I had thought he was in
Geneva or Palma or China or somewhere, but I was wrong. He
had just parked in front of a steamship agency and was buying
a ticket for South Africa. He told me that as far as he is
concerned, airplanes aren't here to stay and he's going to
Durban to open a meat cannery. He's now off to Cannes for a
pre-trip holiday, having phoned Suzy in Istanbul and having
found her eager to join him there. Is Helen on the Riviera and

might you be going there to see her? It's going to be hard for
me to concentrate in boring Montreal, picturing you and
Connor and sundry other fornicators operating on the
Mediterranean littoral this summer. I'm not doing a hell of a
lot these days except dreary preparations for leaving. They may
have to use a straitjacket to get me on the plane. Write.

Bill

San Antonio, July 3

BILL, M'BOY: this isn't a letter, it's a bulletin. i'm off today,
explanation of sorts follows. i'm tired as hell now as i had a
whopping party last night. chicken dinner with rosita,
proprietor of the brothel, and other shady gentry . . . so i'm
sitting in casa garovas now sipping coffee and tapping out
letters and feeling woozy and generally rotten. tonight i'm off
to barcelona – i know, regards to lise – and from there to nice,
from nice maybe to vence, or something. anything moderately
cheap. i cant explain fully why i'm clearing out now but i will
from france. i expect i shall see helen shortly. not exactly a sad
thought. i think she's in st. tropez. i arrive nice sat. why not
drop down for a couple of days?

Mordy

But there was no possibility of my luxuriating in Nice. My
days in Europe were now coming to an end and I had to be off to
London and catch the plane home. But the day before leaving
Paris I made a quick trip to the Louvre. Gazing for half an hour
at *Mona*, I hoped her enigmatic smile would somehow convey to
me an ending – an epiphany, a snapper, a surprise – for that
damned short story. But it was not until four days later that she
revealed her secret.

It came to me, in a flash, at thirty thousand feet, halfway across the Atlantic, as I sat with a Cinzano in the Stratocruiser bar. The story lay not with the thieves who had made off with the painting, or even with the pursuit mounted by the police. In fact there was no pursuit. The story was all in the way the museum handled the catastrophe. In fact there was no catastrophe. A brilliant copy of the *Mona Lisa* quickly reappeared in the empty frame, replacing the perfect forgery that had been stolen in 1927, which in turn had replaced the forgery that had been stolen in 1913, which was the 1893 copy. Mona drove men mad with the desire to possess her. Since the first theft, in 1704, the museum always kept a supply of superb copies on hand. And art experts, who seldom glanced at this tedious cliché of a painting, would never notice that with each replacement the lady's enigmatic smile became a millimetre more enigmatic.

Yes, I would start writing the moment I landed in Montreal. I would call the story "Another Mona" and it would surely be worth every penny of the $250 they were paying for this kind of hokum.

4

I was back in Montreal now and here was a letter from the Côte d'Azur, from Mordecai, to heighten my discontent at finally being home:

Tourrette-sur-Loup

August 3, [1951]

CHER WILLIAM: i've moved. i'm sharing an apartment with jori something, a painter from montreal. she's a friend of jackie sirois. that woman drives me crazy. everywhere i go i meet friends of jackie sirois! helen was here for a wonderful few days. she's staying at cannes. her mother is slightly put off with me. . . . work coming along swell and the book will be finished on schedule. sorry i can't be more amusing, but i worked nine hours today and i'm only writing out of love. i think i'll go to italy sometime in sept. . . . now that you're back home you can ship me the occasional new yorker. helen and i hitch-hiked to grasse while she was here. we also visited the colombe d'or, all the cagnes, and a few other places. there's a wealthy old american bitch out here with a car and she's taking us down to monte carlo one of these days. she thinks we're so sweet. write. all the best.

Mordy

The Jackie Sirois that Mordecai was referring to was now sitting at her typewriter, a few desks away from mine at *Weekend Picture Magazine*, on St. James Street in downtown Montreal. Now married to Brian Moore, Jackie was signing her articles Jacqueline Moore. Part of my new job, at $75 a week, was to edit the copy of staff writers like Jackie ($100 per week), a copy editor being a person who is deemed to know how to spell and who, his superiors suspect, has at least a rudimentary grasp of English grammar, something that is too tedious for the more important editors to bother with.

Carefully I would vacuum the writers' prose, to extract spelling mistakes, solecisms and dangling participles. Then I would make the proper repairs. As the writers were generally older than I was, and considered themselves to be stars, they would now and then curse me out for changes I made that saved their bacon. But fortunately for me, Jackie Moore, a pivotal person in my social circle, produced copy that was consistently lucid, error-free and even elegant, thus sparing me the embarrassment of having to correct her. But, by contrast, there were other writers who could only be described as pains in the ass.

These writers sometimes would get wind of a change I was proposing and would give battle, appealing to the features editor. One such battle revolved around our story about the visit to Canada, in the fall of 1951, of Princess Elizabeth, our future Queen, and her husband, the Duke of Edinburgh. *Weekend* could never get enough of the royal family, and now we were running twelve full pages of photos, including one shot of seventy thousand agitated people welcoming the young couple – she was then twenty-five – at City Hall Square in Toronto. Our writer was very keen on telling us about the Princess's wardrobe, in detail, but one phrase caused great problems for me. "In the evenings," the writer wrote, "Princess Elizabeth lived up to everyone's picture of what a princess should look like. Wrapped in white ermine, her diamond tiara, necklace and earrings sparkling with the jewelled beads on her formal dress, she couldn't be described as 'the girl next door.'"

Now those last four words struck me as being a blatant idiocy. Were we suggesting, I said, during the heated editorial argument, that our readers were so stupid as to think that the Princess might be just like "the girl next door"? But no, said the writer, just look at the next line, which gives meaning to the whole thing: "That is just what fate has decreed she can never be." In other words we were saying that our future Queen was not an ordinary person, this being the kind of philosophical profundity that *Weekend* liked to offer its readers. And so I lost the battle and "the girl next door" stayed in the story.

Montreal

August 25, 1951

Dear Mauricio,

What am I doing? In effect, I'm assistant to the features editor and sit around becoming neurotic about non-sequiturs and idiocy in the copy of highly-paid writers. I jazz up, cut down, rewrite and revolt. I look for dirty words. I help lower the common denominator of 900,000 Canadians. Everybody must help. My boss, Hugh Shaw, is an excellent type and I get along well with him, especially at little sessions when we bitch together at the efforts of writers. He recently observed that a certain lady contributor here writes like a drunken whore at a picnic.

My social life is boring. Alex Cherney and I occasionally seek each other out to talk about Paris, sadly. But today I'm living. A consignment of five packages of Gaulloises bleu arrived in the mail from Paris. It took an hour at the customs house and $1.50 in duty to liberate them, but it was worth it. As I chainsmoke them, the deep, rasping cough they produce and the rupture of the blood vessels of the eye carries me right back to St. Germain.

I've been in touch with your good mother and last night I went around to dinner on Hallowell Avenue, prepared to

perjure myself on your behalf. I found her très sympathique and
a damn good cook. I was very hungry and I wolfed the meal,
eulogizing you between mouthfuls. I gave you 100 on talent
and personality, 98 on chances of success. I gave Helen a big
buildup and was very sincere when I said I regretted your
getting to her first. I gave you 97 for levelheadedness and 119
on sobriety. The latter came up when I was warming to the
subject of Ibiza. I was mentioning the fact that we'd given a few
parties when she said, "He doesn't drink much, does he?" I
gave her a flat No. If she hadn't interrupted me in time, I might
have gone into raptures about those pre-breakfast cognacs,
something that is now sadly lacking in my life.

How's Helen? . . . Do give her my love. If you're a good boy
I'll send you a few New Yorkers and maybe a copy of a new
book called The Catcher in the Rye. Please make Europe
sound lousy when you write. Bien à toi,

Bill

Like Mordecai's mother, my mother was also showing an
interest in her son's drinking habits.

"Is that really necessary?" she said as I told the waiter to bring
me another dry martini before dinner.

"Aw, let him have a drink," my father said. "Tonight we're
celebrating."

It was my return from Europe that was being celebrated by my
parents and me. We were having a bang-up dinner at Ruby Foo's,
the Sino-Judaic pleasure dome and restaurant out on Decarie
Boulevard. All around us, gnawing on the garlic spareribs and
tucking into the egg foo yung, were big shots from the clothing
industry, real-estate tycoons, wily lawyers, racketeers big and
small, and bouffant wives. There was also a substantial sprinkling
of gentiles. My mother had ordered the moo goo guy pan and
Lord knows what other oriental mysteries; my father and I, basically traditionalists, had ordered the gorgeous roast beef with
Yorkshire pudding. Still hungry after my last penurious days in

Paris, I planned to top it all off with a baked Alaska and a green Chartreuse with my coffee.

I was glad to see my parents at ease in an expensive place like Ruby Foo's, finally learning how to spend money. They weren't rich, but they were "comfortable," yet, like many of their generation who had struggled through the Great Depression of the 1930s, they had deep-seated habits of frugality that were hard to overcome. But now, thank goodness, their attitudes were changing and they no longer felt that every penny had to be salted away for some dreadful rainy day. They were even talking about a cruise or a trip to Europe. It was a real pleasure to see them spending and now, in the restaurant, as I noticed Frances, the beautiful cigarette girl, weaving through the tables, I would see if my father would spring for a Monte Cristo cigar for me.

My father, Louis, though threadbare during the Depression, was no stranger to the good life, having made it fairly big during the 1920s before the stock market crash. He'd grown up in New York but fled to Canada as a very young man, mainly to escape his overbearing father. There were cousins in Montreal, but Louis soon left their shelter and headed to Northern Ontario, where there was a mining boom going on. Here he engaged in a number of enterprises that were never quite clear to me, but which I suspect were somewhat shady. I know he sold shares in mines that may have been real or may have been putative. He was always vague about these matters, but he did tell vivid stories of mushing through the snow behind dog teams and drinking rum with prospectors.

Louis came back from the north with enough money to open an office in the prestigious Canada Cement Building, on Phillips Square in downtown Montreal. He drove an Auburn motor car and ate heavy lunches with fellow entrepreneurs at Kraussmann's restaurant across the street (corned-beef hash topped with a fried egg, with hash-brown potatoes on the side, washed down with India Pale Ale). Business was good, selling those beautifully engraved stock certificates, and Louis needed a secretary. An attractive young woman named Mina Blumer got the job, and soon the two of them were married. Less than a year later, on a dark and stormy night in February 1926, I entered the scene.

In the parlance of the time, Louis Weintraub was a "promoter." He developed ideas and looked for partners with money to invest. He advertised in the papers for inventors with great ideas and the office was frequently crowded with clamorous loonies. These were the despair of my mother, but my father enjoyed talking to them and sometimes took them across to Kraussmann's for a beer, where they discussed ventures like rocket-propelled railway trains. One innovator who really impressed my father was the dehydrated-soup man, who knew how to make the stuff, then totally unknown in North America. To my father, the future of this broth was paved with gold. He tried the idea out on my mother:

"You just boil a pot of water," he said, "and then you open the little package and pour in the powder. And presto! In a minute you've got a delicious vegetable soup. Wouldn't you like that?"

"No, I wouldn't," said my mother.

But Louis pressed on, regardless, those being the days before extensive market research. In his shiny Auburn, he set out for the far reaches of the Island of Montreal, places like Ahuntsic, Dorval and Abord-à-Plouffe, where civilization had not yet eaten up the farmland. At each farmhouse he told the farmer that if he bought shares in the Soup-o-Mix Corporation, the corporation would buy vegetables and/or beef from this very farmer, for reduction to powder in its glistening laboratories. The farmer would be skeptical – until my father invited him to luncheon at the Ritz, where he and other farmers would sample the product, the rehydrated soup. With the farmer now very interested, my father would drive off with a bag of carrots, onions, tomatoes and other dehydratable ingredients in the rumble seat of the Auburn.

When the great day came, thirty-seven farmers, awkward in their Sunday best, assembled in a private dining room at the Ritz to toast the enterprise in Scotch and gin. Then they sat down to a lunch like they'd never had before. After the smoked salmon and the asparagus *feuilleté*, accompanied by a nicely chilled

Chablis, the soup was wheeled in, in great silver tureens. And, to a man, the farmers avowed that it was the greatest vegetable soup they'd ever tasted. After the dessert and the *pousse-cafés*, the farmers lined up to buy the handsome stock certificates.

"Was the dehydrated soup that good?" I asked my father when he first told me the story decades later.

"Dehydrated?" he said. "Are you crazy? I told the chef at the Ritz to get the freshest vegetables he could find and make the kind of soup he would make for the King of England."

My father actually went on to produce several hundred packages of dehydrated onion soup, but grocers across the country would have nothing to do with it. As was often the case, he was, in the 1920s, ahead of his time.

The Ever-Warm Safety Suit was another venture that didn't live up to its promise. The bulky suit, in thick black rubber from shoulder to toe, had a dome-shaped metal helmet, making it look a bit like the traditional deep-sea diver's outfit. A nervous passenger, boarding a transatlantic liner, would have an Ever-Warm in his luggage, what with the *Titanic* disaster only seventeen years in the past and still very much on one's mind. Why depend on the lifeboats, which were usually in short supply and, when operative, were crowded with unruly women and children? Instead, you could slip into your very own survival gear as soon as your ship started to go down. In your Ever-Warm, you could bob around comfortably in the icy Atlantic for days on end, there being tasty packets of dried food stashed around the neck of the helmet. When the rescue ship finally plucked you out of the ocean, you'd be as dry as a bone.

My father was very imaginative when it came to public relations and as soon as he got the first Ever-Warms from the factory he decided to display them on the movie screens of the world. He persuaded the Pathé newsreel to send a cameraman down to the Montreal harbour, where a stuntman would put on one of the suits and leap down into the drink from the deck of an ocean-going ship. As the appointed hour approached, the cameraman on the dock signalled that he was ready. But alas, up on the ship's deck, the stuntman had not arrived. My father was there, waiting for him. The minutes ticked by and still no stuntman. There were several big potential investors on the ship's deck and, grimly, my father realized that there was only one solution if the whole Ever-Warm Corporation were not to collapse right then and there. And so, trembling, Louis Weintraub climbed into the Ever-Warm Safety Suit and, as the Pathé man cranked his camera, he leapt off the high deck of the ship down into the cold waters of the St. Lawrence. Bobbing in the water, he waved a rubbery arm aloft to prove that he was still alive, and up on the deck the potential investors applauded and made plans to buy.

But only weeks after this historic event, there came the horrendous 1929 stock market crash. With the Great Depression of the 1930s upon us, Ever-Warm shares were now worthless, as were most of my father's other holdings. As his bank account slowly dried up he was forced to close his office and look for other work. He ended up travelling with his friend Charlie through small towns in Quebec and Ontario, going door to door selling encyclopedias and magazine subscriptions. They travelled in Charlie's rattletrap old Ford and, unable to afford even the cheapest motels, they slept in a tent by the roadside, cooking their meals on campfires. I saw little of my father in those years, and back in Montreal I watched my mother trying to get by on our very thin resources. When we went to the bakery she asked for day-old bread, because it was cheaper. Very fresh bread, she told me, was hard to digest.

Eventually we could no longer afford our Sherbrooke Street apartment and had to move north to cheaper quarters, a second-floor flat on Esplanade Street, accessible by one of those outdoor iron staircases. Here I was only two streets away from Mordecai Richler's St. Urbain Street, but we were not destined to meet until Paris. But in the spring of 1936 we moved again, this time to faraway Verdun, a working-class suburb. My father had managed to borrow enough money to buy a small, unsuccessful business there, a store on Wellington Street called the Verdun Bargain Store. It was a shabby little shop that offered second-rate hair-care products, stationery, bits of hardware and kitchen stuff and Lord knows what – a poor man's five-and-dime. There seemed to be little future in selling this kind of junk, but my mother had an idea. In this poor part of town, women made their own clothes and clothes for their daughters. So why not stock up on yard goods – big bolts of cloth – plus patterns, needles and thread? They did exactly that and, with a flourish, my father changed the store's name to Sunray Silks and he and my mother, who worked long hours beside him, set about learning the business. At home, at dinner, the conversation often revolved around words like crepe, taffeta, chiffon, rayon, organdy and chenille.

In Verdun, at my elementary school, I was the only Jew in the school. At Verdun High, I was one of only three. Jews were every bit as scarce here as gentiles were in Mordecai's Baron Byng High School. And despite dire warnings from friends and relatives living "uptown," I encountered no anti-Semitism. I was even elected president of the Hi-Y Club, where meetings had to open with a prayer, during which the name of Jesus Christ was invoked. I always felt uncomfortable leading that prayer, and I used to mouth those two words silently rather than utter them.

Sunray Silks prospered during the 1940s, and my parents, having moved uptown to a house in Snowdon, were once again in Jewish territory. It was to this house, on the improbably named Jean Brillant Street, that I returned after my fling in Europe. They'd kept my room for me and I'd be incarcerated here until I got enough money together to rent an apartment of my own and buy some furniture. It was hard to imagine anything more leadenly bourgeois than Jean Brillant Street, a thought that tormented me every time I got a letter from that young whippersnapper Mordecai (I was five years older than he), who was living it up at the other end of the spectrum.

Haut-de-Cagnes

August 30

DEAR BILL: You don't really deserve a long letter. after all i'm
still starving and writing on the cote while you are able to drop
into ben's for a sandwich every night. today i installed myself in
a lovely apartment in haut-de-cagnes. . . . a huge window here
overlooks a wonderful view of the "picturesque" hills and the
sea and every now and then i get up from my typewriter
and overlook. . . . another window overlooks jimmy's bar and
barefooted existentialist sex. every now and then i reach my
arm out for a cognac or an existentialist breast. life, as you see,
has its problems. i finished the rotten people about ten days
ago. protter was down here with various other inscrutable
intellectual types and they read parts of the book. protter & co.
have come around: they think i'm stupendous and young and
brilliant. but they also think i'll have one hell of a time selling
the book (the conventional publishers wouldn't read past page
three). it seems i could get the book done by new directions if i
was a homosexual and slept with jimmy. hurray for the literary
life. everybody thinks if i made my next opus a bit more
digestible for the tender bourgeois stomachs i should be able to
sell. all of which – really – is not too much comfort. anyway
the rotten people has been mailed to creative age press. . . . eric
thinks my book is 500% better than my stories and on the basis
of this i ran home and wrote a new story which he says he will
consider very carefully. . . . enough about writing and richler.
i just thought i'd keep you informed. . . . in two weeks – after i
have completed several stories – i move to italy for a month.
i shall work out a presentable draft of my new novel there
and with one hundred pages of copy present it to the
doubleday agent in paris. . . . i shall be back in paris in
mid-october and stay there until i go broke. . . . i hope –
before such ill luck materializes – i will have an advance

on my second book (it will be my first great novel). . . .
i found your letter thoroughly amusing. glad you liked
mama. write soon.

Mordy

p.s. can you lend me $25?

~

HOPALONG RACCOON
PET HAS INTERESTING ACTIVITIES AND FRIENDS

Besides copy-editing, part of my intellectually challenging job
at *Weekend* was to write heads and subheads for photostories like
this one. I also wrote captions for the pictures and in this case
one caption pointed out that "Raccoon's friends include a terrier
pup called Butterscotch, this duck and her family. Hopalong was
brought up with ducks, never chases or frightens them."

While young Richler was dreaming of literary glory on the
Riviera, and writing fiction too obnoxious to be published, I was
earning a living on St. James Street. There, up on the fourth
floor, we knew that Canadians loved animals, and we caught
their attention with snappy headlines: "PORPOISE WITH A
PURPOSE"; "HITCH-HIKING POOCH"; "CUDDLY CAMEL." These
were usually stories with three of four endearing photos, in the
"back of the book," in keeping with the First Law of Journalism,
which is that something must always be found to fill the space
between the advertisements – in those years products like
Picobac pipe tobacco, Odo-Ro-No underarm deodorant, Morris
Minor automobiles.

At the front of the book, there were more substantial stories,
and writing headings for these took much less brain-power than
thinking up things like Otter Biography. How Hitler's Dams
Were Blasted . . . Are Modern Women Happy? . . . Murder in the

Sky . . . Headings like these almost wrote themselves. "MURDER IN THE SKY: Canada's Most Sensational Crime" happened to be one of the best stories *Weekend* ever ran. Jackie Moore worked for more than three years researching the four-part series, which culminated in the hanging of J. Albert Guay, a Quebec City jeweller, and two accomplices. In order to kill Guay's wife, Rita, and collect the insurance money, they had made a bomb with a timing device and put it aboard a Canadian Pacific Airlines DC-3 flying from Quebec to Seven Islands. Twenty minutes after take-off, the bomb exploded and the plane crashed into a mountainside, killing Mrs. Guay and twenty-two other crew and passengers. This event, in 1948, was the first of its kind, in a time before anybody worried about bombs on airplanes. Jackie's story about the lives and passions of the people involved, the detective work that led to the arrests, and the trial that attracted reporters from all over North America was magazine journalism at its best.

~

haut-de-cagnes

sept. 21

DEAR BILL: why don't you write? you cant be working that hard you bastard. i hope you're not browned off because i asked you to loan me $25. it's just that i am – and will be – desperate for money until i get to paris in november where it looks like – among other things – i've got a free apartment. i'm revising my book completely. . . . i leave for italy (hitch-hike) on oct 1 with a beautiful swedish girl. havent been doing much work lately. tomorrow helen is cooking me an arroz a la valenciana in cannes. i saw mavis's story in the new yorker. i'm afraid i didnt like it very much. what do you think?

Mordy

When it started publication in 1951, *Weekend* was a Saturday supplement that appeared with nine newspapers, from the Saint John *Telegraph-Journal* to the *Vancouver Sun*. Over the years more newspapers would take it on and eventually it would appear in forty-one papers with a total circulation of more than two million. In a time when newspapers were strictly black-and-white, *Weekend* provided a glossy splash of colour. In the beginning, in 1951, television had not yet arrived in Canada and photostories, by excellent photographers, gave readers an idea of what the world and its doings looked like. When television took hold, and Canada sank down onto the couch to watch it, photojournalism in magazines gradually became obsolete.

Weekend was a pleasant enough place to work at. The work was not too hard, the atmosphere was convivial, and among the writers, editors, photographers and art-department people there were enough eccentrics to make things occasionally interesting. Detecting and observing the usual peculiar office romances provided amusement for all. There was good conversation at long, boozy lunches where friendships were cemented. If a staffer seemed to be drinking too much, he was called onto the carpet by Glenn Gilbert, the editorial director. "There's room for only one drunk on this paper," he would say, "and I was here first." Gilbert would prove his point on occasion by weaving unsteadily into the office at three in the afternoon, after a four-martini lunch down the street at the Vauquelin. Meanwhile there was also some drinking going on in Europe:

paris, oct. 29

TO WILLIAM W. So i'm back in paris. and it's wonderful! i got in at eight yesterday morning and braced myself with long walks back and forth across the street between the deux magots and the royale for alternate FREE rounds of *fines à l'eau* and johnny walker with fellow bohemian degenerates. . . . until five this morning i went quartier crawling from one den of st. germain sexual perversion to another – with a paris yid friend,

andre bachman. . . . this morning i've got a hangover. i'm
happy tho, (ha-ha) as i'm working again. also my friend terry
[a businessman from Montreal] has struck it rich and is coming
through like a great pal. just in time too, as i'm flat broke.
furnished room in an apartment in etoile rent-free. (we occupy
in ten days). have you ever read Jurgen, by branch cabell?
beautiful book! i hope to have the first draft of my book
finished in two months. . . . the maple leaf forever, i use lux and
god bless america. . . . write. . . . before I forget, I'm going to
write a super-duper triple surprise ending story [for *Weekend*] this
week and mail it to you. scruples collapse with the pocketbook.

                            Mordy

   Short stories with surprise endings were in demand at *Weekend*,
which had been happy to buy my *Mona Lisa* epic, for that wonderful $250. The story appeared, with a beautiful full-colour
illustration, under the title "Another Mona." It was "by Owen
Gray," that being my pseudonym for any works of fiction I sold to
the magazine. It would have been confusing to our readers if my
real name appeared over both fiction and reportage that was
non-fiction. During the next few years, Owen Gray sold a number
of stories to *Weekend*, including the immortal "Dr. Pepin's Beauty
Pill." (Arriving in a French village where all the girls were
remarkably ugly, Dr. Pepin turned them all into raving beauties
with his miraculous beauty pill. All except one girl who refused
to take the pill. Needless to say, Dr. Pepin was soon bored with
the village's vista of unrelieved beauty, so he proposed marriage
to the one remaining ugly girl. There followed a nifty double surprise ending [which will not be divulged here].)
   Could young Mordecai, with his literary integrity, come up
with such sleazy material? I doubted it. But my friend Brian
Moore, ever practical, had no such scruples. I frequently met him
for lunch, where we discussed the art, architecture and con-
trivance of the O. Henry story. He too was selling to *Weekend*,
deft items like "A Question of Command" and "Confession Four."

Brian was still working at the *Gazette*, but he was dreaming of the day when he could break loose and earn his living as a free-lancer, with time enough to attempt some serious fiction. He was often down at the waterfront, covering the comings and goings of passenger liners that plied the Atlantic, and the waterfront was not too far from a restaurant called The Brokers, where we would meet for lunch to devour their celebrated lamb chops *Champvallon*. The Brokers, a stone's throw from *Weekend*, was on St. François Xavier Street, across from the Montreal Stock Exchange. In the heady 1950s, this area was still the financial heart of Canada, headquarters of the great banks, insurance companies, brokerages and enterprises of every description. St. James Street was the Wall Street of Canada, and no one could have dreamed that one day it would be renamed Rue St. Jacques, and that it would tumble into a steep decline.

Lunching at The Brokers, Brian Moore and I would be sur-rounded by money-men discussing stocks, bonds and ingenious swindles. It was an appropriate place for us to plot ways to get that short-story $250 from *Weekend* as often as possible.

4 rue brémontier

paris 17

november 14

WILLIAM, MON CHUM: i'm running into all kinds of snags in my work and love life. . . . a big problem is that i have fallen out with Helen. (she drops round almost every day.) there is also ulla. and sanki. (i hope this doesn't sound just a bit crude but i feel depressed and i might as well take it out on someone who cant hit back for a week.). . . . can you get the man with the golden arm by nelson algren? i read a book of his short stories – neon wilderness – (i'll send it to you) – and i think he is a terrific boy. what's this book by james jones? any good? i hear it's nothing more than ballyhoo and sex. is that right?

everybody tells me that i'm one of the only boys with IT in paris but nobody wants to print my stuff. . . . that's all. all the best. write soon.

Mordy

231 St. James Street West
Montreal

December 12

Dear Mordecai –
Sorry to hear that the Helen passion has cooled. Do you mean we wasted all that time in Barcelona teaching her the niceties of the Spanish language? I liked the way she barked "Venga!" at waiters and hoped you could bring her home so she could do it in the Ritz. Or will you be seeing much of the Ritz when you come back? Don't be silly by coming home too soon. You'll be bored stiff. Stay where you are and soak it up. Even if you have to look for a job or something drastic like that. . . .

You probably know all the throbbing news of Montreal: how Duplessis has closed the gaming houses and insists that pubs close at 2 a.m. (10 p.m. on New Year's Eve). Alex is getting married next month to a girl called Gloria and is going through that routine of buying furniture and looking at chintz. He's enjoying it immensely.

I remember you asking me, a letter or so ago, what I thought of Mavis's NYorker story, saying you thought it trivial. Don't agree. The theme wasn't epic (they seldom are in the NYorker) but the writing was a beautiful piece of craftsmanship. She has a terrific understanding of the language and a definite talent. Maybe someday she'll get around to territory that isn't so Elizabeth Bowenish.

A friend of mine, Harold Dingman, quit last week in Vancouver, with sleeping pills. Age 36. I haven't heard anything that made me feel so bad for a long time. He was a brilliant newspaperman, city editor of the *Herald*, Ottawa columnist, etc. He was a poor, troubled, talented bastard – lost the battle of the bottle. Everybody tried one time or another to help him. I even wrote his column for him once or twice when he couldn't do it himself. Then, today, CP carried a few lines about the sudden death of another Montreal newspaper alumnus – June McFeely. A good girl and a friend of mine. 28. Married and separated and never particularly happy. Jesus, Mordy, you don't know how depressing it is when these things start happening to people you know.

I have no other cheery tidings. Christmas is approaching. Whoops. The cocktail party season. Skiing soon, and that's about all I'm looking forward to. Black Horse Brewery wants me to do its skicast, but I don't know whether I'll take it on. I'd rather ski in my spare time, or drink or read, than pontificate about idiot athletes on the radio. Write soon and copiously. All the best.

Bill

P.S. Is Cora Vaucaire still singing at l'Échelle Jacob? Sentimental Prévert junk that I love. And how are the guitars at the Catalan?

5

A letter from Brian Moore:

Splendid Hotel
Port-au-Prince, Haiti

Saturday night

Dear Palmiro Vicarion,
First of all, there is absolutely no exaggeration in anything I
say. It is all TRUE. Jackie and I have just crept up to bed in our
huge French colonial suite and the memsahib is now among
the bougainvilleas on one of our two balconies while I pen this
note to the accompaniment of a voodoo drum in the hills,
cicadas, screeching animals (unidentified), the scutter of rats
on the driveway by the swimming pool, the chant of mosquitoes
and the wail (incessant) of motor car horns, which is the
predominant sound of the island.

    Today we had a quick drive from airport to hotel through
incredible squalor, huts, women on donkeys, women with
4-ton loads on their heads, a general run-downness and a
noticeable predominance of black chaps. Everyone speaks
unintelligible French. The current is A.C. 110, whatever that
means, so be assured that your electric razor will work here.

From prices here I feel convinced that this is "The Riviera of
the West Indies" (as advertised), but any other resemblance is
purely coincidental.

Room double is $20 a day with meals. However after an
amiable chat with Mr. Alberti, hotel manager, I was promised
an unspecified reduction. . . . Rum and soda is 25 cents. All
other drinks dear. Cigarettes 35 cents, so buy us a carton in
Miami when you come. The temperature: I changed shirts
three times today and showered twice. It is HOT. Bugs aren't
bad. "Les fourmis, vous savez." Seems I am at home. "Vous êtes
chez vous ici," says Madame Maria Fraenckel, hotel proprietor.

Very Maughamish all this "Riviera of the West Indies" stuff.
In fact I am being reminded of Maugham all the time here. But
also of Saunders of the River. Must close now. Those voodoo
drums are getting closer.

Onesime Gagnon

Forty years hence, memories of Haiti would serve Brian well
in the writing of No Other Life, his eighteenth novel, set on a
fictitious French-speaking island in the Caribbean. But now, in
the summer of 1952, he was not researching, he was simply
having a vacation. In a few days I was to fly to Haiti to join Brian,
Jackie and my girlfriend, Betty. But I never showed up. At the
last minute I changed my mind, incurring great wrath from
the three of them. But I had decided, despite the lure of those
voodoo drums, that it would be far more interesting to spend my
vacation in white-bread Toronto.

I had learned that a two-week course in television script
writing was being offered by the University of Toronto, in collab-
oration with the CBC. Television had been flourishing in the
United States for years, but was late in coming to Canada.
However, it would finally get underway – at least in Montreal
and Toronto – in less than three months' time, in September
1952. I was becoming bored at Weekend and perhaps a career in

this new medium would be more interesting. My application for the course was accepted and I took up residence at the Frontenac Arms Hotel on Jarvis Street. While my indolent comrades would be sipping rum and soda around the swimming pool in Port-au-Prince, I would be bettering myself at the university. Surely this was justification enough for my treachery in not showing up to join them.

The syllabus for the course was impressive, promising to cover twenty different topics, from social, economic and ethical considerations in television production to writing "comedy and gags." We would be taught the principles of structure, plot and character in the one-hour play, as well as the requirements of documentary, educational and children's programming. The principles and techniques of making commercials would be revealed to us. It was a formidable menu for a two-week course, with only five hours a day in the classroom.

Our course director and principal lecturer was Gilbert Seldes, a man from New York with an impressive résumé. In his time he had been associate editor of *Colliers* magazine, writer of radio plays, author of books like *The Seven Lively Arts*. But above all, he had been director of the television program department of CBS in New York, responsible for more than fifteen hundred hours of programming. He was a serious man, and at the outset he warned us that if the new medium came to be "filled with junk," we ourselves – the all-important writers – would be to blame. And he went on to scold major playwrights (none of whom were taking this course) for not doing their duty, for being contemptuous of radio and television.

After this idealistic prologue, Seldes quickly got down to the nuts and bolts. As in radio, daytime soap operas would be an inevitable feature of television, so we ought to know how to write them. Remember, he advised, that women characters in the soaps had to be strong and men weak. Action had to be stretched out, and in a serial there didn't have to be more than two or three major events in a year. A man standing on a high ledge, preparing to jump, should be kept standing there for at least ten days of programs.

Seldes was particularly sound when it came to the techniques of the drama, drawing his illustrations from Wilde, Molière and Odets. But ever mindful that we were writing for live television, he warned us to structure our scripts so as to give offstage actors enough time to change their costumes if necessary. And he told us how to specify reaction shots to highlight sudden emotion. He wanted us to be detailed in our scripts, emphasizing what every screenwriter knows – that the director is a prime ignoramus.

Seldes was most intriguing in answering that eternal question: What does the audience want? They want what we give them, he said. There was no public demand for radio before it was invented, or for television or for soap operas or for any great new play. But once it is given to the public, they want it. In the economics of entertainment, supply precedes demand. As for us would-be scripters, he was most encouraging. The field was wide open; in all New York there were no more than twenty competent television writers. At lunch, and at drinks after class, my classmates and I were brimming with enthusiasm and grandiose schemes. We were going to be in at the very beginning, and we would be heard from.

A bright image on a television screen: that's what the future looked like to me in mid-1952. But from the very beginning of the year, over in Paris, there were many clouds on the horizon for my friend Richler. He was impoverished to the point where he felt he would have to get a job when he got back to Montreal, later in the year.

Paris

Jan. 11. 1952

DEAR BILL: i'm pretty damn broke, bill; can you lend me 50 bucks? if not now, soon? i'll pay you back soon after i get home in early sept. i wouldn't ask if it wasn't pretty bad. and another thing: would you keep yr. eyes and ears open for a passable job for me when i get back? anything not too poorly paid and not too demoralizing. . . . does weekend need a proofreader or something? the thought of driving a cab isn't too appealing. if you hear of an opening anywhere put in a plug, will you? this book i'm working on may very well be published (artistically the "gang" swears it merits it) but even then i'll need a job for at least a year. (christ i just realized you're about the only friend i have who really works! how do you like it? why not write a book about it?) i guess that's about all for now, bill. keep well. work good. write soon (especially as regards the fifty). all the best.

Mordy

But within a month Mordecai's mood and fortunes had improved. He had found his way to England, to Cambridge, and was staying with our mutual Montreal friend Sidney Lamb, who was studying at the university.

Cambridge

Feb. 9

DEAR BILL W. i got your $25 okay, thanx, and it came just when i needed it. almost makes a feller believe in gawd again. sid is fine. he commands something of a harem here. i'm working vurry vurry hard and everyone including m'self seems to be thinking i'm writing a damn good book. new story [magazine] will probably run something of it in the spring. . . . also – just to show you that i'm comin up in this world – i'm gonna have tea with e.m. forster next week. and 'ere's a forster story for you (not that i'm saying he's old or senile or something. . . .)

there's a u.s. jet station near here. almost daily the peace-loving jets of america zoom and kazoom about in the cambridge skies. they make a lot of noise. forster likes quiet.

so whenever the planes come over the old boy picks up his binoculars and dashes out on his balcony. he takes down the wing numbers of the planes and sends a letter of complaint to the air ministry. some people say he just sits and sits on his balcony, binoculars on his lap, waiting for the planes to come over.

work six-eight hours a day. pretty tired when it comes time to get letters off. so excuse this if it seems to be put together a little sloppily. anything i can do for you in england???? books?? etc?? the very best. Please write.

Mordy

Montreal

March 15

Dear Mordy –
I'm glad to hear you're working hard. Where does the novel stand now? Hope you're including a few Good People in the cast, not just those sybaritic, syphilitic, nymphomaniacal, alcoholic, venal, schizophrenic, unchristian boys and girls. . . .

Got any good O. Henry plots that I can grind into stories? I pay a cent a thought. I'm also involved in another kind of chicanery these days. Once a week my voice fans out via CBC International to Latin America with a chatty little item called Letter From Canada. I weave a magic loom of bits of gossip culled from the newspapers that is supposed to solace expatriate Canadians who are suffering in Rio and Buenos Aires. It's crazy but it makes a few bucks (which disappear I know not where).

Have you read A. M. Klein's book The Second Scroll? It's really magnificent. Wonderful part about how the ceiling of the Sistine Chapel should be whitewashed and covered with mazzuzoth (is that the word?). You should look for it in the library there, or perhaps I'll send you a copy.

I'm trying to further my knowledge of the toros by reading
Blood and Sand by Ibáñez, but the writing seems to me to be so
lousy that I can hardly go on. Death in the Afternoon recently
got me more interested in the subject than I could become
actually watching those bullfights in Spain. If you get to Spain
again perhaps you can do some shopping for me. I just had
those two old bullfight prints I bought in Barcelona framed and
they look terrific: red frames, grey mats. I'd like some more.
Also several flamenco records. The ones I brought back have
made me a minor hero in the cause of folklore in certain
recherché circles. . . . I'm now a complete Spainophile
(Iberiophile? Espanophile?).

Yes, there is a book you can get me in England. The Film
Till Now by Paul Rotha It's a big bloody book and costs $12 in
the U.S. and God knows how much here, if available. But it's
50 bob in England, still expensive but a substantial saving. Of
course what I would like would be a second-hand copy, but if
you don't come across that I'm willing to pay for a new one.

Be happy, use lots of wax when you ski, let me know if you're
starving and write this very minute. L&K,

                    Bill

I'd always enjoyed movies, but in the last few years I'd become
completely engrossed. I absolutely had to have that recently published Rotha book, said by reviewers to be the best cinema
history yet to appear. I had to quickly become very knowledge-
able as I was now a programmer, selecting films and having them
screened at the Montreal Men's Press Club, which had now
moved to the Mount Royal Hotel. The directors of the club had
been dubious when I first broached the idea, but I eventually persuaded them that we ought to offer members more than just
booze, gossip and poker in the back room. Sunday night would
be Movie Night and wives and girlfriends would be welcome.
We'd get a 16-millimetre projector and the bar would do a
roaring business while reels were being changed. We'd rent

recent films from local distributors and classics from the Museum of Modern Art's library in New York.

Movie Night's first season was a great success and would be repeated during the next few years. Besides selecting the films, with the aid of a committee, I was responsible for writing descriptions for the season's program, with entries like this:

> KIND HEARTS AND CORONETS (Britain, 1949) Alec Guinness plays eight parts with restraint and shows his power as a character actor in this comedy of murder.
>
> KAMERADSCHAFT (Germany, 1931) This film classic deals with a mining disaster on the Franco-German border. Founded on fact, it tells how the miners on the German side go to the rescue of their French comrades. An exceptionally moving film. English subtitles.
>
> ON THE TOWN (U.S.A., 1949) The musical adventures of three sailors on leave in New York and the girls they meet. With Gene Kelly and Frank Sinatra.
>
> LE QUAI DES BRUMES (France, 1937) The great acting of Michele Morgan, Michel Simon, Pierre Brasseur and Jean Gabin is matched by great dialogue in this Marcel Carné masterpiece. Though a murder mystery has to have sordid characters, this one is noted for the sensitivity and tenderness of its portrayal of human qualities.

I could never pass up a film with Jean Gabin in it. No other actor could apply Camembert to a baguette and eat it the way Gabin did. In Hollywood films, no actors ever ate; they might sit around the dinner table and argue, but they never conveyed food to their mouths and chewed it. But eating scenes, in those years, were among the glories of the French cinema. What a pleasure it was, and how hungry-making it was, to watch the French chew with relish, all the time talking volubly and gesticulating with their forks. It was an art, and Jean Gabin was its greatest practitioner, especially when biting into a juicy *saucisse de Montbéliard*.

~

cambridge, march 21

CHER BILL W: was up to london last wkend . . . saw sadlers wells
do sleeping beauty in covent garden. also lyric revue & a japanese
movie. AND EVER SINCE I GOT BACK I HAVEN'T BEEN ABLE TO
DO A STITCH OF GODDAM WORK!!! . . . book was coming along
grand until i set out for london. . . . big do on tonight and i'm
just in the mood to get crazy drunk. feel completely sterile,
impotent, hopeless. oooooh dos arty blues!! papa is sending me
$40 a month now!! also buying me a ticket home (be back sept.
i expect). should i get married? she's a lovely swede. no, i don't
think so. abt. helen, we correspond, but all more palsy than
passion. dont mind explaining why but not in a letter. over
scotches in mtl. sometime, eh??? how abt. you? getting married?
i won't have my book – THE JEW OF VALENCIA – finished until
late summer at best. . . . maclennan's got a bk. coming out here –
each man's son – but i can do without reading it thank you very
much indeed. . . . that's all for now. write.

Mordy

By May Mordecai was in Paris again and he reported that "the
town is swarming with amerkun tourists – wide-eyed, big-assed
idiots from hollowhead, illinois; sophisticated career bitches
from nyork and a whole flock of dungareed googoo-eyed lady-
birds from the village." Again in his letters he spoke of his plans
to come back to Montreal in the fall, and of his need to find a
job. ". . . talking abt jobs," he wrote, "i'd appreciate it if you'd tell
everyone what a great guy i am. i still haven't got a clue abt a job.
have you any ideas?"

By the end of May, he was able to write that he had finished
his book – or at least finished a draft that still needed a good deal
of work.

Paris, May 26

BILL, MON VIEUX: yr. letter (long awaited) was welcome. . . .
looking forward (really) to seeing you when i get back. lots of
things i'd like to talk abt. that just go flat in a letter. saw
rashomon, but i failed to understand it. do you think the whole
film might be a trick?? eric says mavis is in italia, also that (he
thks.) she has sold the Nyorker again.

   i have finished my bk. and i intend to spend most of the
summer re-writing, re-organizing, etc. . . . (i really appreciate yr.
interest in my work, but i prefer not to send out chapters now.
when i get home, tho, i would like you to read the bk. as a
unit.) mike sayers, former editor with faber & faber, pal of eliot
and pound, has made some wonderful suggestions abt. the book.

   i touched up the schoolteacher story and another. atlantic
and harpers, mademoiselle, give me the same fuckingold
runaround – "gee yre great kid! you really shd. be published.
like yr. stuff swell, BUT . . . signed fiction editor. i'm sending off
a couple of stories to rome, they pay well. (mike knows the
editor and i can mention his name) SO MUCH OF IT IS
CONNECTIONS, BILL, AND IT MAKES ME WANT TO PUKE.

   QUARTIER GOSSIP: a guy named dave is gunning for me in
montparnasse. whenever he is drunk (which is always) he takes
to waving around a .45 and asking for this sonofabitch richler.
he swears that he'll get me. i laid his woman, or something.
(dramatic, eh wot?). . . . keep in touch.

                         Mordy

   At those Sunday-night screenings in the Press Club we were
watching John Wayne being heroic in *Stagecoach* and Greta
Garbo being beautiful in *Ninotchka*, both films of 1939. And we
were offering great European actors as well as the more obvious
American stars. We had Peter Lorre to disturb us as the terrified
murderer in *M* (1931), Emil Jannings to elicit our tears in *The
Last Laugh* (1924), where he is the proud hotel doorman suddenly

reduced to being a lavatory attendant, and the incomparable Raimu to make us laugh in *La Femme du Boulanger* (1938), where he portrays the village baker whose wife has run away with a younger man.

Our Press Club was now part of the film society movement, which was flourishing in Canada in the early 1950s. In church basements and auditoriums across the country 16-millimetre projectors would be set up to screen the classics, as well as obscure "art films" that would never reach the commercial movie houses. The screenings were often followed by heated discussions. People who ran film societies exchanged information as to which were the best new films to show and where they could be rented. At one point I attended a convention of film society officers in Ottawa, to which thirty-eight societies had been invited. The talk at meetings of this kind could be very esoteric, there being no snobbery like film snobbery, and to hold my own I was forced to subscribe to *Sight and Sound*, the learned British cinema magazine, and to buy books like *Film Form* by Sergei Eisenstein. From Eisenstein, the great Soviet director, I learned some of the essentials of how to make movies. Before reading him I had never realized that "composition takes the structural elements of the portrayed phenomena and from these composes its canon for building the containing work."

Unhinged by such heady stuff, I persuaded my Press Club committee to let me bring in some far-out short films of the French avant-garde of the 1920s. Among these were *Entr'acte*, René Clair's Dadaist effusion, and Kirsanov's *Ménilmontant*, a bewilderment celebrated mainly for having been made at a minimum of expense. Then there was Fernand Léger's *Ballet Mécanique*, with its mishmash of faces and bits of faces, and pots and pans swinging through space, some of the shots in negative.

A few of my fellow journalists were quite rude in expressing their displeasure at my choice of this highbrow program, but most, especially those accompanied by their wives, simply said that it was all "very interesting." Thus the emperor's-new-clothes syndrome, always protective of modern art, came to my rescue.

Meanwhile, in France, Mordecai had finished writing his novel and was preparing to return to Montreal, where I'd been scouting for a job for him and may have found him one in radio.

tourrette-sur-loup

aug. 15

QUERIDO GUILLERMO MIO – christ, it's hot! but now that i'm sober i must answer your letter. i've been fornicating somewhat earnestly since i finished my book, abt a wk ago. kina and others have been around to lend a helping hand. . . .

i'm sending my lousy book off today. (and really, that's just the way i feel abt it right now!) temko has written bobbs-merrill and they're expecting it.

the job, bill, interests me tremendously! can you send me more information??? also, do you think i have a decent chance of making it??? (you know, of course, that i've never worked in radio). what do you think my pay would amount to??? and thanks, thanks loads, for going to the trouble! – 'you're a bloody good friend,' he said, smiling shyly, as sentiment embarrassed him.

i'll be home sept 13 . . . in some ways it will be nice to see montreal again . . . i wonder, tho, how long the charm will hold out.

see you soon. all the best.

Mordy

While Mordecai seemed headed toward radio, I was determined to get a foothold in the new medium of television. After taking that TV writing course in Toronto, I presented CBC Montreal with several ideas for programs, where I would be the writer. Finally one idea was accepted – the one that interested me least. And in December, only three months after the inauguration of television in Montreal, I was in a CBFT studio, in the old Ford Hotel on Dorchester Street, introducing *Le Club de Ski* – a bilingual program. Once again what I knew about skiing was my entrée into a desirable activity, although I would by now have preferred to be writing about anything other than skiing.

But still, I was learning things. With a CBC cameraman I was out on the Laurentian hills directing the filming of our ski instructor, Louis de Passille. And for Louis, I was writing the essential words: "This stemming, the releasing of the lower edge, will cause the skis to seek the fall line of the hill. . . ." Later, in the studio, I would read narration for action films from the world's ski centres and supervise the weather and snow report for the weekend. At first the television studio was a stimulating place, what with the menacing cameras and other paraphernalia, but as the winter progressed I gradually became bored. Although I realized that there were greater things that could be achieved in television – drama, for instance – I gradually came to the conclusion that this was not the medium for me.

Perhaps I was too easily bored. *Weekend* was certainly boring me by now and in the office I was spending an increasing amount of time writing poems about members of the staff. (Oh, Hughie is a stewey prune/ And Craig's a vague old soul,/ While thirsty Hersey hurls around/ Then hides inside his hole.)

Since bygone university days, I no longer sat with friends and discussed the meaning of life. Was the avoidance of boredom life's real goal, as far as I was concerned? It was about this time that I developed a long-standing feeling of envy for Mordecai. Not only was he fornicating more earnestly than I was, he had a clear, overwhelming *goal* – to write a great novel. Was my puny goal nothing more than to "live an interesting life"?

In 1952 I still had a few friends, like dear old Jack Lieber, who, at the time, were dedicated to the betterment of mankind, mainly through methods laid down by Marx and Lenin. But my suspicions about Uncle Joe Stalin, and my inability to believe in the perfectibility of human nature, kept me from joining them on the barricades. But perhaps I *should* listen to my mother's advice and not be "so selfish." Perhaps I should hearken to W. H. Auden's dictum: "We are here on earth to do good to others." But, Auden added, "What the others are here for, I do not know."

6

I had not seen Mordecai in more than a year, since my sojourn at his house in Spain. Now, as he arrived in Montreal, I was pleased to see that he had dispensed with his beard – not a bad idea, in those conservative days, for a young man looking for a job. As for me, I'd long since gotten rid of my moustache. It had been a blond moustache, a rarity in Spain that aroused amusement and earned me the nickname Rubio (Blondie).

Mordecai soon found his job, as a writer in the CBC's newsroom. After work he would join me at the bar in the Press Club, and it was here that I introduced him to Brian Moore. They were to become good friends and, with Jackie, we would have long, argumentative dinners in restaurants and in the Moores' apartment on St. Catherine Street in Westmount.

But for Mordecai there was an underlying discontent and nervousness. The manuscript of his novel *The Acrobats* (this was its final title, superseding tentative titles like *The Jew of Valencia*) was making the rounds of publishers in New York and was being turned down by one after another – six or seven of them in all. But after six months, good news suddenly came from London. The book had been accepted by André Deutsch, a relatively new publisher who already had an impressive list.

Mordecai, delighted, left his CBC job after about six months to devote himself again to writing short stories and to think about a second novel. He would need photos now, for publicity purposes when his novel was published, and so I took him round to David

Bier's studio. Bier, an old school friend of mine, took some fine pictures of the young author looking earnest and thoughtful.

Finally, after a year in Montreal, Mordecai went back to London to immerse himself in the literary scene. With him, on the Cunard liner *Samaria*, was Cathy Boudreau, a young woman he had met in Montreal and who would become his first wife. Once he was re-established in London, my correspondence with him resumed and I was pleased to see, in his first letter, that he had finally discovered the shift key on his typewriter so that proper nouns were now being capitalized.

Friday, Sept. 11, 1953

BILL, MY OLD: We, three of us, live in a flat on Kings Road in Chelsea. There is Cathy, Florrie McDonald and myself. Our bus stop is called The World's End after the pub two blocks down the street. Two blocks northwards is the Thames.

I saw Joyce Weiner [his new agent] again a couple of days ago. She told me that a big man, I forget his name, from 20th Century Fox was in to see her and asked if she had any Canadian scripts – which are apparently in big demand. I immediately told her abt you, and abt the script you outlined to me one night in the Press Club – remember? the man walking the streets of Mtl. . . . Look, man, wd you take 2 days off from drinking & lovemaking & ideamaking and outline that script? You cd send the copy to me or – if you like – directly to Joyce Weiner. I told her I wd ask you for it. (Fox is particularly interested in a script that wd go over in cinemascope.) . . .

André Deutsch and Joyce have both been extraordinarily kind and encouraging. D thks that a U.S. publisher for my book is a cinch within the next 6 mos while J. W. shows tempered optimism. . . . I won't bore you with details but Mr. D is working hard on it and he and Walter Allen think I'm one big writer, altho the bk is definitely a "first novel." . . . (You know what Morrow said abt the bk??? "All women and wine but no song.")

The bk goes into production within 2 wks, proofs early in Dec. (will send you one). I met the guy who'll do my jacket.

There will be several informal luncheons and drink sessions within the next 3 wks and I'm to meet almost everybody. I sipped a few glasses of sherry with E. M. Forster last week and he'll look at the proofs – voluntarily. Spender is starting a new mag, Encounter, which is supposed to be in the Horizon tradition. . . . Lehmann is also starting a mag. . . .

Will you ask Dave Bier to crop that pic of me smoking and send me 4 airmail. This is imp! And look, I want two more prints of "young author with hand cupped on his chin, having a think." Will you ask Brian what happened to the pics he took? (My public, man, my public!)

All the best,
Mort

Weekend Mag,

Tuesday, Sept. 15

Dear Mort –
Copy boy left at noon for Dave Bier's. It is now 4 o'clock and he's not back yet. The lad has no sense of mission. So I'll write now and send you the pix tomorrow, with the negatives. Thus you will be able to have the next few gross printed over there. What the hell are you doing, anyway, sticking them on poles?

Re the script for Joyce Weiner, I appreciate your intentions, but I don't think anything could come of it except make Miss W. look foolish and waste 20th Century Fox's time, which is worth $1,000 a second. I still think it's a good idea for a film, but not for Hollywood and not for Cinemascope. What I had in mind is a short, half-hour deal realistically done in the style of Palardy's L'Homme aux Oiseaux. The Film Board would probably be the best producer, and someday I'm going to talk to them about it – when I get some more footing in "the medium."

Now you can do me a great favour next time you're in the International Bookshop, 52 Charing Cross Road. Please get me The Technique of Film Editing by Karel Reisz (30 shillings). Also a copy of Les Cahiers du Cinema, the French magazine.

Moore was up to see Dr. Cone today for the big checkup. He had his head tapped and Cone said the case was closed. Nothing to worry about. But he advised little or no alcohol, which there is reason to believe is the good doctor's own private temperance crusade.

All your news sounds good and heartening. Who's this Florrie McDonald? La vie en trois, eh? Ho ho ho. And how's Cathy? My warmest regards. Montreal is dull and anesthetic. Will write you later about my hopes, ambitions, feelings. Have none today.

Bill

Dr. William Cone was the eminent neurosurgeon who had looked after Brian after Brian's dreadful accident. He had been swimming, alone, in a Laurentian lake when he was hit on the head by a motorboat. He was rushed to the Montreal Neurological Institute, where it was discovered he had sustained six skull fractures. He had lost the power of speech and, of course, the ability to write. But he was being treated in a renowned research hospital and after some six weeks his faculties were restored. And he could go home.

It had been work, the writing of his first serious novel, that had taken him, alone, to Fourteen Island Lake in the summer of 1953. Here, in a borrowed cottage, he would find the solitude he needed to start writing Judith Hearne, work that was violently interrupted by a motorboat. But by mid-September he was writing again.

In November, Jackie gave birth to their son, Michael. I went down to the Montreal City Hall with Brian to register the birth. There, on the clerk's desk, were two thick ledgers, one marked "Catholics" and the other "Protestants."

"Which one?" the clerk asked.

"Neither," said Brian.

"Jewish?" said the clerk, reaching into a drawer.

"No," said Brian. "I have no religion."

Frowning, the clerk got up and disappeared into a back room. After a while he emerged, blowing the dust off a very thin ledger. It was marked "Pagans." And it was in this ledger that Michael Moore's birth was registered, signed by his father and witnessed by me. Subsequently Brian asked me to be not Michael's godfather but his mammonfather.

Writing to Brian and Jackie, Mordecai urged them to come to London and visit them, and to bring the baby. "There were many new-born babies on our ship," he wrote. "A few of them were stepped on and squashed, but most of them made the trip okay."

Brian was able to finish the first draft of *Judith Hearne* by Christmas and the final draft by early the next spring. But in London, Mordecai was having less success in trying to forge ahead with his second novel:

sat. jan. 29. 54

Idling abt impotently on a cold night feeling damn depressed. . . . Just happened to pick up yr most recent letter and I thought I'd write. . . .

The book has slowed down on me. These things happen. I know they happen. But each day you sit vacant writing nothing but still a prisoner to the typewriter – each day like that is a special kind of hell. Questions come to you making small wounds. Why are you making this book? Does it matter? Do you believe in it? That's when you get up and have a cigarette and/or a cup of coffee. Then, a short walk. Then

another cigarette. You pick up things. Books you can't
concentrate on. Newspapers you can't understand. So on. Out
again. Up to wander around the neighbourhood bookshops. So
many books! Who – how – why are they written?? Back to the
typewriter. You start again at the beginning, reading from
P.1. . . . I thk art or attempts at art are born of despair. That,
more than vanity or intimations of mortality.

I thk in writing there is no such thing as success. (I don't
have to point out that publication is just a social hurdle and
has nothing whatsoever to do with being a writer.) All writing
is different levels of failure. Nothing really comes off. No.
That's not exactly what I mean. . . .

What I mean is once you go after a truth you can get only so
close – closer yesterday than today, next week than this week,
BUT never there – never the orgasm. Hope of excitement,
sometimes even the excitement itself (inspiration?) but never
the culminating death/birth. . . .

Before I had my first bk accepted and until I began work on
my second I wanted to be famous. Have position. Anecdotes
told abt me. And the rest of it. But now I do not want or think
abt these things very much. They are trifling in themselves.
And, worse still, there is no fame big enough or money bribery
enough to compensate for the pain that goes into the making
of a novel. (Even the mixed joy of publication is paltry, aspirins
for cancer.) So why do I write? I really don't know. I can thk of
a lot of reasons but all of them wd be "thought up" and only
partly true. Nearest I can come to it is "I have to."

Elsewhere: Have ordered René Clair's book for you, shd get
it on Tuesday. Was out drinking the other night with Louis
MacNeice and wife, Kathleen Thomas and John Davenport.
Mrs. Thomas is drinking like a fish. Has been ever since Dylan
died. MacNeice says André Deutsch and Hart-Davis best
post-war publishers. Read Orwell's Homage to Catalonia
tonight. A man of commendable rages. I'll send it on if you
haven't read it. There was a Cocteau festival at Everyman
[cinema] in Hampstead recently. That man is a fraud of frauds.

A poseur of the worst order. Marx Brothers festival begins on Monday (best news in wks!). . . .

Talking abt obscenities, there was a big fuss here. Printers refused to print [*The Acrobats*]. They got a lawyer. André got a lawyer. Richler was called in, charged with obscenity, blasphemy, and worse. Bang bang bang. Several minor changes have been made; e.g., tits to breasts, kick you in the balls to kick you where it hurts, bloody christ to christ. Nothing important really. All most amusing.

Write.

Mort

～

An article I wrote for *Weekend* in 1954 was entitled "The Movie Company You Own," and it was the beginning of my lifelong admiration for the National Film Board and my eventual involvement in its work. Like many Canadians I knew little about this peculiar government agency and what I discovered in Ottawa, in the shabby converted sawmill that housed the NFB, was little short of astonishing.

To start with, they showed me *Neighbours*, a nine-minute film about the perils of greed, made with a brand-new and startling camera technique. Those were the days when movie theatres would show "shorts" before the main feature, but Canadian distributors turned thumbs down on *Neighbours*; Canadian audiences, they figured, would much rather see the usual kind of shorts, like water-skiing in Florida or West Point cadets on parade. "Then, a few weeks later," I wrote, "*Neighbours* won Hollywood's coveted Academy Award Oscar as the best short film of the year. Red-faced, the distributors decided to show it after all."

The NFB's mandate, from the government, was to "interpret Canada to Canadians and to other nations," and for some sophisticates unfamiliar with NFB productions, this meant earnest, dreary documentaries about harvesting wheat and chopping down trees. But the films I was shown in Ottawa were a far cry from that stereotype. *L'Homme aux Oiseaux* was about an unemployed man wandering the streets of Quebec City in search of a job, capturing as never before the flavour of life in the old city. It was humorous and entertaining. *Farewell Oak Street* dramatized the sordid lives of a family living in a Toronto slum. *Angotee* showed us the birth of an Inuit baby in an igloo.

I wrote about these and other NFB films with admiration – and indignation. Why were they so much better known abroad, where they kept winning prizes, than in Canada? At the same time I wondered whether the NFB might not be my ticket out of *Weekend*. Could they use a writer like me? It would be more interesting to work on films like these than on gripping magazine yarns like "Yo-Yo Contest – Competition Is Strenuous in City Championships."

While I was deciding how to approach the NFB, Brian Moore was on his way to Europe, on a ship where he seemed to have stumbled into a nest of singing birds:

ss Maasdam

March 24, 1954

Dear Sir,
On this excellent ship we have a large quota of painters, budding and semi-established authors, one theatre director, a translator quote "of writers of the past and I can truly say I have caught their flavour," one fake Russian countess who sings "Black Eyes," a Mavisish young woman who has written a novel and is taking the boat to show it to T. S. Eliot (he doesn't know she's coming), several interesting and wealthy cripples with their attendants, an Israeli bassoonist who says Denver is God's Own Country, an American brewery worker who is fleeing McCarthyism, which he says is turning America into a crock of shit, a contingent of Latter Day Saints and one pocket book author [referring, of course, to himself]. . . .

Apparently pocket booking is creeping into high places. Gore Vidal, noted young queer author, is writing under the name of Joseph Box. His latest is Death in the Fifth Position. Fellowships ranging from the Tiffany, the Guggenheim, the Fullbright to very small ones are under heavy and constant discussion, we having many semi-finalists aboard. Mostly painters. Trouble is this year juries were apparently "conventional abstract," which left no room for offerings which were subdued abstract, fantasy abstract or abstract advanced. Very tragic.

Many points in Mordecai's vocabulary have been revealed to me as the jargon. All unliked artists are "a trick." Anything unliked is "a trick." People who dance or play bingo are "hilarious." People who drink heavily in the bar are "tourists." There are on the "hilarious" side several American girls of incredible ugliness who are headed for bike trips around Europe. Budget $3 a day. Also some former soldiers going over to Germany where things are well run and you can reach all levels of sexual satisfaction for $5 a night.

Amitiés,
Wade Miller

Brian was on his way to Spain, with stops en route in London and Belfast, his native city, where he would see his mother, sisters and a brother for the first time in six years. In Spain, where he would later be joined by Jackie, he would find a change of scene and solitude conducive to doing some writing. With *Judith Hearne* completed and his New York agent showing the manuscript to publishers, Brian would now get started on his second serious novel, as well as quickly knocking out another of his pocket-book thrillers. With the new baby in the family, it was imperative that he replenish his finances by doing some commercial work. And Spain was the place to do it, Mordecai and I having assured him that it was a splendid place to be and, perhaps thanks to the Franco dictatorship, very cheap.

Brian's next letter to me, dated March 31, was from Belfast:

Dear Marco Polo:

Herewith from the safety of the Irish shores is a scattered report
on the London travels. . . . Mordecai and Cathy are housed in a
basement flat, warm, dingy and not at all uncomfortable in
Hampstead, about 100 yards from the place where I lay in sin
ten years ago with my young Komsomol girlfriend. So the area
and ambience is familiar to me. . . .

Life with Mordecai in Soho and other outposts during the
period I stayed there remains in my mind a confused jumble of
pubs. Thursday to Monday, in and out of the Mandrake, a club
with bearded Britishers, black Little Englanders, all sorts of – to
me – phony lit people. Then the York Minster, other pubs too
numerous to mention, all very jolly, very British. A pity I
cannot love the British. However I liked London fine this time,
mostly by strictly eschewing the numerous second-rate plays
which are on there. Tonight I go to see a great play. Saint Joan.
With the Gate Theatre at the helm, playing in Belfast. . . .

Leave for Spain next Tuesday probably.

Vasco da Gama

Brian's first stop in Spain was Barcelona, where he checked
into one of the cheapest hotels in town. Here large lunches and
abundant wine were militating against his getting any work done.
"I now understand why the siesta," his Barcelona letter said. "The
way things go here I seem to be always asleep. Takes an awful lot
of café con leche to keep me going. I have been trying to struggle
my way through the first chapter of another pocket book. Terrible
going. Barcelona is not conducive to work. I can hear my neighbour's every bowel movement in the hotel and each time I hit the
keys he groans. So very little writing has been done. I have had to
content myself with writing it in my head, a dangerous procedure
as Pernod tends to dull this type of prose. . . . Today I went round
to the cathedral. Magnifico. . . . Everything terribly sombre. Lent.

Preparing for the great orgy. The Spaniards always liked the crucifixion part of Christianity. . . ."

Brian's next stop was Majorca, an island not far from Ibiza, where he found another hotel where he could live for less than three dollars a day. Here he was determined to buckle down to work, having set himself the task of writing a commercial thriller in the genre of James M. Cain, the American writer whose pseudo-Hemingway style produced such page-turners as *The Postman Always Rings Twice.*

Hotel Suizo, Palma

April 20

> I have only now begun to strap myself to my chair and begin the wearisome saga of another Cainman. This entails about four hours' work a day and a hell of a lot of sitting under the awning outside the Bar Jaime, Plaza Mayor, contemplating or endeavouring to contemplate the eternal unverities of the Cainly flight. Action, authenticity, violence, pace, sex and the neurotic wisecrack: all these elements must be kept in a firm simmer on the surface of things. I did nothing in Ireland, London, Barcelona, so now the price must be paid. . . .

But obviously he still found it easy to be distracted, with enough energy left over from his work to write me a letter of six pages, in tiny, cramped handwriting. "I am acquiring a café tan," he observed in the letter, "and a great capacity to have some alcoholic substance – wine, cognac, Pernod, Cinzano – pass through my veins at any of my waking hours. Also, there was the bullfight. It alone was worth price of admission to Spain. . . ." He described the bullfight in some detail, but most of the letter was devoted to ruminations about solitude as opposed to the married state:

> Contrary to all the predictions of male friends, I know I shall have a better time when Jackie gets here. This is perhaps the

final stage of marriage – something that Mordecai certainly, and you possibly, do not understand. One becomes part of the partner and a separation like this is unpleasant, forcing the readjustment to the oneness of aloneness (to be Joycean about it). In any event I am no longer prepared to make that adjustment cheerfully, to do the amount of bonhomie – making strangers like one, etc. – necessary to making the bachelor state tolerable. I have been thinking about this: the central theme in being a single man is pursuit. The male friendships are incidental, easy, based on community of interest in many cases. Take away the sustained motive of pursuit of women – winning their love, affection, being charmed by and engrossed in them – and you have left only a very limited thing: a sexual diversion. For myself I find that now in conversation with women something forces me to bring up at the first possible opportunity the fact that I have a wife – and to speak well of her, also at once. Immediately the relationship changes and – as Bruce [a psychoanalyst friend] would put it – I become castrated – and I am placed in that strange limbo of the faithful married man with whom the lady will tell her friends she had a conversation. . . . The conversation is necessarily short. If you should meet again, the conversation will follow a similar pattern.

So perhaps this is the important thing I have learned by this trip. The days when I went through and stayed in Europe before were not like this. There was always a woman present or at the next stop – or even in imagination she was possibly in the next café. But she was a part of it, she or the possibility of it gave the whole thing taste and smell.

I remember when you came back from England last time you said that it would be the last time as far as going in a tourist status was concerned. One had to have work and purpose in the travel. And for me the corollary is Jackie. She plus work here, plus a real reason for being here, and I could quite contentedly spend a year in Majorca. Or ten years, with the odd trip. . . .

I was irritated by Brian's notion that I had referred to my 1951 travels in Europe as being "in tourist status." He'd gotten that all wrong. Surely I'd been singing for my supper over there, interviewing bootblacks in Piccadilly Circus and dragging myself into radio stations in the Alps to pontificate about skiing. But then again, Brian was always convinced that I never worked hard enough, and I could do nothing, ever, to convince him otherwise. He, of course, was a Stakhanovite at the typewriter, and when he gave thought to the question of where he ought to live it was always in terms of where he could get the most work done.

"Could I do a lot of work in Majorca?" he asked, in his letter. "Or in Paris? I suppose so. But I can do as much or perhaps more work in Montreal with the economic pressures lessened." The question then arose as to whether he could work better in a bourgeois environment or a bohemian environment. He had been reminded of his bourgeois origins during his recent visit to his family in Ireland, where he had enjoyed, as he put it, "seven days of more than solid middle-class comforts, where everyone had a car, good food, wine for dinner. I was an American freak, a bit of a failure, an arty fella off to Spain on a ha'pence. . . ."

A few days later he was gone from these Irish comforts and was visiting Mordecai in London, whose circumstances reminded him of his own bohemian days, before his marriage:

> Looking at Mordecai, I admired the fact that he seems able to work anywhere. I told him he had a good set-up. I meant that. He has – for him. But it would depress the hell out of me, that basement flat, that very small budget. . . . I know, I once lived in that way, in that London. . . .
>
> This is in a very roundabout sort of way a paean of praise for Crescent Street [where my new downtown apartment was located], for Montreal, for the bourgeois values. I've been reading a very interesting book, an exchange of letters between Bowen, Pritchett and Greene, and it all boils down to the very mundanities of bourgeois values. As it does, in the last analysis, with Mordecai. He talks a lot about money, sales, ways and

means. He is satisfied *now*. So would I be myself if I were Mordecai. But I am not . . . I don't know. I haven't sorted it out yet. Once a bourgeois always a B, etc. I want a home in either place. Perhaps in some strange way I've found a synthesis of both in Montreal.

Señor Hoore

His latest fanciful signature, Señor Hoore, was a sardonic reference to his task of writing yet another commercial thriller, work that he thoroughly disliked. But by the time Jackie arrived from Montreal to join him, at the beginning of May, he'd written the first four chapters of *A Bullet for My Lady*. At his request, Jackie was bringing him fifty sheets of onion-skin paper, so he could rewrite those chapters, and four boxes of a medication called Gelusil, to soothe his ulcers. He met Jackie in Madrid and they travelled to Barcelona and Toledo, where they visited ancient synagogues and where the tourist guide refused to answer their questions about the Inquisition, except to say that it had been imported from France. Back in Majorca, Brian wrote to me about the bullfights:

Andraitx, May 18

Dear Hombre:
Jackie has developed an alarming aficion and we are both bull crazy – and I mean crazy! We took a cab seventeen miles to Palma last Sunday and had him wait while we watched some good novilladas. Two ears and a tail for Pedrosa. Ernest Hem is in Madrid now in pink pyjamas for the San Isidro fights. However, although we have missed those the big men will be in Barcelona for the Thursday and Sunday fights and we will be there. Art galleries are taking a poor second to the fiesta brava [bullfights] this holiday.

It is very pleasant here [in Andraitx], although this
Spanish food is killing my ulcer and rendering every meal
an adventure. Ate with Jackie in Palma today, taking the
local bus in. At El Túnel. Soup, beef filet, salad, cheese, wine,
wild strawberries and cream. Price for two 56 pesetas [about
$1.50 at the black market rate]. . . .

Into this idyll the other day floated disturbing news. Letter
from Wing [his New York agent] said Putnams have said no.
Quoted report which said, "I have to send Judith Hearne back
without an offer. This does not make me happy at all because
he is such a very good writer. It seems to me though that the
basic trouble is that Judith Hearne as a character is not strong
enough or interesting enough to support the weight of the
novel." And so on. Also received a listless and unsatisfactory
communication from M. Horniman of A. P. Watt [his London
agents], saying he had the book and "although in the present
state of the market our prospects of success are not as good as I
could wish" he will be glad to offer it to likely British publishers.
This with a dear Mr. M. and a yours sincerely at the end is
about the extent of his communication. This does not satisfy
me, so I plan to spend a few days in London on my way back,
kicking his rear end.

Olé!

Jesus Sanchez Giminez

Brian's agents were making money from his thrillers, and they
kept urging him to produce more of them. But, he felt, they
weren't trying hard enough to place this, his first serious literary
novel. Mordecai, by contrast, was luxuriating in much better
luck. *The Acrobats* was now in the bookstores in England, except
for those that refused to carry it on grounds of obscenity, and the
reviewers were paying attention. The *Spectator* spoke of "Mr.
Richler's distinguished talent" in its lengthy review of this first
novel, set in Spain:

No doubt about it, this is an astonishing little book. As a guide to intelligent, contemporary pastiche it is unique. So let's take a look at The Acrobats.

Here is André, the sensitive but cowardly and ultimately defeated young artist – with whom the author identifies himself to a large extent; Kraus and his sister, the bad, sick German; Barney and Jessie, the sad, sick Americans; Pepe and his wife Maria, the good, simple peasants; Chaim, the inde-structible Jew; Derek, Jessie's brother, the emasculate homosex-ual and ex-artist . . .; Toni, the good, lost whore; Guillermo and his communist friends, tough and brutal and ugly; Juanito, the gentleman turned pimp – here is a whole range of characters all of whom we have, in some guise or another, met before, and yet all of whom are given touches of real life by Mr. Richler.

These are the characters. And the models? The early Hemingway is omnipresent; the Dos Passos newsreel techniques flicker on and off; Miller nightmares pack a few pages with rhetorical, dialogue-free paragraphs; Mr. Norris occasionally changes trains.

This is not to say that The Acrobats is all regurgitation. No, Mr. Richler has a fire and a frenzy all his own which, when they truly take hold of his characters, produce a powerful effect. But what is it all about? Mr. Richler is of the generation which has missed the opportunity (their term) of taking physical part in the good-evil struggle. There have been for him no easy externalisations of his own problems, no Smash the Hun, no Save the World from the Red Tide. But all around him wash the ripples of these simple causes, echoes of clean, harsh storms far out at sea whose origins he can only wonder about. . . . Desperately the characters try to find a truth which means something for them. By struggling they fail; by accepting they win. And it is in Chaim, the old, wise, essential Jewishness, that Mr. Richler finds a temporary peace:

"Chaim, is there any hope?"

"Yes, child, Of course there is."

"Is there?"

"There is always hope. Always. There has to be."

This isn't a brilliant answer. But the failure to find an answer is what The Acrobats is about. And as such – as the work of a worried, whirling, over-read young man of twenty-two who's prepared to face up to *not* seeing the way out – this book should be looked at, and looked at by a lot of people.

Readers of the *Liverpool Jewish Gazette* would probably not be looking at the book. "They've returned a copy of my book with a letter," Mordecai wrote to me. "They said their reviewer could only review the bk in the most scathing terms. So perhaps they'd better just give the bk back. Honest." This was the first of many broadsides Mordecai could come to expect, in future years, from unappreciative guardians of the Jewish flame. But other British critics were more open to the book. After listing what he felt were its shortcomings, Arthur Calder Marshall, in his BBC Radio program, said, "*The Acrobats* couldn't be such a bad book if the author hadn't got the makings of a major writer in him. His faults spring from the richness of his imagination, from his desire to pack into a single novel the thoughts and ideas which could have gone into several. . . ." The *Glasgow Herald*, noting Mordecai's age, said "there is so much maturity in some of the writing that it is difficult to believe that it is a young writer's first novel."

In Canada, the reviews were generally positive. "Richler has written a good book," the Toronto *Telegram* said. "His next book will be better and the one after that – perhaps great. He's a hard, powerful, original (but he will gain more originality) novelist and the criticism will not bother him." But if it didn't bother Mordecai then, he might come to agree with some of it in later years, when he was happy to see *The Acrobats* go out of print.

For the moment, though, he was exhilarated by the reception the book was getting. It would be published in the United States later in the year, and his agent had sold translation rights in Norway, Sweden and Germany. Now he was in Paris, looking into the possibility of finding a French publisher.

paris

11 p.m. may 14. 54

BILL: Sitting up here on the fourth floor of the Hotel de
France, rue de Vaugirard, grateful for the breeze (after a
blazing hot day), puffing on a Gauloise, and grateful,
too, that the traffic on rue Monsieur le Prince has
slowed down. . . .

Honest, Paris is shit. I've had this city, but GOOD.
American one-year crap artists now drink at Le Tournon,
near Jardins de Luxembourg. Paris Review and Merlin crowd.
Everyone an editor, a writer and conforming non-conformist.
Ibiza, our old Ibiza, is now their suburbia or where-you-
take-her-for-a-week's-fucking. Richard Wright pops in
every night for a go at the pinball machine, a chuckle and a
beer. . . . Pergola now a queer joint. Mabillon tamed down.
More galleries than grocery shops between Seine and
St. Germain. . . .

I've finished first draft of novel No. 2. Joyce thinks
very highly indeed of embryo ms BUT I'm not so sure
at all – except that it will get me in good trouble in
Montreal. . . . Oh yeah, this'll kill you, man. Warner
Bros. thks I'm one hot-shot writer. Most of Acrobats,
they say, wd be censored, but what am I thinking of
doing next???

Can you send me two copies each of Sat Night, Canadian
Forum, other imp Can reviews? Swedes, Norwegians
want them. Did Surrey [a Montreal friend] get copy
of bk Deutsch sent him? Answer all questions pronto.
You're slipping, man. You haven't written coherently for
some time. . . .

All the best
M.

Montreal, May 21

Dear Mort,

The day at Weekend has put me in a foul mood, so I think I'll take it out on you. In your recent letter, for instance, you say that I'm slipping, that I haven't written coherently for some time. *I'm* slipping! Jesus, man, clairvoyance would be a help in deciphering some of your mail. For one thing, I seldom know if or when you received letters I send you. That's because you seldom acknowledge or comment. Did you write your last letter (all caps, Uncle Bernard, hotel bill, etc.) before or after receiving *my* last letter? Also I went to a bit of trouble finding out about opening a bank account here for you, and I sent you a card to fill in. But since then, no card returned and no mention of what you want done about the account. . . . Mind you, your system makes for some delightful surprises. In the past week I've received from you (I guess it was you) two large parcels of books and a number of clippings of reviews from provincial papers. No mention of these in your correspondence, however, so I guess you want me to hang on to all these things. On the other hand, no Cocteau book, which you mentioned several times. Did you send it? Is it lost? I don't want to be pompous, but for chrissake Mort don't become so much of an artist that such details are beneath you.

I'm astounded when you say "Paris is shit." God, man, what do you mean – the little area bounded by Dupont's, the Mabillon and the U.S. phonies? You should have stayed in a hotel at Bastille or République or somewhere and eschew St. Germain. I don't see how you can judge a city on the strength of the fact that the writers you have met are cruds and the Americans are revolting. For chrissakes (I really am in a foul, pompous mood), I hope your future travels don't always gravitate to the local Soho, wherever it is. You probably don't agree with me, but I think the people writers should avoid are other writers. The Canadian Authors Association recommends that one mingle with Real People, even Workers, and keep the Writer's Storage Batteries filled with Material.

My news: I'm finally getting into the film game, which is much more interesting than the newspaper game (though not your literature game). Yes, the Film Board phoned me from Ottawa and asked me to do a script on Dr. Hans Selye, the medical researcher here who is an expert on stress, world-famous, new theories, etc. They consider it one of their more important film projects. I said OK, and I'm going to spend a week in Ottawa talking it over, getting to know the Film Board, seeing what I can learn, etc. I managed to get a week's holiday from Weekend because I'm way ahead in my work.

If I haven't insulted you too much, please write immediately.

W. W.

Paris

May 24 54

DEAR BILL:
Yr letter of May 21 to hand.
Wow! Christ!
But yre right you know. Your blast was deserved. I write incoherently, rapidly, and without many factual references. Sorry. Will try to turn over a new leaf. Or leaf over a new turn. . . .
Yes, I sent you two parcels of books to hold for me and to read and I will continue to send the odd bundle of interesting stuff as I read thru it. I honestly can't remember whether I sent you the Cocteau book or not. I'm afraid it may still be lying around in the room. I'll check with Cathy. The bank deal is important and your sending the card is much appreciated, only last time I was down American Express way I forgot the goddam card, will go again on Friday. Oh yes, I wrote that last letter – all caps – *before* receiving yr long letter.

I'm studying German pretty hard these days, going to
Munich on June 8. Had a long, friendly letter from the Krauts
[his German publishers] saying how nice they'll be to me when
I get there. They have $225 for me there and Joyce has another
$300, or will have it in a few weeks. I still hope to have new bk
done by Sept (will work hard on second draft in Munich).
Figure I have enough money to keep me until November, by
which time I shd get or hope to get new advances. ALSO,
Simone de Beauvoir is now reading Acrobats for Les Temps
Moderns – or so Ellen Wright [a Paris agent] tells me.

Mort

~

My education in practical filmmaking, as opposed to studying
the opaque writings of cinema icons like Sergei Eisenstein, began
in that old converted sawmill on John Street in Ottawa. There,
people at the National Film Board were kind enough to pause in
their work to explain what they were doing and why. I spent
hours in one of the cutting rooms, watching miles of celluloid
rattling through the moviola, with the editor intently watching
the images on the little screen. Now and then he would jam on
the brakes, reverse the motion and then go forward again, frame
by frame, until he found the place to cut. Making that cut, then
another, and then extracting a short strand of film from the
rushes, was, I felt, an act of great courage, akin to a surgeon
slicing into the living flesh. I could never bring myself to do it.
Then the editor would take two other strands of film hanging
from his rack and splice the three pieces together. He would run
this spliced section through the moviola to show me the effect –
and it was magical. He had created a tiny story. It was like the
process of writing, where what you're doing, basically, is selecting
words and stringing them together. Dear old Comrade Eisenstein
would write six metaphysical pages about the principles involved,
but all Dave, the editor, had to say about his creation was, "Do

you think it works?" "Yes," I said, reverently. "It works great."

In another cutting room, I watched a sound editor adding sounds to otherwise silent footage. Making footsteps fall in a convincing way was a great art, especially when the high-heeled lady went out of frame and we were to imagine her receding in the distance, off-screen. In the recording theatre I heard an orchestra recording music, especially written for the film, with the composer nervously watching and listening for the right chord to fall on the right image on the screen. Then, finally, in the mixing theatre, I watched them combining the three elements – picture, sound and music – into one harmonious whole: a movie. It was delicate, painstaking work and mixing a half-hour film could take a whole day. In later years, when I was involved, working in the cutting room and in the mixing theatre always struck me as being much more stimulating than being out on location with the camera, hopefully pointing it at something that might be interesting.

It was during this visit to Ottawa that I met Grant McLean, a man who was later to become director of production at the NFB and a close friend of mine. Grant had joined the NFB as an assistant cameraman back in 1942, three years after the board's founding. Before long he was in the Arctic, filming Inuit hunting whales, polar bears, walrus and caribou. Then he was in a Lancaster bomber, flying across the Atlantic to shoot the film *Target-Berlin*. In 1946, he was travelling all over China as a cameraman-director on loan to the United Nations to film relief efforts in areas stricken by flood and famine. He was the first western cameraman to film the background of the Chinese civil war, meeting leaders of both sides, including Communists like Chou En-lai and Mao Tse-tung. In the cave city of Yenan, Grant argued about politics with Mao, telling him he was too doctrinaire, that the end did not always justify the means. The excellent film that resulted from all this, *The People Between*, was suppressed by the Canadian government for fear of upsetting the Americans, who didn't want to acknowledge that part of China was now being ruled by Communists.

Besides Grant McLean I met other filmmakers who liked to talk about their adventures on location – mostly about things that went wrong, like cameras that froze and had to be thawed out, canoes that sank, crews that got lost, idiot directives from headquarters that had to be ignored. The documentary directors and cameramen I met struck me as being mavericks, great improvisers, young men of derring-do – people like David Bairstow, Bernard Devlin, Stanley Jackson, Ian MacNeill, Gordon Burwash. I heard their stories when I met them for a beer after work or at parties in the evening when the wine flowed freely. It didn't take me long to conclude that this was the life I would like to lead.

While the wine was flowing in Ottawa I presumed it was also flowing – probably Rhine wine – in Munich, where Mordecai had arrived at the invitation of his German publishers. He wrote me enthusiastically about the city, which was still showing much bomb damage. "Food remarkably cheap and plentiful," he wrote. "Huge (and I mean huge) ham omelet with one pound of potatoes and one pound of sauerkraut and one quart of beer costs 2 marks 50, or 60 cents. Will be able to live quite well here on 100 bucks a month. Nightclubs cheap as Spain, honest." He quickly found his way to Schwabing, Munich's Montparnasse, where he listened to Freddy Bockenheimer's New Orleans Jazz Band. "Munich thick with American soldiers," he wrote. "Have already been to the American Way Club, where you can get Western sandwiches, nothing harder to drink than Coke, big racks of comic books, latest hit tunes, barn dance tonight, pingpong every night. Hostess there, one Coreen from Texas, offered me a sundae, which I refused."

In Montreal, for my first NFB assignment, I was visiting the laboratory of Dr. Hans Selye, who was anxious to show me some of the unpleasant things he was doing to rats. He was the world's authority on stress, which he defined as the strain on the body associated by any attack by disease, injury or mental pressure – including the hectic pace of life in the 1950s. I spent several days with Selye at the Université de Montréal, trying to fathom what he was telling me about hormones and the roles of the adrenal glands and the pituitary. This wasn't easy, as I was completely illiterate in matters of science, but I managed to grind out a script where Selye could voice his contention that many diseases have no single specific cause, but are largely due to nonspecific stress. Like many NFB documentaries, it ended with the notion that much has been done, but much remains to be done. I feared that the whole thing was tedious and that, even though it was only ten minutes in length as a short for theatres, it would send the audience out to the lobby and the candy counter. But the board was very pleased with the film they made from my script, titling it *Stress*, and they asked me if I would now like to write a script about heart surgery. I wouldn't, being squeamish, but I needed more experience in film craft, to say nothing about the money, so I accepted the assignment.

~

Munich, July 8, 54

DEAR WEINTRAUB: Lissen, you're making terrific progress filmwise. Honest, I'm delighted. Christ, if you can get a feature film script done. . . . Maybe, hey, we'll do the Great Canadian Film together one day. . . .

News by way of Canada: R. Weaver, CBC, is gonna pay me $75 for first broadcast rights for "Secret of the Kugel." Will you settle for $25?? [This was a short story Mordecai had written, based on an idea I'd given him.]

Munich news: Literary editor of Munchner Mercur phones last week to ask if I would be kind enough to allow an interview. And I was. . . . Scene: home of Herr Arenz, editor, author, etc. Also, Peter Paul Althus, big poet. And the lit ed of Abend-Zeitung. Cognac, much gin.

This, man, was the funniest evening of my young life. Two men taking down all my opinions, pronouncements, prejudices – ho ho ho. Kids traipse in and will I autograph books. Wd I like this, wd I like that? (I'm never coming home – never.) Then Arenz pulls out a letter congratulating him on his bk on Stevie Zweig. Letter is signed "Albert" – from Princeton, New Jersey. Now if you can out-lifeman Arenz you're in!

AFTERWARDS, drunken Richler staggers into Fiat station-wagon and is whisked off by two Georgia gals to Officers' Club for gallons of Scotch, etc., and where I made one of my best anti-U.S. speeches. . . . I have been adopted by Special Service girls of U.S. Army, Karslplatz, Munich. They steal onion-skin paper and carbon paper for me. Also the Army orders of the day. They bring gifts – lighters, Planter's mixed nuts (chewing 'em now) and, still better, American cigs at $1 a carton and Gordon's gin at $1.50 a bottle – only if I *feel* like paying. (Pardon while I light up a Chesterfield. King size, you know.)

I'm halfway thru a bk abt Montreal, with a ghetto background. . . . I'm trying to trace the development of the ghetto from the scholar-poet to authoritarian to liberal to money leadership . . . e.g., 50 yrs ago my grandfather, a Chassid, was a leader of the ghetto: today he'd be a "character" in the same community. I'm not interested in passing judgments or shouting – I'm simply observing. . . . The only people who could consider this bk anti-Semitic – there are, of course, good and bad people in it – are those Jews who are very frightened. I don't consider myself a Jewish or a Canadian writer. I am a writer. I'm not interested in the fact that Jews can't get into certain hotels or golf courses. I'm interested in Jews as individual persons – and I'm not writing a "Jewish problem" book. Briefly, you can put it this way: I think those who were murdered at Dachau should not be mourned as Jews but as men. (The distinction, I think, is important.) I don't believe there is any such thing as a Jewish outlook or a Jewish Problem or Jewish Spokesman. Each man has his own problem (part of that, of course, might be his being a Jew).

This book, coming, is a much "quieter" one than the first. Also longer. And Bigger. Joyce has read half of first draft and considers it a big improvement on first bk.

Acrobats is out in Denmark and Italy. Gabriel Marcel is very
interested and may publish in France. An Israeli firm, run by a
family named Persitz, is likely to do Hebrew edition. Will be
published in Sweden by Bonnier, biggest and best house there.
In Norway Glydendal will publish in their Yellow Book Series.
Hemingway's first book appeared in that series, also Faulkner,
Steinbeck, Greene, etc. Here in Germany it's Kindler und
Schiermeyer Verlag, a post-war firm. I thk I'm one of the few
(only??) Canadian novelists to be translated into so many
languages. However, nice as it is, advances average only from
$150 to $200. No royalties for at least 18 months. Working
very hard here. Still hope to have bk done by Sept., but I'm
damn worried abt how good or bad it is. . . .

Have finally straightened out the bank deal. Royal Bank of
Canada, St. James Street, has opened an account, Savings F
16523. When you've got time, would you see Mr. M. E. Stack,
Savings, there, give him the eight bucks, and say I'll make a big
deposit in Sept (I hope).

Write.

M.

After two months in Munich, Mordecai went back to London
and in August he and Cathy were married. He had planned a big
party for the occasion and I decided to phone my congratulations during that party. In those days, making a transatlantic
phone call was an ordeal. You had to book the call with the operator an hour or two in advance, and when you got through the
connection was often bad. And these calls were very expensive.
I'd never made one before and didn't know anyone who had; if
there was any urgency in those days, you sent a cable. But now,
finally, I was talking to Mordecai.

"How's married life?" I asked, thinking this an amusing
opening for the conversation.

"I can't talk to you now," said the bridegroom, and I heard
loud party noises in the background.

The conversation soon petered out and I hung up, anxiously wondering what the phone bill would be. A few days later Mordecai wrote to me: "Yr wild phone call still the talk of London's literary world. Actually, it was a bit of a bore. I was in the middle of a conversation when you made your transatlantic interruption. Also, you never did tell me what the weather was like."

In letters that fall Mordecai kept urging me to come to London to work. He was meeting people in the film world and, he told me, "They're hungry for stuff, man, and you've got lots more in you than most of the guys around here. Why not make the break and come to London? You cd make your expenses and way better than that on TV alone. Think about it. And what about British rights to yr Weekend stories? Have you got an agent working on them?? You might get 100 bucks apiece, you know."

In October, Mordecai delivered the manuscript for *Son of a Smaller Hero* to André Deutsch. "I'll try to see that you get a copy of the ms. in December," he wrote to me. "I'm anxious for you to read the bk. There's a lot of 'dangerous' stuff in it, and André and I will see a lawyer abt possible libel suits. . . .

"I'm off on a three-month money kick starting tomorrow. Hope to get me and my missus to Continent by end of Jan. Then, onwards to novel No. 3, already half outlined. . . ." By a "money kick" Mordecai meant a burst of commercial writing – short stories with trick endings, TV scripts and, above all, a paperback thriller. Brian Moore had given him some tips on how to write thrillers, but when Mordecai said he was weak on plotting he made a deal with Brian whereby Brian would supply the plot and Mordecai would write the book. For his trouble, Brian would get 25 per cent of the proceeds.

Meanwhile, that summer, André Deutsch had accepted *Judith Hearne* for publication, the manuscript having been brought to his attention by Mordecai. Thus Deutsch would become the first publisher of the first of Brian's nineteen literary novels.

7

Nineteen fifty-five was, for me, an excellent year, a pivotal year. I finally broke away from *Weekend* and resumed the freelance life, so I could do more film work. And I could travel. For the first time in my life I would venture farther west than Toronto, crossing Saskatchewan with a lion tamer and his travelling carnival. I would also cross the Straits of Gibraltar to Tangier, where I would sip Cinzano with Paul Bowles and his young Arab boyfriend. I would write more documentary film scripts and would take up residence in London, from where I would watch my friends Moore and Richler make ever bigger literary waves.

At the beginning of the year I was living on Crescent Street, between Sherbrooke and St. Catherine in downtown Montreal. It was a five-minute walk to the corner of Peel and St. Catherine, which Montrealers firmly believed was the crossroads of Canada. Nightclubs like the El Morocco and the Samovar were a stone's throw away. A block or two to the east of Crescent were elegant restaurants like Chez Ernest or Café Martin, and only a bit farther east one could find the solace of smoked meat at Bens or a one-dollar rib steak at Curly Joe's. With Brian and Jackie, it was often the Club Room in the nearby Lasalle Hotel, where our ancient Teutonic waiter would hobble over with the legendary braised short ribs of beef.

Now, with more freelance money in my pocket, I could afford to take a girl to dine at Chez Stien, where the likes of Pierre

Trudeau and René Lévesque, not yet famous, might be seen eating their *blanquette de veau*. I could take her to Her Majesty's Theatre, just three streets away from home, to see a Broadway play on tour. Or, in a more frisky mood, we might go a bit farther afield to St. Lawrence Boulevard, to enjoy Harlem Night at the Montmartre ("Always the Best Coloured Show in Town").

Crescent Street, in 1955, was quiet, tree-lined and purely residential. My apartment, with its big bay window, was on the third floor of Dr. Ruddick's three-storey townhouse. The elderly doctor, father of my poet-psychoanalyst friend Bruce Ruddick, lived on the second floor and had his office on the first. The doctor would turn in his grave today if he knew what happened to his Crescent Street as the century progressed. Trendy bars and restaurants would come to clutter the street, and the former Ruddick residence would now house a condom store, with signs boasting that they were available in all colours and flavours. Today's patrons of that store would never believe that in the 1950s condoms were simple, monochrome affairs, with no exciting corrugations or ticklers attached, and were available only in drugstores, where they were kept behind the counter. We bought them surreptitiously and with embarrassment.

On January 3, 1955, Mordecai sent New Year's greetings from London. "You and yours should have only from the best," he wrote. "I must get back to Montreal in 56. Figure on settling there eventually. It's the place I know and can write abt best. I have no choice . . . I guess we'll all be together in Mtl in 56 . . . or in abt 18 mos. That wd be nice. . . ."

The winter of 1955 brought some disappointments to 26 Park Crescent, London W.1, where Mordecai and Cathy were now living. On January 28, he wrote me that *Maclean's* magazine had turned down *Son of a Smaller Hero*, which they had been considering for serialization. Mordecai quoted the letter a *Maclean's* editor had written to his agent: "The consensus here was that a number of considerations, technical and otherwise, made it impossible to publish the book in magazine form without to some extent distorting the material itself. . . . In confidence, I think we're making a mistake. I think Richler has created an extraordinarily fine book and deserves every possible encouragement. He'll probably find my comments baffling. There's not much one can say when one is returning the most brilliant book we've ever rejected. . . ."

That last remark did not mollify Mordecai. "Shit," he wrote, "I'm not so much disappointed as angry. What business have they got pretending they are interested in promoting serious writing? Anyway while they're so embarrassed and gooey and gushing for more material (they want to see everything I do, the dears) I'm going to hit them hard with a 'funny' short story plus a letter saying take this or nothing more from Richler ever. . . ."

Although 1955 was a good year for me, it started poorly, taking me in and out of hospital, for several weeks, with complications following minor surgery. On February 5, Mordecai wrote:

> DEAR BILL: Brian wrote yesterday to say you were back in the hospital again. What bastard luck! Cathy and I were both disturbed by this latest bit of news. . . . Remembering yr injunction abt being – or playing – the comic with one's bed-ridden friends, I'll keep this letter straight. No hospital jokes. I've been in twice myself, both times for operations, and I know just what a bore and discomfort the whole thing is.
>
> Is there anything we can send you??? Bks, records, mags? (I can still make arrangements to have things sent from England. In fact, I've written Derek to send you the Wingate bk, Celluloid Mistress.)

A few weeks later, Mordecai got some bad news from New York. "Putnam has given me the old heave-ho," he wrote. "No contract. No nothing." Putnam had published *The Acrobats* in the United States but didn't want *Son of a Smaller Hero*. Mordecai's letter to me quoted what the Putnam editor had written to his agent: "We haven't any doubts about Mr. Richler as a writer or about his future, but we simply don't think that we can sell this particular book in this country to any great extent. We had some good reviews but a rather dismal sale for *Acrobats*, and in all honesty I don't think we can afford to do another book of Mr. Richler's about which our sales experts are so pessimistic. . . ."

In March, Mordecai wrote that after two months of concentrated thinking he had just finished the first outline of a third novel. "I intend to start serious work on it beginning of May and I thk this one – my first truly original – will really be good." Meanwhile he was busy with a number of money-making projects: stories, articles, a radio play. And from Paris, there was a tempting offer: "Can get 200,000 francs [about $600] for a pornographic novel from Obelisque Press," he wrote. "Another 300,000 to follow if bk reprints. Worth thinking abt. Altho, right now, I'm trying to get Cathy to write it."

When Mordecai got the proofs of *Son of a Smaller Hero* he sent me a set for my comments, which I conveyed in a letter:

Montreal, June 4, 1955

Dear Mordecai,
This is a difficult letter to write, because I have to tell you that I was very disappointed in the book. I must reread it soon because, as I went along, I kept hoping that it was I who was at fault, not you, that the deficiency lay in my understanding rather than in your presentation. But you say you want my immediate reaction, so I'd better not beat around the bush. I'd be less of a friend if I didn't give you my honest opinion.

I think you have an important and interesting story to tell, but you spoil it through faulty technique. It was this, plus some matters of taste, that kept it from succeeding as far as I was concerned. We can't argue about taste, but I wish we had a chance to discuss technique. By this I mean construction, accuracy, pacing, proportion, economy and relevance. I don't want to be pompous, but I think it was the sum of all these factors that kept me from becoming totally immersed in the book, from being terribly concerned about the outcome and from really believing in the central character.

Let's start with accuracy. This cannot be very important to you, because there are so many easily-avoided errors of fact. When Brian writes his thrillers, he surrounds himself with street maps, directories and reference books; the result is a compelling sense of authenticity, high accuracy about the physical properties of places he knows far less well than you know Montreal. Yet you don't seem to have done as much in writing a serious book, a book in which (excuse the expression) "local colour" plays such an important part. You want to be documentary, but your documentation is so often wrong.

It's not Atwater Street (p 27) it's Atwater Avenue. On page 46 Theo went to Magdalen, College, Oxford, but on 51 it's Cambridge. That's really awful. It's a BB gun (p 56) not b-b gun. And it's not Kick Cola, it's Kik (that was the charm of it); the painter was Jackson Pollock, not Pollack.

My letter went on and on in this vein. I felt it was my duty to give him these notes, but I hated myself for doing it. Surely I was nothing more than a shabby drudge, niggling at the work of an artist I envied. I was the stuffy old pedant, secretly admiring his carelessness, his dangerous, high-flying frenzy, while I plodded along safely, somewhere down below, looking for spelling mistakes with my magnifying glass.

Besides errors of fact, my letter, which ran to seven legal-size pages, took issue, among other things, with the book's choice of words ("Can you honestly say that a woman like Leah would use a word like 'consummated'?"). I listed a few clichés ("her scarlet mouth," "I love you best when you are angry") and I wondered about his hero ("The startling thing about Noah is that he doesn't seem to have any problems – with money, with sex, with social barriers."). I detailed how I couldn't believe in many of his characters and I questioned his lack of compassion for almost all of them.

Forgive me if I'm wrong, but your denunciations come so thick and fast in this book. I wouldn't be writing like this, if I didn't think you could stand the criticism and that it might be of some use to you. I am convinced that your next book will be much better, especially in view of the fact that you say it is to be non-autobiographical. In that case it should be more detached and disciplined. (I think you put too much stock in being "angry" as a form of motive power.)

Also, it seems to me that there are some almost incredible lapses of good taste, or am I being effete? I couldn't believe my eyes when this "drunken Irishman" (God, what a cliché) was introduced as Moore, and a Mavis was brought in. I don't think Brian will be annoyed, but it's such a bad joke.

Having said all this, I realize that I haven't said enough about the very fine, even wonderful, parts of the book – Shawbridge, the crane, the Zionist meeting, etc. It's these fine bits, I guess, that make me resent the neighbouring bad sections. As for the book as a whole, I sincerely hope that I'm wrong and that Walter Allen is right.

Love to Cathy, please don't take offense, and write soon.

Bill

Walter Allen was an English critic who had read the manuscript for André Deutsch and, in recommending it for publication, had said, "Richler is the first Canadian who is also a novelist. His book exists on many levels. The city [Montreal] comes through brilliantly . . ." The book, however, did not lack for detractors, especially in the Jewish press. A review in the *Congress Bulletin*, organ of the Canadian Jewish Congress, spoke of "the genre of self-hate" and said that the book was "a caricature of Jewish life one might expect to find in *Der Stürmer* [the Nazi newspaper]." In the *Montreal Star*, a Jewish reviewer, denouncing the book, wrote that it was "definitely batting in the wrong league. It should have been clothed in shiny paper jackets and sold under the counter at the corner newsstand."

But in England, the critics were appreciative. The *Times Literary Supplement*, in a lead review, said: "Mr. Richler's admirable novel recreates the teeming streets, the frustrated passions, the furious inbred life of Montreal's Jewish quarter. The plot is rather shaky: a Jewish boy trying to break free from the tight jackets of religion and family, takes a Christian woman from her husband and lives with her; but he cannot push rebellion to the point of revealing that his own father entered a burning building in the hope of finding cash rather than holy parchments. Mr. Richler has not yet quite the art to deal with such ironies. What he does give, in *Son of a Smaller Hero*, is a picture of various Jewish characters – the patriarch, his feebly cunning son and honestly intransigent grandson, their patient and long-suffering or frankly acquisitive women – and the stiflingly rich background of sex, religion and food from which they emerge. Some of the characters are memorable, but the background is more memorable still. Jewish writers are always in danger of becoming fascinated by the problems of Jewry to exclusion of all other interests, so that Mr. Richler's next novel will be awaited with anxiety as well as with hope; but there is no doubt of his prodigal talent."

~

By the end of February, I was fully recovered from the indignities that had been visited on me in the hospital by my surgeon, Dr. Butterfingers. A mistake with medication – his mistake? a nurse's mistake? – had made me much sicker and had greatly prolonged my stay in bed, but eventually I managed to escape alive.

April, with my health restored, was a momentous month. I quit my job at *Weekend*, started a six-month contract with the NFB, got married for the first time, got rid of my old Smith Corona typewriter and bought an Olivetti Lettera 22. That

Olivetti was the most beautiful portable ever created, so beautiful that the Museum of Modern Art added it to its collection of great product designs of the twentieth century. Armed with this machine, how could I miss as a freelance writer?

My marriage to Bernice Grafstein was destined to last only four years. Like me, she was a film buff and we'd met at a film society meeting. She'd recently gotten her doctorate in physiology at McGill and was now continuing to do research there. During the evenings of our courtship I tried not to think of her afternoons in the lab, putting electrodes into the brains of cats.

I'd always been squeamish, anxious to avoid the sight of blood, but I couldn't avoid seeing a bit of it when the NFB sent me to research l'Institut de Cardiologie de Montréal, at the time the only institution in Canada devoted entirely to the study and treatment of heart disease. The doctors there thought I ought to witness a bit of surgery, and I did, reluctantly. "Beating heart is exposed," I wrote in my notebook, looking away. Later, sitting with the doctors, they explained it all to me and I filled my notebook with terms like mitral stenosis, systolic murmur, pulmonary edema, oxymeter, pulmaflator. If I ever made sense of all this, my film would be able to baffle the audience with science, something the NFB always liked to do.

The script I wrote turned out to be not a pure documentary but a "docudrama." An actor played the role of Charlie Harris, a garage mechanic I invented and on whom I bestowed a heart attack and who was to undergo an operation. An actress played his wife, Mary, and another actor played Dr. Dupont, who was looking after Charlie. Dupont also explained the surgical procedure to Norman Kihl, our interviewer-narrator. One part of the script I was particularly proud of was when I called for the camera to give us a BCU (big close-up) of Dr. Dupont's hand as he said, "Ah, here it is. It's the special little knife the surgeon may use. You see, he wears it on his finger, through this ring. Then he passes it into the heart to the diseased valve. When it's in place, he pulls it like this to cut."

During the filming, the real doctors would perform real surgery (not on actor Charlie, of course), but they would have no speaking roles, except for the director of l'Institut, who would tell us how to avoid heart disease: don't get fat and avoid worry and overwork. This being several decades before the invention of exercise, he didn't order us to get out there and start running.

The operation, needless to say, was a great success and Charlie was able to crawl back under the cars at the garage where he worked. The film was called *New Hearts for Old* and despite its bit of hospital drama I thought it rather dry and didactic. But we were all very pleased when *Variety*, the show-business weekly, gave it an enthusiastic review, saying, "If the rest of the 26 stanzas in the National Film Board's telefilmed video series titled "Perspective" are up to the quality level of "New Hearts for Old," Canadian television audiences are in for a standout circuit of documentary shows for the next seven months. . . ."

I was living in England by the time the film was broadcast, and Brian Moore, in Montreal, made a point of seeing it and sending me a critique that was at odds with that of *Variety*:

> The essential dichotomy between the narrative technique and the non-Aristotelian agape, implicit in the opening scene where the Hero, as symbol of Angst, is shown grappling futilely with the essential nature of the tragic muse in the ineffectual logos of Verdun, is never resolved in the penultimate setting. Kihl, or Chorus, obtrudes, shattering the three verities. The Hero's Penelope, bearing magazines and other trivia [wife Mary's visit to the hospital], obtrudes a curious note of luxe, calm, volupté into the simple ordre et beauté of the Hero's plight.
>
> Was this intentional, pertaining to the Satiric? It is greatly feared that it was not; ergo, unintentional. "Art is the conscious mastery of materials to produce a given aesthetic verity." – Holdebrunner.
>
> Therefore the verdict, pro tem, is regretfully, contra.
>
> Rev. F. X. Moore, S.J.

~

For my next script, I would not be interviewing people like Dr. Gagnon and Dr. David. This time I would be talking to the likes of Chicago Red, Stuttering Dutch, High Pockets McCarthy and Humbug Mike. They were bally operators, grind operators, gazoonies – in a word, carnies. They worked for the World's Finest Shows, a travelling carnival that visited small western towns, where their arrival in the summer was one of the great events of the year. Farmers and their families came from a hundred miles away to ride the Tilt-o-Whirl and see the Headless Woman in the Freak Show.

The carnival travelled in its own train, a long string of boxcars, flatcars and sleeping cars, all of them painted bright silver. The train would stop at small towns, where the show would be set up for a few days and then torn down, to move on to the next venue. I joined the show in Melfort, Saskatchewan, and would travel with it across the width of the province to Lloydminster, and into Alberta as far as Vermilion.

I got on the train late at night and was shown to a lower berth in one of the sleeping cars. I fell asleep to the rhythm of the wheels as our mighty steam engine pulled us across the prairie. I awoke in the morning just in time to see the occupant of the upper berth clambering down, the Man with Two Faces, the star of the Freak Show. It was not a pleasant deformity to suddenly encounter at the crack of dawn.

The sleeping car had been refurbished, rather crudely with unpainted wood, to suit the needs of the carnies. At one end there was a big wood stove where the two Globe of Death motorcyclists were frying bacon and eggs. To one side there were a few slot machines – one-arm bandits – where two early-morning gamblers, midgets, were standing on boxes, feeding quarters into the slots and pulling the levers. It was all a bit bizarre, to say the least, but when one of the motorcyclists asked me if I liked my eggs sunny side up, I started to feel at home.

A few hours later the train pulled into a town called Lloydminster and the unloading started. Trucks rolled off the flatcars, laden with equipment and workers, and they headed for an open field, a mile away, where the show would be set up. On the trucks were the parts that would be assembled to make the Moon Rocket, the Rolloplane, the Octopus, the Ye Olde London Ghost Ride. One truck carried a large sign saying DANGER – LIONS, TIGERS. At the fairgrounds – the show was part of the annual county fair – Hank Blade, the show's assistant manager, was driving stakes into the ground to show where each attraction should be located.

"This will be the north end of the Freak Show," Hank said. "The front will run down here for about a hundred feet, where I'm going to put the shooting gallery. Now I'd like to put the Midget Show right next to the Freak Show, but you can't put two ballies together, can you? If I had a grind to put between them, that would be okay, but we don't have any grinds this year."

A bally, I learned, was a show where there was a platform in front of the tent where a barker would exhort the public to buy a ticket and come in. He would tell them, in the most lurid terms, what they would get for their money, and would show them a few "samples," like Freddie, the Armless Wonder, who would come out onto the stage and who, the barker promised, could thread a needle with his toes. A grind, as opposed to a bally, was a show where the barker talks but doesn't offer any samples.

"A grind is something simple," Hank Blade told me. "A monkey show, a snake show, a rat eater. Things like that."

By now the trucks were arriving from the train and the carnies were setting up the show on the streets that Hank was laying out. The merry-go-round would go here, the stand where Annie Moonshine would sell her indigestible candy floss would go there. Hot-dog counter over here, Penny Arcade over there. It was all done with speed and precision, like a military operation. As I watched, I noticed a number of young boys from the town, eager to volunteer to carry planks or help drive in the tent pegs. They were awestruck by all this, the most glamorous thing ever to happen in towns like Lloydminster or Melfort. Every so often a teenager from a town would befriend some of the carnies and run away with the show. A letter to his parents would explain that he was finished with school and had found his career. There was a big turnover in carnival labour and a husky farm boy was usually a welcome recruit. If he was shrewd, so much the better. He knew the ways of country people and he could help the auctioneer, a great pitchman, swindle buyers of junk jewellery, cheap watches, tinny cutlery.

The whole elaborate show, with its many "attractions," was set up in less than five hours, including the big ferris wheel that towered over everything. By mid-afternoon the crowds were coming through the gates, ready to be thrilled on the rides and entertained in the tent shows. On the platform outside the Freak Show, a big bass drum was being beaten to attract customers, while Johnny Bananas, billed as an African pygmy, was leaping about and eating fire from two torches he was brandishing. When people started gathering, the drumming subsided and Cliff Kay, a dwarf, started spieling into his microphone:

"It's all here, folks, it's all here, the greatest collection of strange human beings ever gathered in one place. . . . So c'mon down front here and watch what we're gonna do now. . . ." Along the front of the tent were picture-banners showing what could be seen inside: Fantasma, the Rubber-Skin Girl; the Man with Iron Feet; the Headless Woman.

"Yes, ladies and gentlemen," the dwarf barker was chanting, "you'll see her on the inside – the Headless Woman. You'll see her exactly as she has been living since her head was severed from her body in a street accident in Toronto ten years ago. You'll see how medical science has kept her alive – and happy! – through a system of pumps and tubes. All for the price of twenty-five cents. That's only one-quarter of a dollar, folks. . . ."

This spiel, and others like it, went verbatim into my shooting script. Documentary filmmaking in those days, before the advent of the highly mobile, lightweight camera, was very different from what it is today, when most shooting is done without a detailed script and where interviews are impromptu, with much of the structuring being done in the cutting room. But in the 1950s, the camera we were using was the heavy, ungainly Auricon, which always had to sit immobile on a tripod. As in a feature film, everything was scripted, including the questions an interviewer would ask and the answers he could anticipate. With *Carnival* and other films in the series, the interviewer was Fred Davis, a radio announcer doing his first work for television. Davis would later become famous as the quick-witted host of *Front Page Challenge*, the long-running TV show. But now there would be no ad-libbing in the interview I wrote for him and Terrell Jacobs:

SEQUENCE SIX.

80. Two-shot Davis and Jacobs.
We see the bars of the Steel Arena cage behind them. They are in the cage.
Davis turns to look behind him.

JACOBS: Yes, I've been in the business thirty-six years.
DAVIS: How many lions have you tamed, Captain Jacobs?
JACOBS: Thirty-five hundred lions, fifteen hundred tigers. . . . Say, you're not nervous, are you?

81. MLS reverse angle. We see the cause of Davis's trepidation: it's Monarch, who is sitting on a perch in the cage behind him. (This is the only shot where Davis and the lion are in the cage together. It's merely suggested in the following shots.)

DAVIS: N-no. You're sure it' safe?
JACOBS: Well, you wanted to get the feel of animal training, didn't you? So don't you think it's best to be in the cage?
DAVIS (very nervous): I guess so . . .
SOUND: Monarch roars.
JACOBS: As I was saying, I've broken five thousand lions

and tigers, more than a hundred polar bears and about a hundred and twenty-five leopards and pumas.

82. As 80.	DAVIS: Have you ever been hurt? JACOBS: Five hundred and eighty-six stitches, both arms and both legs broken, one shoulder broken in one place, the other in two places, thirteen ribs broken and I lost my right eye.
83. Davis turns and looks over his shoulder. We see the nervous look on his face.	DAVIS: If you had your life to live over again, Captain Jacobs, would you still be a lion tamer? JACOBS: I must certainly would not. . . . Say, what's the matter?
84. MS reverse angle. There are now *two* lions on perches "behind" Davis.	DAVIS: I thought there was only *one* back there. JACOBS: Oh, it's nothing. It's just a friend of his . . .

In the script, as the interview progresses, more lions keep appearing in the cage until there are four of them on their perches, all of them supposedly behind Davis. Fred never forgave me for asking him to go into the cage with Monarch, but I felt it was his NFB duty. The sequence was effective, but it would have been much more so if I could have included something Captain Jacobs really said, in answer to one of my questions when I was doing my research. After he told me about all the cuts, bruises and broken limbs he had suffered, I asked him whether he would do it all over again, if he had the choice. He didn't answer by saying, "I most certainly would not," as I wrote in the script. What he actually said was, "Are you out of your fucking mind?" Not suitable for television, of course, proving once again that the documentary film can, on occasion, veer a few inches away from absolute truth.

8

Late in the summer of 1955, Bernice and I sailed to England, where we planned to spend a year in London. She had a fellowship to do research at University College and I would write some film scripts and magazine articles. After much wearisome house-hunting, we found a congenial furnished flat in Ladbroke Grove, not far from Notting Hill Gate. And we were not far from Mordecai's flat, where I could now join in the poker games that included three other expatriate Montreal writers: Ted Allan, Reuben Ship and Stanley Mann. Also, we later learned, our flat was only a few hundred yards from Rillington Place and the former residence of John Reginald Halliday Christie, a mild-mannered man who murdered six women, burying some of them, in that fine old British tradition, in his back garden. They hanged Christie just two years before we arrived in London. The proximity of Rillington Place and the heavy fog that sometimes enveloped London in those days gave our Victorian street a pleasantly spooky feeling.

I didn't go into all that in my letter to my parents in Montreal, advising them that we were very well housed. "The living room is in the back," I wrote, "and it looks out on a private park, to which we have a key. The central heating seems to work (it often doesn't in England) and there's lots of hot water. We are a five-minute walk to the subway, and from there it's about ten minutes to the centre of the city. Down the street is a delicatessen where they have frankfurters flown in from Vienna, olives flown in from Israel and pickled bamboo shoots from China . . ."

My mother wrote back advising me to be careful in that delicatessen, lest I put on weight. She also said that she and some of her friends were reading Brian Moore's book and they all found it depressing. In this they were in agreement with the Toronto *Telegram*, whose review of *Judith Hearne* said, "It is a shame to see Brian Moore's obvious talent so prodigally spent on a pointless theme of bitter misery."

But other reviewers saw it differently, this story of a very poor, lonely old maid living in a seedy bed-sitting room in Belfast. "The way in which this young Canadian author, Brian Moore, has managed to project himself into the soul of a middle-aged Irish spinster is awe inspiring," said the *Globe and Mail*. "Judith is authentic down to the last shoe button. Her thoughts, her movements, her speech are as real as if this was an autobiography instead of a novel – and a first novel at that. Judith is drawn with gentle understanding, with tragic and compelling insight. We live with Judith, we understand her, we pity her, we ache to help her. . . ." The *Globe* review concluded by saying that *Judith Hearne* ought to win the next Governor General's Award for fiction – which it didn't. Instead the award went to a forgettable novel entitled *The Sixth of June*, by another Montreal writer, Lionel Shapiro.

When Brian's book was published in the United States, under a new title – *The Lonely Passion of Judith Hearne* – the Washington *Post* called it "the discovery of the year." The *New York Times Book Review* said that "the craftsmanship and powers of construction shown in this book are such that only astonishment can greet the fact that this is the author's 'first serious novel.'" *Time* called the book "an authentic tragedy" and went on to say that "the struggles of Judith Hearne in her lace-curtain destiny are those of a gladiator caught in his net."

These reviews conferred sudden celebrity on Brian and in Montreal he was being lionized and sought-after for interviews.

While in London I learned of all this from his letters. He wrote the first of these, playful as always, in the form of a news dispatch:

CBC LITERARY PANJANDRUM

MAKES PILGRIMAGE

TO SEE IRISH AUTHOR

Robert Weaver, described by the Times Lit Sup as one of Canada's real critics, is at present on a literary pilgrimage to Montreal. Weaver, a scholarly-looking man in his late thirties, held a literary soiree in the Ridgewood apartment of Robert McCormick, a local CBC official, Saturday night, to which he invited the little-known recluse and hermit Bernard Mara [one of Brian's pen names]. Mr. Mara, in his usual churlish manner, refused the invitation, saying it was impossible for him to go out on a Saturday night, it being against his religious beliefs (Child Worship). The noted Toronto critic then offered to visit the Author in his home on Saturday afternoon.

Weaver proved an indefatigable conversationalist and beer swiller, tossing in names like James Baldwin, Mordecai Richler, Edmund Wilson, Malcolm Cowley, W. A. Deacon, Morley Callaghan and Hugh Garner, all of whom are known personally to him. An eager sleuth in matters literary, he said, "It is a small country and I have discovered one of your pseudonyms and have read two of your Bernard Mara books." He also said that A. Knopf, in a Toronto lunch with the Critic and Callaghan, spoke glowingly of Hearnebk but denigrated SOSHbk. To remedy this, when the Critic asked me what I really thought of Richler, I presented our London Correspondent as a combination of St. Francis of Assisi and Moses Maimonides. "He is a very lovable fellow," I said, at which the Critic winced.

The Critic was not aware at the time that the Author, having fasted all that day, was completely inebriated on three rye whiskies. Finally the Author, having delivered himself of his opinion on literary conferences, the Critic's radio programme "Critically Speaking" ("I don't want to be rude, but who listens to it?") and various other subjects and, the Author's sentences starting to slur, the Critic wisely took his leave. . . .

Jackie Moore had mixed feelings about her husband's sudden renown, and she conveyed these to me in a letter. It gave a good picture of what authors have to put up with.

Montreal, Dec. 20, 1955

Dear Bill Weinfraud:

Last Saturday, well-known Montreal novelist and wife took courage in hand and ventured to annual Press Club buffet. This year good red wine flowed at the buffet table which heightened enjoyment no end. . . . Brian Moore caressed by many ladies who "had a good cry" over Judith Hearne. Moore took all this in his stride by glaring at the wall over various ladies' heads and muttering under his breath. Mrs. Carlo Italiano among conquests. Also Mrs. Franklyn, Mrs. Poland, Mrs. Newton. Me good girl. Me not jealous. Me just upchuck.

Brian has new ulcer pills. They work miracles. He can drink. And does. He can go to cocktail parties. And does. He is a new man. Said Dave Willock: "I never saw Brian look better, so thin and so much more amiable."

Sunday night went to posh establishment on Trafalgar Avenue for evening of documentary films. Miss Fleet, elderly upper-class sister of host, came up to Moores: "Which one of you has written the book?" she asked. I pointed mutely. "How nice. Is it about Canada?" Author said no, about Ireland. "How delightful. I simply adore the Irish. So romantic." Constance Garneau told Author she thought it was a very happy ending. "After all, poor Judith won't have to live in a horrible boarding house any more. She'll be well looked after." Author speechless. Another lady said she didn't understand ending. Would author please explain. All in all, I realized I was out with a PERSONAGE. When we got home, Author said he now understood why we remained hermits all year. . . .

Love to you both,
Jackie

"In my last film, *La Gran Siguiriya*," the Spanish delegate said, "I tried to mould time by means of light, making light vibrations tangible. Then I stumbled on relief, for time is space in relief. I was not looking for this, I was looking for the expression of time through the life-throb of the universe in which we are engulfed."

Listening to this, I realized that I was the wrong man in the wrong place. I have always felt uncomfortable in the presence of extremely deep thinkers, and when the time came for me to give *my* speech I'd never be able to match the profundity of Señor José Val del Omar. The affable Spaniard was addressing the First Meeting of Experts to Promote International Cooperation Between Film and Television, being held under the auspices of the United Nations Educational, Scientific and Cultural Organization (UNESCO). I, oddly enough, was representing Canada, as one of the "experts." My unlikely appointment to this position had been engineered by my pal Grant McLean, who was in charge of production for television at the NFB. Seeing I was already in England, Grant thought I could easily nip down to Tangier, where the conference was being held. All I would have to do is write a report, which nobody at the NFB would read, and I could have a good time for two weeks in this exotic corner of Morocco, the International Zone of Tangier, surely one of the most weird cities of the world.

I flew into Tangier the day before the conference was to begin and was pleased to find myself billeted in the Rif Hotel, at the expense of the City of Tangier. It looked like a fine hotel to me, until I met, in the lobby, J. B. Bhownagary, the delegate from India.

"We must get out of this hotel immediately," Bhownagary said. "We must stay at the El Minzah."

"Why?" I said. "We're on the beach here, aren't we?"

"This is a three-star hotel," said Bhownagary. "El Minzah is the top, five stars."

He immediately got on the phone to the conference administration office and after a long discussion got us moved to Hotel Velasquez-Palace, the El Minzah being full.

"The Velasquez is four stars, better than three, I suppose," said the disappointed Bhownagary, who was to become my principal adviser in the days to come. He was a seasoned "conferencier," veteran of many such meetings the world over, and he knew that international organizations like UNESCO always wanted the maximum in creature comforts for hard-working delegates, with easy access to the best bars and restaurants.

In the report I eventually wrote for the film board I thought I should start with a description of the conference's opening ceremonies: "The day dawned clear and warm, with some bewilderment in the air," I wrote, "as we delegates hadn't expected the formalities to be quite so splendid. We stood on the steps of the Legislative Palace and watched the consuls of eight nations arriving in Rolls-Royces and black Cadillacs. It is a committee of these consuls that constitutes the government of the International Zone.

"As the local police band played unknown anthems, a ferocious-looking guard of honour stood at attention, Arabs wearing white capes and carrying long spears. Finally, arriving in the biggest of the black cars, was His Excellency the Mendoub, local representative of His Sharifian Majesty Sidi Mohammed Ben Moulay Arafa, Sultan of Morocco." (It is interesting to note that the old sultan himself arrived in Tangier a few weeks later, in an armoured car supplied by the police to protect him from his hostile subjects. With Morocco in turmoil, this was the beginning of the sultan's exile.)

"After the outdoor ceremonies," my report continued, "dignitaries and delegates went into the Legislative Palace to listen to welcoming speeches. Here, in the Grand Chamber, was where our meetings would be held, around a huge horseshoe table. The rich mahogany and brass appointments in this room, and the luxurious carpeting underfoot, would have done justice to the headquarters of the United Nations in New York; it was surprising to find anything so grand in a small North African city. But it was only one of the many anomalies of this curious little enclave that has no flag, no elections, no census, no income tax – and where, to mail a letter, you can choose between the British, the French or the Spanish post offices, each with its own stamps.

"Why were we granted the use of the palatial Legislative Palace? Because the local Chamber of Commerce was eager to play host to a world conference – any world conference – figuring that this would somehow elevate the reputation of a city that is known chiefly for smuggling, sin and international financial fraud."

Tangier is located on the northwest tip of Africa, on the narrow strait where the Mediterranean meets the Atlantic. Looking across the strait, on a clear day, you can see Europe – Spain and Gibraltar. Approaching Tangier from the sea you can see that it's really two cities: the European section, with its tall modern buildings, and the old Moorish quarter, the medina, with its mosques, minarets and its maze of narrow streets winding up the hill to the kasbah. There were some 170,000 people living here in 1955 and some ninety banks to serve them or, to be more accurate, to serve foreigners with shady deals in mind. In those years, all European countries except Switzerland had strict currency controls, but there were none in Tangier. Here you could legally do things that would put you in jail in Britain or France, like change large amounts of hard currency into soft at free-market rates. Also the banks dealt freely in gold and you could conceal your hot money in a secret numbered account. For my part, I did my own minuscule amount of money-changing at the Moses Pariente Bank, a Jewish institution founded in 1844. Moses's family had been moneylenders as far back as 1796, and it was said that they helped finance Admiral Nelson's preparations for the Battle of Trafalgar.

In Nelson's time, Tangier was notorious as a home base for the vicious Barbary pirates, who terrorized British, American and other shipping in the Mediterranean. There was no piracy in 1955, but the Tangerine tradition of skulduggery at sea was being kept alive by diligent smugglers. Their cargoes were mainly American cigarettes, highly prized in Europe, highly taxed and very expensive. In a good week, in Tangier's bonded warehouses, there might be up to ten thousand cases of tax-free Lucky Strikes and Camels waiting to be loaded onto speedy ships – often war-surplus submarine chasers – that would whisk them over to remote shores in Spain, France or Italy. In one short trip, a smuggler captain could clear $50,000, provided he could elude or bribe the customs police and get his cargo ashore.

Shady banking, smuggling – and sin. Stories about sin in Tangier, the Chamber of Commerce protested, were highly exaggerated. But all you had to do was sit down at a table in a café in the Zoco Chico, the marketplace in the old town, and after a few minutes a man would approach you saying, "A beautiful girl, sir? Or perhaps a sweet young boy?"

In Tangier that year, there were sixteen European brothels registered with the police and fifteen Arab brothels. Registered prostitutes had to undergo regular medical examinations, but the medical status of the squads of unregistered freelancers was less certain. Many of the girls, we were told, were working to save up money for their dowries and would eventually marry well. For the truly exotic, we were advised to visit the famous and luxurious Chat Noir, where, for 400 pesetas, three naked young women would give us a private performance of *tableaux vivants de l'amour érotique*.

It was against this gaudy background that we delegates were holding our high-minded conference. Our purpose, a UNESCO document informed us, was "to assist in developing international cooperation and exchange of educational, scientific and cultural programmes among producers and distributors of films and television organizations." In most of the sixteen countries represented at the conference, television was very new, but it was already obvious that films would be very useful in satisfying the voracious appetite of this frightening medium. Much of the conference palaver concerned how television stations could get hold of films as cheaply as possible, and I was impressed by how such a crass topic could be couched in such elegantly abstract verbiage.

We were also supposed to discuss new techniques for making films especially for television, and I thought I might learn something in this area that would be useful for the NFB. But none of the other delegates seemed interested in this; old-style producers would just keep on producing in the traditional, cumbersome ways. I tried to tell them how the film board was making its television half-hours – research and script it in two weeks, shoot it in two weeks, edit it in two weeks, make it fast and cheap with small, mobile crews – but the Belgians, the Poles, the Cubans and the others just weren't interested.

At the screenings, however, the NFB films were generally considered to be the best of all, and *Neighbours*, the Academy Award winner, got the most applause. But Mr. Andreev, one of the Soviet delegates, told me *Neighbours* was far too violent. I asked Mr. Andreev and Mr. Jouravlev several questions about Soviet television (it was magnificent), but they had not a single question about what we were doing in Canada.

I have never found it easy to stay awake at committee meetings of any sort, and it was especially difficult in Tangier, when we had to convene at 9:30 in the morning after very late nights of official and unofficial partying. Fortunately we were working on the Spanish system, with a siesta from 1:00 p.m. until 4:00, when we resumed until 8:00 in the evening. Also, it was possible to doze off during the screenings, especially during documentaries from the Communist countries, which were often of the Boy Meets Tractor variety, or How We Built a Dam.

The conference, needless to say, concluded by passing a resolution calling for the establishment of a new international organization to promote whatever it was that we had been talking about, a lofty goal. One could surmise that Mr. Fulchignoni and Mr. Cassirer, big wheels from UNESCO in Paris and the ringmasters of our conference, might have had this in mind from the very start. They surely would be the bosses of the new organization – IOFCTV? UNTVFC? – and there would be lots more conferences, in Tahiti, in Bermuda, in Singapore. Mr. Bhownagary of India, Mr. Pugliese of Italy, Mr. Szancer of Poland would all be there – and maybe even Mr. Weintraub of Canada. It would be nice to meet these fine fellows again, in the best hotels, although in Tangier the local eccentrics I met around town were much more interesting than the conference delegates.

Hotel Velasquez-Palace
International Zone of Tangier

September 22, 1955

Dear Judith Hearne,
Last night I partook of couscous at the apartment of Mr. Lamar Hoover, editor of the Tangier Gazette, the English-language weekly. Mr. Hoover is your nice average American, but his wife, Anoushka, is very odd, like most expatriates here. She is a sweet little gamine who two years ago got on her bicycle and pedalled to Kabul, Afghanistan. Alone. The sinister Dr. Feldstein, delegate from the Czechoslovakian People's Republic, was also present at dinner, as was a Dr. Pichard, psychoanalyste from Paris.

During the course of the couscous I mentioned that I had been to the bullfights on Sunday, where the crowd had laughed at the inexperienced young matadors and the kills had been messy. Anoushka said she didn't understand bullfighting, whereupon Dr. Pichard explained it to her. "Madame, je vous assure que la course de taureau est simplement de la bestialité sexuelle," he said. "Je connais personellement une centaine de matadors qui m'assurent qu'ils ont joui [had an orgasm] au moment de la mort de l'animal." Does Hemingway know that? Do you, as an aficionado?

As for the UNESCO conference, it is preposterous. It is now siesta time and I sit typing in my private Louis XIV sitting room. My balcony overlooks the sea. I can see Spain. The other delegates are taking their leisure. The observer from the World Health Organization is no doubt allowing the supple hips of the Hotel Rif barmaid to take his mind off the universal misery. The gentlemen from the German Federal Republic are down at the beach. The ominous Dr. Feldstein is no doubt transcribing his notes. The representative from Warsaw is probably at the bar, drinking Royal Kebir and laughing hysterically, which is all he has done since his arrival. Monsieur Braunberger of France, producer of that great classic Un Chien Andalou, is talking money with some fellow producers. ("I make one fortune with that picture, but I do not make much with L'Age d'Or.") There are some other dropworthy names here: Kurt Oertel, a German's German, who made that Michelangelo film, and Henri Storck of Belgium, who made Rubens, which you will remember we showed at the Press Club.

Tomorrow night I will be throwing a party in my Louis XIV sitting room. I have invited Paul Bowles, whom I met the other evening through Christopher Wanklyn, McGill contemporary and great pal of Norman Levine. Christopher, a writer who has been living here for a few years, occupies a little Arab house in the heart of the medina for which he pays $11.38 monthly. Bowles seems to be very pleasant. (I think you agree that his Let It Come Down and The Sheltering Sky are very fine novels.) He spends his summers here and his winters in his house in Ceylon. Tomorrow night he will bring Ahmed, a young Moroccan who I presume is his boyfriend. Paul does not live with Mrs. Bowles, who is also here and who remarked to me, "I

now drink in the mornings. I must stop it." She was very
upset because some friends of hers moved into a new house
here and so far have found two vipers in it. "It's nothing,"
said Paul (he and his wife are still bad friends), "they're only
baby vipers." Presumably they're not the big, slithery ones
used by the snake charmers, up in the kasbah, when the
tourists come round.

To my soiree tomorrow night I have also invited M. le
Vicomte François Merle des Iles, who tells me he is quite
unused to western garb as he spends most of his time sitting in a
mud hut in the Sahara. However he has come to Tangier
because he feels it is time he widened his circle of acquaintance.
M. le Vicomte assures me that the authentic native dancers
from the desert, who performed at the UNESCO gala on
Saturday night, were actually prostitutes rounded up in Tangier
on 48 hours' notice and quickly rehearsed. The real dancers
have to stay in the desert for political reasons.

I tell you this town is crawling with odd people and strange
sights. I still can't get used to the veiled Arab women or the
handsome Berber women, who come down from the mountains
every morning with heavy loads of charcoal on their backs. They
spend the day in the market selling the charcoal. Then they buy
food with the proceeds and walk back home with it, many miles
away, getting there in time to spend the night making the next
day's charcoal. It's gruesome to see them walking along the road
as the Cadillacs whiz by, almost knocking them over.

As you must know, there's rebellion brewing in neighbouring
French Morocco and Spanish Morocco, where the locals want
independence. The other day the Vicomte took me to a very
out-of-the-way Arab coffee shop of the most desperate order.
As we came in, some rough-looking characters, sitting at one
of the tables, immediately lapsed into silence. The Vicomte
told me, in whispered English, that they had probably been
planning some bad things to do to the French, with dynamite,
and they might be thinking we were spies. "Why don't we go

somewhere else," I suggested hastily. "Why don't I buy you a drink at the Velasquez?"

My party tomorrow night should be a good one. Sorry you and Jackie can't be with us. L&K,

Tangerine

I was fortunate to have seen Tangier during the last year of its existence as an international zone. In 1956, both France and Spain reluctantly relinquished their hold on almost the whole vast expanse of Morocco, which now became an independent kingdom. The little corner of Tangier also became part of that kingdom and was "de-internationalized." Thirty years later I went back to Tangier, to see what had become of it in its new status. What I found looked sad and dusty to me. As in most post-colonial cities, the tidy office buildings of the European quarter were now in seedy disrepair. Paul Bowles was still living there, and a few other diehard expatriates, but most of the eccentrics had gone. And the old sparkle was gone. But Morocco had its independence. Now, as in most "developing" countries, the people would no longer be oppressed by colonial masters but could enjoy being oppressed by dictators of their own race.

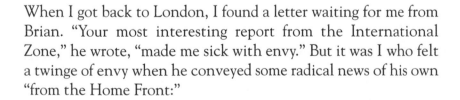

When I got back to London, I found a letter waiting for me from Brian. "Your most interesting report from the International Zone," he wrote, "made me sick with envy." But it was I who felt a twinge of envy when he conveyed some radical news of his own "from the Home Front:"

First of all, we have a home. Seven rooms, plus basement. Living room, dining room, large hall, kitchen, pantry, basement (three rooms) and upstairs are four bedrooms. Plus garden. Price $15,500. In Westmount, on Lansdowne. Number 498. $7,500

on 5½% Mortgage. A very good buy with privilege to pay off
$5,000 in five years and then dump down the rest without inter-
est. Having new roof put on for $300 and have had painters
(German) do whole house, much white and grey, for $300.
Moving next week. Jackie's mother has pitched in with some
expensive Bronzoni stuff, sofa and chairs. Incredible, really, how
all this happened to us. Now I am a man of substance.

I am not coming to Europe this fall, although that has little
to do with the housebuying. I decided shortly after you left
that I must cultivate my garden and apply myself to second
book. Mort writes that he has three times started his third,
getting up to eighty pages the last time. Well, I have him
beaten hollow. I calculate that I have been seven months at
work on mine and last month I started all over again, completely
anew. I now have a grand total of forty pages – or fifty – but I
am, I feel, on the right track. So my plan for this winter is to
write it, leaving all other distractions aside. . . .

I cannot tell Mort any news of Melzack's sales as I have not
seen Melzack [owner of the Classic bookstore on St. Catherine
Street]. But Mort's book is on a separate table in Eaton's. Book of
the Week. Many copies in all stores. More than Judith Hearne.

We had dinner with Cherneys and their Uncle Abe Rother,
four feet six inches tall, tougher than Hemingway, killer of
elephants, lions and all sorts of wild game. Pretty interesting.
Like myself he is in the real estate business.

Success to your ventures, and keep me advised.

Marechal Juin

~

My next venture was a minor one, but it did provide me with
some amusement. Back in Montreal, *Weekend* wanted me to do
some articles in England and one topic they suggested caught my
fancy: Savile Row, the men's tailoring capital of the world. I
started my research immediately and discovered that we were

in the midst of the third great style trend since the war. First was the Drape Shape, or Gorilla Look, with its beefily padded shoulders, narrow hips and necktie knot the size of an orange. Then came the Edwardian Look, with its narrow shoulders, four-button jacket and nipped-in waist. But now it was going to be the Daddy Long Legs Look, with trousers tighter and jackets shorter. "We will be showing a lot more leg," the manager of Gieves & Hawkes, No. 1 Savile Row, told me.

Savile Row was actually a short, undistinguished-looking street, but here and in the streets around it there were about thirty master tailors, operating in quiet, dignified shops. In the old days, you needed a formal introduction before they'd even take your measure, but now they were looking for the Yankee dollar, and all you needed was a bankroll. Elsewhere in England you could get a made-to-measure suit for $25, but in Savile Row the cheapest three-piece job was about $100. And you could pay up to $200.

For this you would, of course, get the finest materials. To measure you, the tailor would likely assign a jacket expert for the top of you and a trouser specialist to work below. (This man would ask you, discreetly, whether you preferred left dress or right dress, a question more important than ever now that pants were to be worn very tight.) Most of the sewing was done by hand and you would get at least three fittings, although some Savile Row establishments were known to provide twelve fittings before both customer and tailor were satisfied. The end product was supposed to be as much a part of your personality as your skin and would look better after a few months' wear than when new.

All this I noted down diligently for my article, but I struck real gold when I went round to interview the editor of *Tailor and Cutter*, the bible of the trade. He was the world's most feared authority on men's clothes and his comments were reprinted worldwide, especially when he attacked the famous, like when he denounced Sir Winston Churchill's homburg hat for making the great statesman look like "an impish jelly baby." *Tailor and Cutter* had been after Churchill regularly since 1908, when it took a whack at his wedding suit (the sleeves were too short). Now it was the new prime minister, Sir Anthony Eden, who was causing despair. Once he had been a fashion plate, but now, *T & C* sighed, "he seems to have lost all interest." Recently the magazine had the dreary duty of pointing out that Sir Anthony had been seen wearing black shoes with a brown hat. It was a sad day for England.

When I called on the magazine's editor, the aptly named John Taylor, he gave me some excellent tips on how to dress like a gentleman. How many suits would I need? At least seven: one for each day of the week, and rotated so that each suit gets a week's rest. Shoes should be on a two-day week and no tie should be worn two days running. One should always carry two handkerchiefs – "one for show and one for blow."

For my interview with John Taylor I'd dressed very carefully, putting on my best shirt and the suit that I used to wear when applying for a job or getting married. Finally, I mustered courage enough to ask him the question.

"What do you think of *my* clothes?" I asked.

"Stand up," he said. "Let's have a look at you."

I stood up, sneakily trying to polish the toe of my shoe on the back of my trouser leg. But he caught me.

"That won't do, will it?" he said sternly.

"No," I agreed, "it won't."

"And here," he said, yanking at my sleeve. "One ought to let one's shirt cuffs show a little, oughtn't one?"

"Yes, one ought," I said. "But tell me, Mr. Taylor, what advice can you give me about my clothes in general?"

He looked at me thoughtfully. "Why don't you burn them?" he suggested.

Bingo! With that remark I knew that I had my story for *Weekend*. I would provide readers with a good laugh at myself – always a popular approach.

I wrote to Brian at length about my exploration of Savile Row, but he showed little interest in my findings. Years later, however, when he was a regular visitor to London, he started

being measured for his suits at Huntsman's, his shirts at Turnbull
& Asser's, his shoes at Lobb's. That was when he was really in
the chips. But even now he seemed to be making very good
money. In New York, Dell was going to bring out his new thriller,
Intent to Kill, with an initial printing, they told him, of 300,000
copies. It would bear his new pen name, Michael Bryan. And
Gold Medal Books, possibly in the spring, was going to print
250,000 copies of *This Gun for Gloria*. The thrillers that he
would come to despise and disown were making for a very comfortable life. And, of course, that new house.

498 Lansdowne Avenue

Westmount, Nov. 4

Dear Paty du Clam,
Well, old man, I have nothing to talk about that isn't real
estate these days, so here goes: I don't know if I've told you this
before, but owning a house in Westmount produces subtle
changes. Shouldn't be surprised to see myself voting a sound
government in. First, all tradespeople who come to the door
call you sir, much more politely than ever before. We are above
Sherbrooke Street. That counts. Life is different on the higher
altitudes. Our neighbour is a McGill man, unpronounceable
Mittel Europa name, formerly taught at Harvard. Young wife,
name of Honor Sharrar, famous American painter, has her
work hung in the Whitney and Mod. Museum. Sold one once
for $9,000. . . .
    Strange changes have set in. Imaginez vous that you are
sitting in a house, all of the inside painted white, bamboo lamp
in dining room overlooking garden, Noguchi lamp in hall, a
few tasteful (framed) reproductions. You walk into your living
room, real bookcases (not bricks and planks), fireplace, all
white (tout est blanche chez nous) and you sit under pull-down
lamp from ceiling (Kanter-Erickson) on sofas (two by
Bronzoni) looking at black officer's chair (Bronzoni) and

expensive little table lamp (K.-E.). Everything the best, man. I mean, it isn't real. I look and I say what am I doing here? All old furniture banished to study and basement. What's happening to me? The Kanter-Erickson men will be here next week with bamboo blinds for dining room and hall.

As Jackie says, Weintraub would never believe it. That is all. We miss you very much. Come home.

Yours,
Alfred Knopf

Hotel Madison, Paris 6

December 31, 1955

Dear Alfred Knopf,
We are in the City of Light for a ten-day year-end holiday. And, as Walt Whitman would have said, I sing of cheese! The other day, in the paper, the French Minister of Agriculture asked, rhetorically, "How can a nation ever die that is able to produce 327 different registered cheeses?" Inspired by this, we last night repaired to the restaurant of H. Androuet, Maitre Fromager, at 41 rue d'Amsterdam, where we were disappointed to find that they offered only 200 of the 327 cheeses. However we made the most of it, asking them to bring on the cheese, platter after assorted platter of it, rendered digestible by choosing from among the 130 different wines in their cellars. Let me assure you that what we ate was not the mundane Camembert and Brie that graces your Westmount table. No, here we had Chabichou from Poitu, Pelardon de Ruoms from Languedoc, Broccio from Corsica, and on and on – an all-cheese dinner. Ecstasy, it was, leaving me this morning feeling too ill to leave the hotel room.

Nothing much to do in Paris, as you know, except gormandizing. Some theatre, but nothing outstanding except

Molière at the Théâtre Nationale Populaire. This was tremendous. New Aymé play about a man who changes people into birds. Funny, less than great. Little avant-garde play by Ionesco, but it was no Godot. Lots of imports, translations, like Les Sorcières de Salem, by Arthur Miller. With Simone Signoret and Yves Montand this was histrionic but good.

Magnificent Etruscan art exhib at the Louvre, where we dropped in to check that the Mona Lisa was still there. Musée de l'Homme a discovery. Wonderful shrunken heads and a fine collection of South American Indian ceremonial penis knots.

We attended a stirring mass meeting featuring Pierre Mendès-France debating with Jacques Duclos. Latter brought thousands of vehement Commie supporters to heckle Mendès-France. Great mob scenes. Thousands of police with walkie-talkies, truncheons, rifles. Bernice and I somehow found ourselves in the midst of the Communist cheering section and were almost crushed to death.

We have also, finally, succeeded in doing a bit of what young travellers dream of, i.e. Meeting French People. We looked up our shipboard acquaintance Grenier, who you will remember played the younger man in that Dostoyevsky play L'Eternal Mari in Montreal. He bought us drinks and then took us out to lunch at the home of some friends in the country. It was a remarkable day because lunch lasted until after midnight, with pauses for cognac, champagne, dinner and the French elections. Magnificent house, built by Mansard for the Maréchal de Noailles. Mozart once stayed there. Present incumbent a short-film producer and his millionaire mistress. Civet de lièvre served for lunch, with 1947 Pommard, Vosne Romanée and Gevrey-Chambertin. Oh, it's the life I love.

You will find enclosed the new list of forbidden books from the Olympia Press (which is just around the corner on rue de Nesle). Tender Was My Flesh, by Winifred Drake, sounds good, doesn't it? And how about Humphrey Richardson's The Sexual Life of Robinson Crusoe? And this Lolita, by Vladimir Nabokov, hot off the press. As the brochure says, "Its very existence

suffices to shatter the present moral order." But still, the
puritans are winning out everywhere, even here in the City of
Light. As noted, Henry Miller's new Sexus is the first
English-language book ever to be banned in France. However
Olympia Press will fill your mail order from abroad. But I jest.
In your new haut bourgeois status on Lansdowne Avenue you
will probably throw this brochure right into your wastepaper
basket, your Kanter-Erickson bamboo wastepaper basket
imported from Mozambique.

Happy New Year to both of you and to young Michael!
Please write frequently and copiously.

> Yr. Obt. Servt.
> William ("Bill") Weintraub

9

In London, the Angry Young Men were at work, making the city a stimulating place to be in 1956. Novelists like Kingsley Amis and John Wain and playwrights like John Osborne and Arnold Wesker were telling us about frustration and rage in the working class, stories seldom heard before in class-ridden England. In May, at the Royal Court Theatre, we saw Osborne's landmark play *Look Back in Anger*. In this, the embittered Jimmy Porter's ranting and pacing about in his shabby one-room flat was radically different from what went on in the usual West End play, where gentlemen wore dinner jackets and sweet young things said, "Anyone for tennis?"

In a different vein, in that very good theatrical season, Dylan Thomas's *Under Milk Wood* was a real treat, while Ionesco gave us two remarkable one-act plays. In one of them, there was a large family in which every single member, male and female, is called Bobby Watson. These people conversed at length with lines like "Oh, you must mean Bobby Watson." "No, I mean Bobby Watson, Bobby's son. Not Bobby, Bobby." Like much of Ionesco, the play was a bit long – but engaging.

For me, however, the most memorable theatre took place on a February afternoon when I managed to wangle a ticket to the Members' Gallery of the House of Commons. Here the troublesome question of capital punishment was being debated, amid a national outcry for its abolition. For more than two years now there had been a growing suspicion that one Timothy Evans had been hanged for a crime he did not commit. And other cases were being cited where the innocent might have been executed, ample reason to do away with the gallows. Britain was fascinated by the case of Evans, who had been convicted of killing his wife and baby daughter. But three years after his execution, the remains of six more bodies were found on the premises where he had lived – 10 Rillington Place, North Kensington, not far from the Notting Hill flat where Bernice and I resided in 1956. Evans had been living in the same building that was occupied by the monstrous Reginald Christie, who was tried and executed for the six murders. Now it was widely believed that Christie had also been responsible for the killings for which Evans had been hanged.

In the House of Commons, in the capital punishment debate, the Evans case was being vehemently cited as a reason for abolition, while the home secretary and others on the government benches, with equal vehemence, insisted that justice had been done in this case and that Evans had definitely been a murderer. The members who spoke had obviously studied the Evans and Christie cases in detail and, in effect, the two trials were being refought on the floor of the House, with verbatim quotes from testimony, Conservatives for the prosecution and Labour for the defence. It was a long and angry debate, but it was conducted with such eloquence that it made me realize, once again, that the English language was really the property of the English; it was *theirs*, and the rest of us could only approximate it. That afternoon in the House, the venerable chamber rang with sarcasm, invective, great wisdom and great stupidity, and it was, for me, the season's greatest theatre.

But I should not overlook another performance, one that took place at the Candlelight Theatre Club, in Chepstow Villas, a street very close to where we lived. Because of the play's theme, I thought Brian Moore would be interested, so I wrote to him about it:

48 Ladbroke Grove
London, W. 11

February 27, 1956

Dear Skinny [he had recently lost weight],
Here culture abounds everywhere, even around the corner. On
Saturday night we attended a play at the nearby Candlelight
Theatre Club. This has been a very cold February, and the
heating in the theatre was minimal. Like other members of the
audience, I was wearing an overcoat and gloves throughout
the performance. The room seats about 120, but there were
only 20 of us shivering souls in the audience.

The play was Midsummer Irish, a comedy by M. J.
Fitzgerald, produced by Joan Quinlan. We'd been given tickets
by our jovial landlady, Mrs. Eland. As it turned out M. J.
Fitzgerald was the pseudonym of Mrs. Eland, and Joan Quinlan
was another pseudonym for Mrs. Eland. And Mrs. Eland
played the part of Maggie Murphy, the village postmistress.
The action takes place in County Tipperary, which I'm sure
you know well.

The part of Cathleen O'Connell was played by Cynthia,
Mrs. Eland's ripe, busty daughter. Part of my motive in going
to the play was the hope that Cynthia might be wearing
something tight, but in this, and in most other aspects of the
evening, I was disappointed. The only really interesting
character in the play was the priest, Father Fitzgerald, who
after the dance went round with a whip, rooting young people
out of the haystacks. Does this really happen in Ireland?

After the final curtain we applauded bravely. Then we
walked home with Lt.-Col. R. I. P. Malcolm, our Scottish
upstairs neighbour, who had some nasty things to say about
Mrs. Eland, our impresario-playwright-actress-landlady. "Does
she think she's fooling anybody with that Irish accent?" he
said. "She certainly didn't have it before she turned Catholic

four years ago." I am thinking of lending Mrs. Eland Judith Hearne. That will sober her up.

Meanwhile we are caught in the crossfire of hatred between Malcolm upstairs and Eland down. Thistle and Sham-shamrock make most devastating remarks to us about each other and it is becoming harder and harder for us to maintain neutrality. This has become exacerbated since Colonel Malcolm's ceiling fell in during the current freeze, gravely endangering his stamp collection. As you must know, it can be damn cold in this country. The thermometer in our bathroom read 43 degrees F this morning. I would not have thought it possible, in such an indoor clime, that human life could be sustained, let alone baths taken.

As for the top floor of our abode, things have been less stressful since Mrs. Gransden's girlfriend was sent to Holloway Women's Prison for stealing money from Mrs. Gransden's Postal Savings account. However we understand that Mrs. Gransden may have to vacate as a result of having "black men with hobnailed boots" (Colonel Malcolm's phrase) stomping about in her quarters at 3 a.m. (Thought you might like this bit of Ladbroke Grove folklore.)

As ever,
Even Skinnier

In Montreal, Brian was also preoccupied with the theatre. At the request of a Broadway director, he was adapting *Judith Hearne* for the stage. For Brian this would be a fruitful and rewarding year, but it would not be without frustration.

He would compete his second novel, *The Feast of Lupercal*, and during one four-month period he would see the publication of three of his books: *Intent to Kill*, a thriller by "Michael Bryan"; *This Gun for Gloria*, a thriller by "Bernard Mara," and *The Lonely Passion of Judith Hearne* (the renamed American edition) by Brian Moore. One author, three names. There was the satisfaction of good financial reward in all this, but the year had its irritations – all stemming from that play, with the many quibbles of the Broadway people and the rewrites they wanted.

"There are MANY parties this year," one of his letters to me said, "but day in, day out, including weekends, the playwright toils. I have never worked so hard on a thing, if only because plays demand a different routine from other writing. In other things, I work best at a certain number of hours a day – then forget about it until the morrow. But the play is the sort of thing you work nights at too – then go to sleep, get up and start all over again. And somehow you do so many versions that you forget what's gone before. I have been a month on this latest version and plan to spend two weeks more before sending it off. . . ."

I was not unfamiliar with the agonies of dramatic creation, having just written *Is It a Woman's World?*, a non-documentary drama, a fantasy actually, for the NFB. Now, in a letter to Brian, I was able to advise him how to find respite from the pressure of work:

> Dear Eugene O'Neill,
> From Mordecai's abode there are muffled cries of birth-agony. These echoed through his phone call to me at noon today, as he urged me to accompany him to an afternoon movie, where the barren typewriter could, momentarily, be relegated to blessed oblivion. Mort argues that Monday is too early in the week to start working, and that if one can get nothing more out of the day than an iron resolution to work hard the rest of the week, it is still quite an accomplishment for a Monday. I must say this makes sense.
>
> But oh, I have those free-lance blues. I know what it is to await the mailman. I especially await news about my possible trip to Russia (you got my last letter, eh?). Editor cables that he is writing me on this, but he writeth not. Meanwhile I will be doing a Weekend piece on Lady Docker, who rides in a gold-plated Daimler. Confidentially, I would rather

be writing something GREAT, but I cannot think of anything great to write. Maybe I should go out to Elstree and get some joe job and learn something about the feature film biz. Maybe I will.

Write.

Orson Welles

~

After the Queen and Princess Margaret, Lady Docker was the most talked-about woman in Britain. My first interview with her was over lunch with her and Sir Bernard in their elegant Mayfair apartment, where the butler poured the pink champagne and the maid served paté de foie gras with truffles the size of your eyeball. In my first question to her, I asked how she had managed to become the women's marbles champion of the world.

"You need strong knuckles – and lots of practice," said Her Ladyship, showing me her knuckles. It had been an uphill struggle, with long hours on the floor practising. She took her marbles with her wherever she went, to her country estate, to her house in Jamaica, to her yacht in the Mediterranean. She asked the British Marbles Board of Control for a few tips, but that august body icily retorted that marbles was a man's game, and she wasn't welcome. But she persisted, and even got a few experts to coach her, including the eighty-four-year-old captain of the Cupthorne Spitfires Marbles Team. Finally she was ready for the big day, for the tournament against the championship team of Yorkshire factory girls. She arrived for the tournament in her gold-plated Daimler, knelt down on a gold cushion and sent a wicked marble spinning into the fray. The rest was history. And needless to say, the British press loved it.

But there was a price to pay, she told me. Sir Bernard was head of a huge company that produced, among other things, Daimler automobiles, and his board of directors was embarrassed by not only the marbles, but also other japes that garnered great publicity, like the Dockers' occasional fights in nightclubs. The company directors also wanted to know why Lady Docker's gold dress, her wild-mink stole, her sapphire mink bolero and other sundries had all been charged to the company. Sir Bernard said it was invaluable publicity for Daimler. As the boardroom battle raged, Lady Docker sent thousands of autographed photos of herself to shareholders. In the crisis, Sir Bernard told me, "Norah behaved like an absolute brick" – the highest compliment a British husband can pay to his wife. And Norah demurely told me that she had learned the rules of the financial jungle, "Never wound, kill."

But it was all in vain. Sir Bernard was booted out of the company and Norah had to relinquish her beloved Daimler, the Golden Zebra, for which she had designed the decor. All the metal fittings, inside and out, were gold plated – wheels, windshield wipers and the cocktail bar facing the back seat. Upholstery was courtesy of six real zebras and there was a man to brush it every day (the more you brush zebra skin the silkier it gets). The confiscation of the car made headlines, and a nightclub comedian wrote a song entitled, "When My Hair Has Turned to Silver, Will My Bumpers Still Be Gold?"

I had expected Lady Docker to be tough and brassy, weatherbeaten by night life and scuffles with the International Smart Set (when she bopped Prince de Faucigny-Lucinge in the Monte Carlo Sporting Club, the slap echoed up and down the Riviera). But lunching with her and Sir Bernard I found her to be very gentle, feminine and soft-spoken. She had soft hazel eyes, a smooth complexion and a trim figure that made it hard to believe she had just turned fifty.

When she was sixteen, she'd been a shopgirl selling hats in a Lancashire town. But she managed to meet the right people, and her first husband, when he died, left her half a million dollars. Her second husband, when *he* died, left her twice as much. And now, her third husband, Sir Bernard, was still rolling in money after being kicked out of Daimler. The most important thing in life, they told me, was to have fun. Recently, having decided to let nothing interfere with that and figuring they had twenty-five or thirty years left to live, they divided their capital by thirty and decided to spend that much for each year.

Their flamboyant behaviour shocked the upper classes, but the poor seemed to be not in the least offended. "When I went to open a charity bazaar in the slums," she told me, "I purposely wore a mink coat and drove up in the gold car. They loved me for it. The women kept looking at my coat and saying, 'Can I touch it, love?'"

I asked her how she felt about people who criticized her extravagant ways and she was emphatic in her answer. "It's very fashionable to pretend not to have money. That way you don't have to give any away." The Dockers, on the other hand, were said to be very generous with their charities, although they seldom made these public. "I took up marbles because it was a benefit tournament for cancer relief," she said. "A lot of my friends had cancer, and my mother died of it."

The Dockers' greatest extravagance was their yacht, the *Shemara*, which, at the time, was the largest owned by any Briton. She had a cruising range of seven thousand miles and a crew of thirty. When I went aboard I was shown nine luxurious bedrooms, seven tiled bathrooms, a cozy lounge with a fireplace, a machine to make ice cream and enough champagne for a six-month voyage through the most thirsty latitudes.

Of the many parties they gave on the *Shemara*, the most famous was the one for thirty-three Yorkshire miners, whom they'd met during a visit to the mines. The miners were picked up by a fleet of limousines and driven across England to the yacht. Waiting for them were three saddles of beef, plus salmon, lobster and pheasant. And so many cases of champagne, whisky, gin and brandy that one observer noted that the yacht basin might be rendered unnavigable by the empties. To entertain the miners, Lady Docker danced a hornpipe for them.

All this, and more, went into the article I wrote for *Weekend*. And I ended the piece by saying, "For many Britons, the Dockers seem to be a symbol of vanished splendour. Recovery from the war has been hard, and life has often been drab. Quietness and carefulness have been post-war virtues in Britain, but the Dockers just don't have those virtues. Instead, they make a bright splash of colour in the greyness of everyday life; some people revel in this, others are revolted. And many have a mixed opinion, like the socialist writer who watched the goings-on aboard the yacht when the miners were being entertained.

"'It was vulgar,' he wrote. 'It was reprehensible. And, in its old-fashioned way, it was splendid.'"

⟞

498 Lansdowne Avenue
Westmount, Quebec

January 10

Dear Wanderer:
Strange doings in Land of Plenty: Larder of Lansdowners, deriving from Christmas gifts, now includes smoked grasshoppers, alligator soup and rattlesnake sauce. Also French snails, rare spices. Also, bar at Lansdowne now includes Pernod, Pastis, Byrrh, Scotch, Rye, Izarra. Reason: Host's sudden return after years of pain to drinking form. Weight this morning: 166 pounds.

Lansdowners are filled in with incisive word pictures of life in London. In particular a breathtaking description of the Young Palace Set at Kensington High Poker Soirees. R. Ship, T. Allan, B. Weintraub and M. Richler. It seems Weintraub always loses. Mort always wins. True to form? . . .

48 Ladbroke Grove
London W. 11

January 29

Dire Sire:

About those poker games, you've got one small detail wrong:
it's Weintraub who wins, Richler who loses.

Today I am recuperating after yesterday's recuperation
after Friday's Mortoparty, at his place, in honour of
his attaining the age of 25. This thought, plus the
imminence of my own tri-decade anniversary, led to some
serious imbibition.

A gay fiesta, on the whole, with the presence of some 30
souls, representing the Canadian colony, various Bolshevist
factions and certain indigenous intelligentsia. One guest was a
culture lady on a mission from the People's Democratic
Republic of Poland, who spoke of the sweetness and light
prevailing in that land. Made jokes about Stalin and generally
spoke in a way that indicates that the Party girdle is loosen-
ing. As you know, the Red Menace, at this distance, is neither
as Red nor as menacing as it is at home. However, it was startling to hear somebody say, "When I was in the agit-prop
school with Tito's son. . . ."

Yours for world peace,
Trotsky

Letters from Brian, that year, were getting longer and longer,
making me wonder, as a slow writer myself, how he could have
time left over for his prodigious output of professional prose.
Some of the letters were four pages long, typed single-spaced and
with narrow margins. Now, more than ever, he kept bringing me
up to date on *Weekend* office gossip, as brought home to him by
Jackie, who was still working there:

January 30

Now Hear This:
Weekend has taken over NANA syndication service
officially. Glenn Gilbert, Weekend prexy, is installed in
sumptuous apartment at One Beekman Place, NYC,
commutes once weekly to Montreal to run Weekend. Craig
quote to JMoore: "Money is very big now." New deal
makes McConnell empire international, muchly big, with
prospects for all staffers, globegirdling, in near future. First
rumblings are: Clark to London, A. O'Brien to Cortina for
Winter Olympics. . . .

February 15

Hear Me Talkin' to Ya:
About INTENT TO KILL [his new thriller]: I have received
advance copies and the book is a honey, boy, a honey.
No sex at all in blurb, treated as straight novel with suspense
note, and GET THIS (because they paid a lot for it) the
cover was done by the same artist who did the cover for
Not As a Stranger, which cover was used by MGM in all their
promotion, etc., and on movie marquees. And, son, my cover
looks damn like that one. So mine may sell like hotcakes
or it may fail because people think it's the soft cover edition
of Not As a S. Is that quite clear? Carry on. I am sending
you a copy forthwith.
   Again there have been airmail special deliveries flying to
and fro, between Fifth Avenue 522 and Lansdowne 498.
I have been countering the promotion department of Dell,
who have discovered about Judith Hearne and want to use
my real name in promoting Intent to Kill. It comes out on
Feb 9. However I have, I hope, scotched that by direct
violent letter writing. . . .

March 12

Diary of a Smaller Hero:
I have just read Lucky Jim, by Amis, about three years after
everybody else. But get it, read it, it is the funniest book since
early Evelyn Waugh. Funnier in some ways. Do read this.

Met with Canada's Ed Sullivan, the mountainous Nate King
Cohen [CBC broadcaster and television producer] in his
Laurentien hotel suite. Nate wants to make hour dramas
budget $11 thousand each one. Said Mort had sold Acrobats to
him. Offered him Intent to Kill. While I was there, 4 writers
called, offering him scripts. He says he has had calls from 30 in
all since appearing in town. Nate Europewards this spring to
record England's lit life, great men before recorders and T.V.
cameras, interviewed by your genial host.

Leaving Nate, went to meet in Press Club with Norman
Levine, who is staying here at the home of Mort's mother and
who emplanes for Ottawa tonight – I hope. He was full of
questions, suggestions, etc. Gather his book will be titled (by
me) Across Canada on a Promise to Pay. Or Journey Without
Travellers' Cheques. He wants to model his opus on Greene's
Journey Without Maps and has some interesting thoughts such
as staying for a weekend with Vincent Massey and then writing
about him as a little man who looks like a Martian. Tried to
dissuade him from this bit of imagery, but you know these
creative people when inspiration strikes them.

Norman was warm on Mort, cold on Weintraub, freezing on
Weintraub (feminine gender). Said Bill was a nice fellow but
no get up and go. Coming from him that was, I felt, a damning
indictment of you, old slug. . . .

No get up and go? How could I let that canard go unanswered?
Moore had passed on that wretched remark of minimalist Levine
with obvious glee, finding in it further support for his conviction
that I was bone lazy. Nothing I could do would ever change his
mind. If I sent him a ten-thousand-page novel that I'd written in

a week, I'd still be a slacker. And look at my recent efforts. I had, in addition to the usual stuff, written – and sold! – a one-hour television play, based on my old *Mona Lisa* story, nicely recycled. To be called *Million-Dollar Smile* and to appear on London ITV. I was about to fire off a blistering retort to Brian but then decided to play it cool, low-key. Perhaps my mentioning the figure of $4,000 would make an impression:

March 21

Mon ami,
Thank you for passing on Norman Levine's warm salutation.

Yes I have read Lucky Jim and agree that it is the funniest. Kingsley Amis in person was not quite so hilarious at a party where we met him recently. High as a kite and made an improper suggestion to my wife.

Not that you asked, but I now have work lined up to keep me busy until about May 15. By that time I will have been in London for eight months and will have made about $4,000. This covers my contribution to our budget for the whole year with enough left over to buy a car. But to make this dough I have had to ply the old rackets – Weekend and Film Board, mainly – with a few other uninspired odds and ends. What I haven't done is hang around the film studios, try to write a feature script (although I did write two shorter dramas). In other words, I haven't progressed very much. And not much time remains to do that sort of thing, according to our original plan. Only two and a half months, at which time we embark on our two-month auto tour of the Continent – a trip we've been planning for years.

Why don't you and Jackie join us in part of our Grand Tour, which departs from Brussels on August 6 at 9 a.m. The powerful automobile will roar down the Rhine Valley, stopping only for refreshing draughts of 52 Riesling Trokenbeerenauslese, and traffik in contraband photographic equipment. Out of the Rhine into the Black Forest. Munich. Short putsch and then turn left to Salzburg, Innsbruck, Brenner Pass, Venice, Trieste, Belgrade, Split, Something or other, Macedonia, Salonika, Athens, Rhodes, Lesbos. If funds permit, by short air-hop to Istanbul. Return via Athens, Brindisi, Roma, Florence, Pisa, Torino, San Remo, Monte Carlo, Cannes, Avignon, Dijon, Chambertin, Pouilly Fuissé, Montrachet, Pommard, Beaune, Paris, Calais, Dover. Golders Green by 9 a.m. October 6.

Come for a month of this, or any part you like. You could recoup the cost and more by doing research for the next tome by Bernard Mara or Michael Bryan. Is either of those authors familiar with The Glory That Was Greece? You could skulk through the sinister back streets of Salonika and familiarize yourself with the ways of traffickers in drugs, armaments or illicit olive oil. Jackie too could make the trip profitable by doing a mag piece on the oppression of whatever group of people we find being oppressed, as we drive along, through country after country. Do come. I can pick up passengers at any sea or air terminal in western Europe. Please advise.

Baedeker

Brian wrote his next letter to me before receiving my itinerary for the Grand Tour, so there was no response to my invitation to join it. Instead he wrote in great detail how he had been approached to write a biography of Sir James Dunn, recently deceased. Dunn had been head of Algoma Steel and one of Canada's richest men. His widow, it seems, was a great admirer of *Judith Hearne*. In his discussions with Lady Dunn's secretary, Brian gathered that a very favourable biography was required and that the fee would be $30,000 (about $200,000 in 2001 dollars). "My father's Catholic conscience fought with Greed," Brian wrote, "and conscience finally won. Let me tell you, it was quite a day. Not every day you turn down $30,000. Everything seems dull since, as though I had been playing in a dollar poker game and had been moved back to penny ante. But I gave it up and was glad. I hate to think that money can buy everything and hate more than that the idea of giving two years of my life to being Lady Dunn's lapdog and writing a shameful eulogy of one of the Greatest Bastards this country has ever produced."

I read Brian's words with a mixture of admiration and irritation. His probity often irritated me, this time forcing me to wonder whether I, dilettantish hack that I was, could have turned down that $30,000. But when Brian's next letter arrived, I got some comfort from the seeing that now it was he who was irritated – by a letter of mine, the one where I'd invited him to join me in Venice, Athens, etc., etc.

March 31

Dear Baedeker:
Please do not, repeat NOT, continue this insidious listing
of pleasure trips. Let me explain: I have a wife, a two-year-old
boy and a house. I have not made any dough since last October
and I have not finished work on my second book. I am
determined to finish it properly and cultivate my jardin. So
when I finish it – next month I hope – I will have to buckle
down and make the usual handsome Moore allowance of
commercial dough. If and when I do this, I will have bucks, will
travel. That would be in the fall, late fall, at the earliest, and
the travel would have to be purposeful. Meaning Ireland
and England and possibly one pocket-book research place. But
also it would be for the minimum amount of time as my boy
Michael is at that golden age when he speaks but comprehends
not and when I am to him a great mother figure [Jackie being
downtown at work all day] and he does not like it if he does
not see me each day. To keep his trauma from danger I cannot
leave him for too long.
    Michael is a great fellow these days. He is all sunshine and
trust. A pity it will not last. But he is much fun to be with. He
can identify your photo as well as pictures of Joyce, Proust,
Gide, Dostoyevsky, Flaubert, Yeats and O'Casey. He can identify
pictures by Picasso, Klee, Rouault. I taught him these little

lifemanship tricks and am now starting him on secondary
painters like Surrey, etc. It goes over pretty good when people
like Jean Palardy are around. (Especially when the guest can't
identify the people concerned.)

~

"What am I doing here?" I used to ask myself when work took me
into unlikely situations, like when I suddenly threw a Vampire
jet fighter into a steep dive, not far from Exeter, in Devon.
Fortunately the pilot quickly took the joystick away from me and
brought the plane back up to where it belonged, somewhere
around thirty-five thousand feet, I guess. I had had no idea that
the controls were so sensitive; just an inch or two too much with
that joystick could send you plummeting down to perdition. The
pilot had asked me if I'd like to fly the plane for a bit and I'd been
foolish enough to say yes. The experience would be useful for my
Weekend story. The pilot and I were seated side by side, in this
fighter-trainer, having taken off from the Empire Test Pilots'
School at Farnborough. The ride across the width of England
was exhilarating, up there above the clouds. Until I took the
controls and tried to annihilate us.

That question, "What am I doing here?" came up again a few
months later, at the Cannes Film Festival, when I woke up suddenly from a sound sleep during the screening of a boring
Russian film entitled *Poème Pédagogique*. I had been accompanied
to the screening in the Grande Salle by Anne Hébert, the
Quebec novelist, but my snoring during the movie presumably
blotted my copybook with her forever. I also managed to alienate
an official of the Soviet delegation, sitting in the seat to my
right. It was a sharp jab in the ribs from this apparatchik's elbow
that woke me up.

What indeed was I doing at this festival? As the days went by,
I couldn't seem to figure out what to write for *Weekend*, which had
been extravagant enough to send me down to Cannes. I was there
to do an "atmosphere" piece, not to review the films, and in any

case the films that were being premiered, except for a very few, weren't very good. Only Ingmar Bergman's latest, *Smiles of a Summer Night*, struck me as being a masterpiece. *Et Dieu Créa la Femme*, with Brigitte Bardot, was also interesting, if only to check out the press release's contention that Bardot had "the sex appeal of Marlene Dietrich, the glamour of Ava Gardner, the oomph of Jane Russell and the pep of Marilyn Monroe." Most popular of all was *The Swan*, because it starred Grace Kelly, who was now Princess Grace, having only a few days earlier been married to Prince Ranier in nearby Monaco. Thirty million people were said to have watched the "storybook wedding" on television, and at Cannes the festivaleers peered out at the Mediterranean to see if they could catch sight of the 147-foot yacht that Onassis had given the young couple as a wedding present.

With my press pass, hunting for an angle, I made the rounds of the cocktail parties and the late-night galas, attired in my new dinner jacket. At these booze-ups I fell in with the British contingent, which was led by actor Peter Finch, a heroic drinker, and was graced by the presence of beautiful actress Belinda Lee. Finch and the other Britons assured me that it was infra dig to actually attend the screenings, which interfered with partygoing and lying on the beach. A quick reading of the press release was all you needed if you wanted to be prepared to discuss a film intelligently.

But what could I cook up for *Weekend*? There was a symposium on the aesthetics of the cinema at the Hotel Majestic, with thinkers from several countries vying with each other to attain new levels of incomprehensibility, but this would hardly be of interest to readers of the *Moose Jaw Times-Herald*, one of the twenty-seven leading newspapers that were now carrying *Weekend* as a Saturday supplement. With a circulation of 1,500,000 – the largest of any Canadian publication – *Weekend* had to cater to a common denominator that was not too high.

Desperately searching for an angle, I interviewed Irina Skobtseva, the Soviet glamour girl, but all she could tell me was that in the new Soviet cinema it was no longer just Boy Meets Tractor but also Boy Meets Girl. This interview led nowhere, and in the end I was obliged to find my story at Eden Beach – *la Plage des Vedettes et la Vedette des Plages* (the Beach of the Stars and the Star of the Beaches).

"That's where the action is," an American journalist advised me, and he was right. Arriving at the beach at noon one sunny day, the first thing I saw was a terrified girl in a bikini cowering in front of a photographer who was brandishing a live baby alligator, about eight inches long. "He won't hurt you," the photographer was saying, but the girl didn't seem to believe him. Another photographer explained it to me. It seems that the pin-up industry had become highly competitive and the men of the navy would no longer settle for simple photos of girls in bathing suits. Now there had to be something unusual in the picture, like a little alligator sitting on the girl's shoulder.

Nearby a beautiful Danish blonde was posing with a parrot perched on top of her head. "Hurry up!" she was saying to the photographer. "He is eating my hair." Here, I realized, would be my story for Saturday readers of the Timmins *Daily Press* and the other twenty-six papers. I would explain to them how at eleven o'clock of every festival morning, beautiful girls of many nations, in the briefest of bikinis, would arrive at the beach and array themselves on their towels or stroll up and down, insouciantly. The hope of each girl was to be discovered by a film producer, but while waiting for that happy moment she would willingly pose for the cheesecake photographers of many nations who were swarming the beach.

Somehow I managed to get a story out of all this, to be fleshed out – if I may put it that way – with appropriate girlie photos. My masters in Montreal liked it very much, and thought it quite humorous, but when I saw it in print, accompanied by a photo of myself talking to Kim Novak, I could only hope, vainly, that nobody I knew would ever see it. It was, to put it plainly, silly. And it got me to brooding again about how could I be wasting my life concocting such tripe. Was it just because I was desperate to see the world, at any price? But if I had to see Cannes at festival time, why wasn't I writing a piece for some obscure little journal denouncing the meretricious sham of these caviar-and-champagne film festivals? Why wasn't I up in the mountains, where, hopefully, I might find some peasants who were starving?

I was still brooding about this sort of thing when I got back to London, after my festivalling. And my world was made to seem only more trivial by a letter that Mordecai passed on to me. It was from Brian and was addressed to both Mordecai and me:

April 11, 1956

Dear Mortbill,
Am addressing this Round Robin to show you that you are wasting your time in that England backwater you live in.

Yes, I spent two and a half hours with Graham Greene yesterday, right here in Montreal, and imbibed a hell of a lot of doubles in the process. Graham had just been taken on a city tour by two Jesuits and today he is flying back to the Old World to have a look at the Grace Kelly–Prince Ranier nuptials. "Can't resist it. Love Monaco."

G. G. told me he is half way through my book and likes it very much. Told him I liked his too and we had a very nice chat about books and films. I must say G. G. is pretty good in this dept. I mean he says pretty sensible things about the filmic medium: "Sell your story outright and stop worrying. You can never collaborate successfully and they will change it. The alternative is to write the script yourself and allow no changes. This is wearing." He then kindly cast my book for me, with Robert Taylor in the lead and Irene Dunne as Miss Hearne. Both have lots of money but each thinks the other one will only take him/her if they think he/she is poor. Eventually they get together for a happy ending. "Do not worry," G.G says. "If they do it that way your consolation will be that you will get lots of doubloons."

He told me some pretty good ones about what they did to his books. Very witty fellow, very pleasant, very intelligent and reasonable. Would like to see him more often but I suppose I shan't.

What's new in your neck of the woods? This morning from
Winnipeg Norman Levine cables: "Please send $50. Reply
at once."

I don't care if no one knows what Feast of Lupercal means.
Do you know what Sun Also Rises means? Anyway, you
ignorant bastards, read your Shakespeare. J. Caesar.

Told Graham Greene I liked Heart of the Matter. Favourite.
He said: "Oh, God, it's quite my unfavourite book."

Never know what to say to authors, do you?

As ever,
Scobie

~

As the year progressed, the accolades for *Judith Hearne* kept
pouring in. In one of his letters, Brian told me that he had been
invited for drinks by Hugh MacLennan and he quoted a paragraph from MacLennan's letter of invitation: "That is an utterly
wonderful novel you've written, and even with a small body of
work to follow it up, it's just about certain to live. It's my guess
that a very large body of work will follow it up, for if anyone is a
born novelist, it's you. I think you've got just about everything,
including an absolute grasp of your medium and that kind of
ability to ride a bicycle on curves around a tight rope that simply
can't be learned. That book of yours is like music with melodies
returning and returning."

Besides quoting MacLennan, Brian's letter also quoted from
the jacket of *The Other Paris*, Mavis Gallant's first book, a collection of her stories, which had just been published: "Her people
are observed with a stereoscopic eye, a neat sense of detail, and a
comprehension as deep as the sea. She laughs and cries at the
right places."

In July, after the American edition of *Judith Hearne* had been
published, Brian sent me a clipping from the *New York Times*,
where a laudatory review by Orville Prescott said: "Seldom in

modern fiction has any character been revealed so completely
or been made to seem so poignantly real." But in his letter
that accompanied the clipping, Brian was less than thrilled by
this praise:

> The Times does one book a day and Orville Prescott is their
> Führer. There must be something really wrong with my book if
> that crap artist likes it. But it is BIG to get his word, they tell
> me. I am not impressed and neither should anyone else be. . . .
> I can't send you other reviews as I have only one copy of them
> [these being the days before photocopy machines] and must
> keep them to show to the Theatre Guild people, but here is a
> pastiche of some of them: The Washington Star made the book
> their lead review, with 2-column cut of author. "Powerful First
> Novel by New Irish Author." Review by one Carter Brooke
> Jones, full column – "a serious, mature, well-organized novel."
>
> The Washington News has a two-column feature by one
> Tom Donnelly headed "More Shadow Than Substance" (a
> reference to Shadow and Substance, a well-known Irish play)
> and starts off with a fine dig at Little, Brown [the publishers
> who insisted on a new title for the American edition]:
> "Look beyond the title, which might suggest an emotional
> smorgasbord with pathos laid out on the table like a platter of
> cold cuts, and you will find Brian Moore's The Lonely Passion
> of Judith Hearne a novel of rare and biting excellence." He
> goes on for eight paragraphs.
>
> "Remarkable First Novel, Sardonic and Intelligent," is the
> Worcester, Mass., Telegram's contribution, ending up with
> "This is the best novel we have read this year." 2-col cut
> of Baby Face Moore. Boston Globe: "Compelling sense of
> presence. Judith Hearne is here to stay." Boston Herald:
> "Exceptional first novel." Also similar stuff from Cleveland
> Plain Dealer, Erie Times and papers in Connecticut, Utah, etc.
> West Coast papers not in yet.

~

In the Canadian Film Awards that summer, *Saskatchewan Traveller*, for which I had written the script, won first prize in a new category: films made especially for television. I was particularly pleased by this, because in none of the other films I wrote for the NFB's "Perspective" series did the research give me so much pleasure. It was a simple story I wanted to tell: the tribulations and satisfactions of a travelling salesman visiting small Prairie towns. I started out in Yorkton, where I met a number of salesmen who were happy to tell me about their experiences. One of them, a somewhat tired, middle-aged man named Harold, agreed to take me on his weekly rounds of small towns in his old Chevrolet. He was selling grocery products, in a time before supermarkets, and he took me to Dressler's Store in Churchbridge, Anderson's Store in Saltcoats, Dad's Grocery and Gas in Waldron, Kammermeyer's Pool Hall and General Store in Langenburg. I listened as Harold made his pitch to the merchants – "I've got a real good special on canned tomatoes for you this week, Fred" – often being interrupted by shoppers, who always had priority. He would wait patiently to get the storekeeper's ear again and then have to put up with bad temper on occasion or, more often, good-natured joshing.

I'd had no experience of small towns, and was fascinated by places like Goodeve, Fenwood, Mozart and a hamlet actually called Tiny. The blacksmiths' shops, the grain elevators, the enormous prairie sky with its stars at night – it was all so strange, and somehow exotic. I even liked the seedy old hotels we stayed in, where the fire escape from your second-floor bedroom might consist of a coil of rope, with one end attached to the radiator; if a fire broke out you'd simply throw the rope out the window and climb down to safety.

For this film, I persuaded the NFB to let me leave the interviewer out of it. Instead, it would be a straight drama, with an actor from Toronto playing the salesman. All the other parts would be taken by the locals playing themselves, Mr. Dressler in Dressler's Store, Mr. Anderson in Anderson's Store and so on. In my instructions to the director, I wrote: "The atmosphere should be rural but not hayseed; the people involved are all quite civilized. What is not intended is that twangy, Toonerville-trolley rusticism that is so dear to the hearts of certain Prairie writers. It just doesn't exist in this area." The director, Don Haldane, later told me that he felt *Saskatchewan Traveller* had achieved a Chekovian flavour. I wouldn't go that far, but it really was a pretty good half-hour.

Besides our winning the award, there was another piece of good news from home that summer. The National Film Board was about to move from its rickety old Ottawa headquarters to a spanking new building in Montreal, with state-of-the-art editing rooms and recording theatres, as well as a huge sound stage, suitable for making feature films. One of the great benefits of this move, for me, was that I would no longer have to go to Ottawa for meetings and could thus throw away the small grey booklet that had been issued to me by the Liquor Control Board of Ontario and was labelled "Individual Liquor Permit." It seemed that anybody in that strange province who wanted to buy a bottle now and then to take to a party had to have one of those permits. Inside the permit were pages where the store clerk would enter the date of your purchase and the amount of booze you bought, be it a bottle or a half-bottle. Presumably if there were too many entries you'd be called onto the carpet, somewhere. The booklet carried a page of warnings: don't drink and drive, of course, but also "It is an offence to permit drunkenness in your home or hotel room." For a Quebecker like myself, that little grey booklet epitomized the soul of Ontario. And now I wouldn't need it any more.

If I needed anything to remind me of the difference between prim-and-proper Ottawa and my old Montreal, it could be found in the next letter I received from Brian:

> The Vachons [friends from New York] and we went to a night-club the other night and stayed from 11 to 3 a.m. without any stop in the show and never a repeat item. This show had six strippers, an ice review, then a talent contest for amateur singers (great), then a magician, then a Negro show, then again six

strippers, which is where we came in. Vachon, experienced in North American nightclubs, said he never saw anything like it in his life. It was the old El Patio on St. Lawrence.

. . . I was 35 last Saturday. A very sad day. Got very drunk Friday night, to keep the record straight. Last fling of youth. Life more than half over. Remember this when you are 35. It is a sad birthday. . . .

That letter was forwarded to me from London to Altaussee, Austria, where Bernice and I had just arrived during our seven-week Grand Tour of the Continent, driving in our new British Ford Zephyr. In Altaussee, an alpine village, we were staying with my old McGill friend Charles Wassermann, who, with his wife, Jacqueline, was occupying his ancestral home. From this base, Charles was doing broadcasts for CBC Radio and was currently working on a series called *Iron Curtain Journeys*, describing his forays into Hungary, Czechoslovakia and Poland. He was also broadcasting for the BBC, and in German for Swiss, Austrian and German radio. While I was writing for the *McGill Daily*, way back then, Charles had been learning his trade at the McGill Radio Workshop. These activities had been much more important for us than the academic side of university life.

In Altaussee, I was surprised to find the locals addressing Charles as "Herr Baron." It seems that long ago Charles's father, Jakob Wassermann, a celebrated Austrian novelist, had been offered a baronetcy by the Emperor Franz Joseph, but had turned it down. But that was enough for the proud villagers of Altaussee to forever consider that Jakob and his son, Charles, were true noblemen, deserving to be called baron. We had a very pleasant stay with the baron and the baroness, rehashing old McGill days and, as I advised Brian in a letter, "He sets a fine table, with wine by the cask and savory wild mushrooms picked by a retinue of local peasants."

From Altaussee we drove to Vienna, where again one saw depressing signs of the economic recovery that was making Europe more expensive for tourists. But Tito's Yugoslavia was still dirt cheap, and in Zagreb you could get that wonderful Gavrilovic salami or a tangy Schweinspaprikas for next to nothing. We got as far south as Rijeka, on the Adriatic coast, but by then it was time to turn around and head back homeward. Athens, the Greek islands and Istanbul would have to wait for a later trip.

Heading north and west, we stopped for a few days in Venice to take in the film festival. I'd been hoping there would be a new Fellini film, having recently seen *La Strada*, certainly the most brilliant film in many a year, but there was no Fellini on the program. Claude Autant-Lara's *Traversée de Paris* was very good, as was *Der Hauptmann von Koepenick*, a German entry, but by and large most of the films – or the ones we managed to see – were as lacklustre as those at Cannes.

Back in London, I reported on my trip to Brian, especially as to its cost, as he and Jackie were thinking of a European tour in the spring.

London, Sept. 18, 56

Dear Strindberg [he was still writing his play],
The White Cliffs of Dover are really grey, and belong to the realities of this world, unlike Venice and Beaune, of blessed memory. You will be interested to know that yesterday morning, as the car ferry approached these legendary cliffs, I felt a lump in my throat, mainly because I was at the stern, looking back at Boulogne.

But enough is enough. As you so sagaciously note, we have had a reasonably extended junket and all things must end. For your future guidance, you may want to know the vital statistics of this Third Crusade:

Number of days away . . . 49. Number of countries visited . . . 8. Number of miles covered . . . 3,450. Total cost . . . $875. Average cost per day, including gasoline, food, lodging, everything . . . $17.85. With economies it can be done for less than $15, I think, but we didn't try too hard. Hell, one scriptie and one Weekender paid for it.

I am now thoroughly sold on car travel. Much cheaper than
by train and you see a hell of a lot more. One of the greatest
bits was the glory road from Beaune to Dijon, passing fabulous
road signs that say Corton, Nuits St. Georges, Chambertin,
Vougeot and I won't torture you with any more. We must all do
this *slowly* some day. We visited several cellars and the free
tasting is magnificent. Straight from the barrel, Monsieur, and
shall we see how the Savigny-les-Beaune 53 is doing?

In Paris for three days. It's changing, slowly and sadly,
although it will probably take a good few decades before it looks
like Murray's in Montreal. But it will. Even since you were there,
things have happened. That little tabac near the Madison is now
bright moderne, with fluorescent lights. Spoiled.

But back to London and more serious considerations.
Winchester Road [where Mordecai was now living] most
impressive these days – a real lit factory with George Lamming
batting out a novel in guest room, Mort polishing novel in
front room, and Cathy doing script-typing job for Reuben Ship
in kitchen. I am angling for office space on the landing, hope
to set up shop soon. I have a few original or semi-original ideas
for feature scripties, and am going to work hard on one or
another of these in the months ahead. Will do a few
Perspective and Weekend items to pay the rent.

Thanks for yours of recent date. Please write again
soon. Really looking forward to seeing Novel 2. Will I also
see playscript?

W. W.

In the fall of 1956, London was preoccupied by upheavals in
Europe and the Middle East. In Ladbroke Grove, we got a first-
hand account of the aborted revolution in Hungary from Charles
Wassermann, who came to dinner during a visit from Austria.
Charles had been in Budapest as a radio reporter when the
turmoil began, and he told us how he had seen corpses hanging
from lampposts. He watched as a mob swarmed over a statue of

Stalin that had been knocked off its pedestal, with people hacking away at it with steel saws to get souvenir fragments. One man rushed over to Wassermann, kissed the Union Jack on his car and handed him a small piece of Stalin. But then the Russian tanks started rolling in, to suppress the rebellion, and one tank major shouted to Wassermann, "I give you thirty seconds to get behind that barrier, or I shoot."

At the same time, in Egypt, things were boiling over around the Suez Canal, and this prompted a heated letter from Brian:

> Total horror and abhorrence here for the British-French action. The Commonwealth has been rifted and Albion has once again proven her perfidy – aren't they bastards! . . . The unspoken question here is Israel's part in all this. Liberal opinion is too polite to say it, but generally people – including me – think the Israelis are fools and possibly scoundrels. They've established some sort of record as the number one victims of aggression showing that now they can line up in collusion with the old-line capitalist powers. A point forgotten by almost everyone is my small Irish one. Egypt is Nasser's country – he is a hero to his people, he ousted the monarchy, he blustered but at least he freed his country from foreign rule. How on earth people can call him a Middle East Hitler is a masterpiece of doublethink. It's his country, for heaven's sake, it's his canal. And don't tell me Eden [the British prime minister] went in to protect Israel. Eden must go. Provocation of border incidents is no excuse for going into a war of this kind. Ben-Gurion [the Israeli prime minister] must go. . . .

The "border incidents" Brian was referring to were months of repeated Egyptian commando raids into Israel, a state that had now been in existence for only eight years. In an effort to put an end to these incursions, Israel sent troops into Egypt at the end of October. Advancing toward the Suez Canal, the Israelis quickly routed the Egyptian army. A week later Britain and France invaded the Suez area, to reassert control over the canal. This

lifeline between Europe and the Orient had been controlled
by Britain for almost a century, before being nationalized that
summer by Gamal Abdel Nasser, the Egyptian president. Now
Britain and France feared that Nasser might close the canal to
their shipping, cutting off the supply of oil from the Persian Gulf.

Brian's letter about these events elicited a reply from me:

> In your letter you seem to feel that I must be a fan of Perfidious
> Albion. Sir, may I remind you that I am a veteran of last
> Sunday's "Eden Must Go" march on Downing Street. Yes,
> Mordecai and I attended that meeting in Trafalgar Square, to
> listen to Aneurin Bevan (wonderful speaker) lambaste Sir
> Anthony. Then the mob decided to march on Downing Street
> to express its sentiments. We went along, and it is strictly a
> page for the Memory Album. About 20,000 people jamming
> Whitehall. Mounted police charging. Scuffles. Placards
> knocked down. Everybody screaming "Eden must go!" We were
> right up front, with the horses plunging around, and for a
> minute it was quite dicey. Some of those coppers' Black and
> Tan faces, wow. Ambulances clanging in and the crowd yelling
> "Shame!" Yet it was all played by sporting rules; had it been
> Paris and the Garde Republicaine there might have been some
> corpses. Or with the Montreal police, even. As it was, there
> must have been 500 bobbies on hand, and it took them more
> than an hour to clear the street. Very patient.
>
> Yes, Eden Must Go, yet I think as of today his stock is going
> up a bit. Very interesting to note Gallup Poll figures: 40 per
> cent of Britons were for this Suez thing, 43 per cent of
> Canadians. . . . As for Israel, of course they shouldn't have
> done it, but I guess it must look a lot different from Tel Aviv,
> with those noble Arab commandos dropping in for a party
> every night, and the Ilyushins pouring into Egypt, and every
> Arab screaming that Israel must perish. And, worst of all,
> Britain, Russia and everybody else patiently lining up to kiss
> Arab asses and press gifts of tanks into their hands, in return
> for all that lovely oil.

> After eight years, the Israelis must have felt that Somebody
> Up There Don't Like Them, and the first kind word from Paris
> must have sounded very nice. There's something sad about old
> Ben-Gurion saying, "At last we have an ally."

My correspondence with Brian about the Suez Crisis went on
for several weeks, with Brian insisting that Ben-Gurion's action
in invading Egypt had destroyed Israel's "moral position" and
that this saddened him. Britain, he said, had kept its troops in
Egypt for decades, propping up the corrupt monarchy of King
Farouk, and it was only Nasser who had freed his people – and he
got no credit from the western world for doing this.

My response to this was to say that Nasser was just another dem-
agogue who replaced one form of corruption with another. "Being
Irish," I said, "you seem to give 95 marks to anybody who kicks
out the British, but I only give 60. I'd give him the other 35 if he
let his people vote, and bought the poor bastards food and medicine with their cotton crop rather than bombers to 'defend'
them from a country that has never stopped asking him for a
peace treaty."

By Christmas time the Suez furor had abated somewhat and
our letters could get back to the usual topics, like money, publishers, editors, agents and – of course – how stressful our work
was, poor drudges that we were. It was time for Brian to again
give me an inventory of the bottles in his bar, and I noted that
since his last listing, back in January, he had added several more
kinds of wine, plus cognac, Strega and Kummel. Also, he
informed me that in the St. George's School Christmas play,
Michael had been given the role of the Infant Jesus. That surprised me, because back in September Brian had written to me
with an account of a parents' meeting at the school, where he
learned that despite being the youngest child in his class,
Michael was the class bully. "He's given to biting little girls'
behinds," the proud father reported. "That's my boy!"

10

498 Lansdowne Avenue
Westmount, Quebec

January 2, 1957

Dear William:

Let me open this season of mists and morning frightfulness by
wishing you a very good New Year. I say, with all the weight of
Old Moore's Almanack behind him, that this year will be
known as the Weintraub Year, the Year of the First Canadian
Feature Film.

Well here I am opening a new year with an empty desk
and unlimited freedom to think idle thoughts. The play
version [of *Judith Hearne*] has once again, Dec. 31, winged
its way southward and there is nothing to do but write letters
for a day or two.

Partying: last Saturday to the Bieler annual – many
hundreds of people – slightly boozed Hugh MacLennan
telling me how much he loved me – then on and upwards
to the home of Prof. Frank Scott, where the assembled
guests dined in Westmountian style, served by parlour
maids. On hand, Prof. Catlin, British political scientist
and stalwart of Labour Party, ex-Cornell, Magdalen
College, Princeton and U. of California. Speaks

donnishly and wears three-foot-high collar. Knows Ike
well, also knows the Kabuka of Kabaka and Queen of
Tonga. After donnish winemanship discourse on wine,
cigars, etc., said he smoked White Owls. I said, "Your
academic record may be marvellous but, sir, White Owl is
a lousy cigar." So, as you will note, the old Moore bludgeon
is still loosely swinging in all directions.

Prof. Scott's wife said Frank saw Mort on TV, then went
upstairs at once, saying, "I must write a letter." Must say
that of people there, F. Scott is by far the brightest and
best. A very fine chap, much more on the ball than his
son. He is now fighting the Duplessis Padlock Law before
the Supreme Court and is also defending the Indians
against the Seaway. He came down in moccasins during the
evening and announced that he was on poking terms with
Mrs. Chief Poking Fire. This made Prof. Catlin's eyebrows
mount, and also those of his wife, a small mousy lady
who has published 22 books and is known in the trade
as Vera Brittain. She was not very interesting. Except
when it came to publishermanship. She was pretty good
on that.

Then on to New Year's Eve at Frank Coleman's, your genial
host. Large room full of luscious young things, dancers, TV
girls. Many abstract painters spitting at Frank's $900 Kisling.
A Negro queer kissed me and said, "I just loved Judith, man,
lo-ved her."

Horrible tendencies develop in me at this time of year. I
fondle bottoms, kiss girls and am regarded as obscene. Was in
sofa clutch with Coleman's wife when husband showed. But
enough – shudders! My wife stayed sober so that she would be
able to tell me in detail next day just how disgusting I was. A
woman at the party said, "You're 35? My God, I thought you
were 45." An abstract painter called me a Rotarian because I
said I had seen some pretty good museums in Europe. All
very Montreal.

Thanks for Christmas kiddie books, which Mike likes
and which he forces me to read to him so often that I now
loathe them.

> Yours,
> Sam Shubert

> 48 Ladbroke Grove
> London, W.11

> January 8, 1957

Dear Brian,

Thank you for your letter of Jan. 2, which arrived yesterday. I
was much cheered by your Old Moore's Almanack prediction
that this will be Weintraub's year. I hope it was an omen that
your prediction arrived when it did, as yesterday was a Big Day
for me. Now I can no longer hide from you the solitary vice
that I have been practising in the privacy of my own room. Yes,
it was yesterday that I completed, on schedule, the first draft of
a book. This covers 215 pages this size, double-spaced, so I
guess that's over 80,000 words.

I can honestly say that I have never nourished a secret
dream to write a novel. But on the sleepless night of
November 23, the idea hit me. In the normal course
of Weintraub events I would have discussed this copiously,
dawdled, dallied, procrastinated and finally forgotten about it. I
don't know what came over me, but I started work the next
morning. Dropped all other projects, resolved not to tell you or
Mort unless – or until – I got a rough first draft. Thus wrote fast
and finished in six weeks. I figured discussing it would inhibit
me, make me feel silly. Bk is abt boy attempting to grow up in
Montreal. Not sentimental, tries to be comic. This, of course,
raises the question of what happens if it ain't funny, McGee?

Answer: It falls on its ass with a special kind of clang, and we shall seek no points for effort or goodness of heart.

I haven't had the courage to read it through from end to end yet, but I've just glanced at a few pages and it looks pretty bloody awful. I will now put it away for about ten weeks while I replenish my finances by writing a couple of documentaries. If, on April 1, WEINBK (code name) still looks at all possible I will start reworking it. If it looks like anything at all after reworking, will show it to you and Jackie and will solicit your most candid opinion.

Told Mordecai abt this last night, and he was surprised. He had vaguely thought I was working on a TV play. Maybe he's right. If it ain't a bkie, maybe I can TV it. Mort sez not to burn WEINBK without showing it to him, like he burned the first book he wrote.

Glad you felt up lots of girls during the festive season. Me, it came out in another way. Discovered that under the influence of drink I am quite an abandoned jitterbug dancer. Terpsed wildly on Xmas and New Year's Eve. Fell down several times.

Please write.

Mazo de la Roche

January 12, 1957

Dear Bill:

When I began to read your letter this afternoon my eyebrows rose and I registered ONE UP in the utter surprise division. This is great news – great. I cannot tell you how pleased and delighted I am. If we can only get you into the club we will all rejoice in heaven.

Everything about this beginning is, to my mind, right. First of all you have done a first draft without, as you noted, any of the usual Weintraubian Fabius Cunctator syndrome. This is a good augury, is it not? Secondly, six weeks – whole first draft – means that you ran into no troubles, and that there is something there. The theme, what you mention of it, and the fact that there is a comic element, sounds to me like something I would like to read. And, as I have always said, you have taste and ability, and a good deal of technical knowledge. I predict that once launched you will be the great moneymaker of us all. As long as you will be content to leave agenting to your agents and control your promotion ideas.

This may all sound very incoherent, but really your news is the most cheering of the new year. As you said, I think you are most wise to keep the fact of bookwriting to yourself and wise not to show it until you are good and sure that you can do nothing more with it. Also I think that if you decide to write a book there should be only one editor; it is the antithesis of scripting and unless you can stand by your own judgments from the beginning you had better get out of the chair and take up golf.

So learn from Old Moorski – publisher mauler – and heed this advice. First of all, keep it to yourself and do not talk the book out instead of writing it. . . . Secondly, if you can at all avoid it, I would not do what you now propose to do. That is take ten weeks away from it. Ten weeks is too long. Two weeks is enough. Then start again, more slowly and keep doing a bit every day. I find the morning the best time. After breakfast the censor is at work and there are no bright ideas. It will look bad then, which is when it is most likely to be improved by cold-eye reworking. If you take ten weeks away from it, you may go stale and not want to begin again. And if you are as immersed as you must have been to do a draft in six weeks, then the sooner you do a second draft the better. Later – this summer – that is the time to lay off for a month or two and then go back cold as a new reader. Right now, if you're doing your documentary script, why don't you still hit a para or two of Weinbk each morning?

Now to point number two, which is always a good one when you are writing into a void. I am in a very good position at the moment to push your manuscript. I have found that the author is mistakenly regarded by publishers as a likely tipster for unknown writers. These guys always ask, who do you know who might have an MS? I can get you in immediately for a high-level reading at Atlantic, with Macmillan of Canada, as well as Little Brown of Canada, pally now with Jack McClelland. And there are others, believe me.

Mort writes he works until eleven at night. You have squirrelled away six weeks – a book. I am doing nothing! Rather a reversal of the normal routine, don't you think?

Come home. Ticker tape parade down Peel Street.

A Broadway Has Been

Much as I wanted to get on with work on a second draft of my book, I had to give precedence to more practical matters, like learning how an English gentleman of the eighteenth century went about taking snuff. There was, it seems, a right way and a wrong way to do it, and the first dose had to be put into the farthest nostril, not the nearest one, with the thumb. All this was being explained by Mr. Howard-Williams to students at the Royal Academy of Dramatic Art, where I was taking notes for a documentary. Bernice and I had decided to stretch our year in London into a second year, and this meant that funds had to be replenished with more scripts and magazine pieces.

"Now if you're waiting for me to sneeze, you'll be disappointed," Mr. Howard-Williams told the class, after demonstrating the complex nostril technique, essential to actors in Restoration comedies. "If you're addicted to snuff, as they were in the eighteenth century, you just don't sneeze. When you're finished, you continue the motion, like this, with the little finger pointing gracefully outward. It was all very studied, and done purely for effect." After the class, I told Mr. Howard-Williams that I'd like to try some snuff and he gave me the address of a little shop which, he told me, used to supply snuff to Queen

Victoria's mother. "We were also purveyors to the Kings of Hanover," Mr. Sedgewick said in the snuff shop, and it was encounters like this that confirmed my wisdom in deciding to stay in London for another year.

There were four young Canadians enrolled at the Royal Academy of Dramatic Art, and my script followed them through classes like that of Miss Boalth, who was showing them how to move ("To get up, you *melt* off the floor and *radiate* into the surrounding air"). Most instructive to me was Miss Morrell's voice production class – "No, Helen, you're not doing the 'o' properly. It's a very difficult sound for Americans and Canadians. It's 'o', not 'owe.' When Americans try to imitate English people they say, 'Owe, noe!' But that's not English. It's 'Oh, no!' Now everybody say 'ee-ee' – and don't smile when you say it."

In London, at RADA, the emphasis in an actor's training was on technique, in the most minute detail. But in New York it was The Method, as promulgated by Lee Strasberg in the Actors Studio; an actor didn't "act," instead he projected his own inner emotions as he identified with the character. Brian Moore had recently experienced the theatre scene in New York when he went there for a few days to work on the script of his *Judith Hearne* play. He would work with Daniel Petrie, the young Canadian director who was determined to bring the play to Broadway. In writing to me about this episode, Brian seemed to want to show me how unimpressed he was by the bright lights of Broadway. But he was, of course, just a bit impressed:

> Dear Wm.,
> My tale begins with an order to the Playwright (that's me) to attend O'Neill's Long Day's Journey Into Night, currently packing them in – three and one-half hours of O'Neill. Burt Lancaster sits one seat ahead, getting adoration. Then on Saturday morning, right next to Mus of Mod Art in ancient mansion, meet with Mr. Petrie – still looks just like a Nova Scotia boy. Upstairs we use the Louis Quinze chairs and impressive bathroom facilities of Miss Theresa Hellburn

while we get down to it – getting down to it means start at
ten – couple of pipple drift in and out say hello – hear you're
great – and then Petrie continues reading my script aloud –
interrupts now to find out on phone when Rod Steiger is
available and where he is – unlisted phone number given at
Hotel Warwick – then back to play – "Now Judith says –
excuse me." Phone. "Hello, Rod, Dan. Rod, what are you
doing? (count five) – Yeah, well lissen we have a play, it's about
the Hiss-Chambers – dynamite – Roger Stevens is the money –
he's very strong on it – open on Broadway say February. Now,
Rod, at a meeting the other day we decided that you would be
the man to play Chambers. (count two) Yeah, Stevens. (count
two). Of course it's the lead." Turns to Playwright (me). "Had
to play it cool. – Franchot Tone turned it down, also Johnny
Forsythe." Picks up script. "Now in this scene, Judith –"

Out to P. J. Moriarty's Chop House for lunch. Much hello
Mr. Petrie stuff. Actors come up to shake hands humbly. Petrie:
"This is Breean Moore – he's writing my next play." Actors
huge smile. "Well, that's great – great – anybody in mind?"
Petrie: "Shirley Booth." Actors sag. "Oh?" So back to work –
work until seven interrupted only by the following – messenger
service to bring Dan's long-playing record over to Dinah Shore
at Century – my script to Dan's agent who was with Perry
Como at Ziegfeld – and four calls from people playing in
Dan's little TV spectacular Dec. 23 – colour – starring Pat
Munsel, Vic Damone, the Four Lads, Basil Rathbone and God
knows who else. Dan: "I thought I'd like to try a musical." Last
interruption was while he phoned Sardi's. "Hello, Dan Petrie.
Table for three? (count two) Upstairs? No! (count one)
Call me back."

At seven p.m. Playwright and Dan head down to station
wagon waiting with six-foot blonde woman in it introduced as
Dorothea – mother of his kids and casting director of Theatre
Guild TV department. Off to Sardi's on wet Sat night. Drive
up, money to doorman, park it. In table downstairs next to
Leo Genn, who is feeling an eighteen-year-old girl's tits and

drinking Chablis. At eight thirty-seven walk out, car waiting –
takes taxi instead over to theatre where we are to see last night
of a play starring Luther Adler and Syl Sidney authored by one
Robert Alan Aurthur, a TV hacklet – a quick-folding play.
Meet Producer Herman Shumlin, Viveca – get that – Lindfors
(Dan's comment, "That bitch"). We watch this abortion on
stage, which dies for all time to professional cooing sounds of
"Wonderful – just wonderful." At first intermission walk out to
lobby, handsome young lad prances up. "Dan! Dotty!" Kisses
Dotty. Looks at me. "Who's he?" Dan says this prancer is John
Cassavetes – a movie or stage boy, not sure – and that I am
"the man writing my play." Cassavetes: "Oh, indeed –?" Flashes
enormous smile. Dan: "John, there's no part for you in Breean's
play." Cassavetes: "Well, in that case I can be my usual shitty
self." Walks away.

Inside again people are weeping at this crap. I ask Dan
whether he likes this play, called Special Baby. Dan says no.
After final curtain we march to lobby with Dan saying loudly it
is just wonderful. Then young man – your age with grey
touches – handclasps Dan. Dan: "Breean, meet David Susskind,
he produced tonight's play." Breean (learning fast): "Wonderful
play." Susskind: "Are you the guy who wrote that Irish –?"
Playwright nods. Dan: "He's my boy. We'll be in your shoes
soon." Susskind: "God help you." Now a man waddles up,
looking remarkably like Playwright in his fat phase wearing
similar Brooks Brothers suit plus midnight-blue suede slippers.
Dan: "This is Bob Aurthur – wrote the play. Meet Breean
Moore." Bob: "Hi." Breean: "Wonderful play!" Bob (with
renewed handclasp): "Well, that may be horseshit, but I
like to hear it."

Backstage then to meet Luther Adler in his drawers. Other
actors fall on Petrie spouse with cries and kisses (she is casting
director, right?) and she tells them all they were wonderful.
Beautiful young girl shakes my hand and offers to kiss me,
saying, "Wonderful, wonderful – the critics should go to
stoopid school."

Outside, station wagon comes mysteriously out of darkness and we pile in and onto parkway to Dobbs Ferry, to Petrie ranch house. To bed. In morning, coffee, coffee ring, two blond kids briefly presented and then wife removes them – an oiled machine of a home, this – and we go to work – work – work – tray lunch – Bas Rathbone calls – he is terribly worried. Work – work – work. At six – break – finish – Playwright tired and hoarse from declaiming and being stopped for notes. Big bar open – Dan never touches it. Enter blonde wife who touches vodka gibsons. Some talk about play at last. Consensus. Third act "most moving." Other acts "need work." Mrs. Dan – expert eye – is big for this play, keeps treating Playwright as though he were young O'Neill – asking him who he would like to have in it – her suggestions Peggy Ashcroft or Wendy Hiller. And leave us not forget that Hume Cronyn has read book and loves it for Jessica.

Evening we go downstairs to play ping-pong with several thitter visitors. All beat me. And so to bed. Next morning train to Grand Central, emplane in afternoon to home. Dan was really impressive in play department. Full of good ideas – sensitive – a master handler. I am now convinced that I am writing a great play. Must rewrite first two acts, fix third. "Take your time," says Dan. "No hurry. A month? Okay." So I have no time to be writing these long letters.

That was at the end of November. Two months later Brian wrote to me about the results of his work. "I am crushed, all washed up," he said. "I have now reached the stage of my final exams and have failed once more. Ten amateur critics in New York have read my play and not one liked it. So Dan Petrie flew to Montreal and has just spent a harrowing weekend with me in which he told me that all the work we have done is kaput. The shattering thing about these thitter pipple is their utter lack of confidence in their own ideas. As you know, I was labouring day and night under the illusion that I was following expert advice. And now – phutt!"

Yet always the professional, Brian was about to embark on yet another stem-to-stern rewrite. This time he would follow his own instincts, disregarding "expert" advice. "So now I am to sit down again and start writing a play," he said, wearily it seemed. "I am also to think about a new novel."

~

My second year in London continued to provide pleasant discoveries. Not only was there Mr. Sedgewick's little snuff shop, there was also the Reading Room of the British Museum. I was doing some research on an obscure historical subject and, with some proper letters of introduction, I managed to get permission to work in the Reading Room. Here it quickly becomes apparent that this is the greatest library in the world, and as you sit there, going through the volumes they bring to you, you wonder whether your chair might possibly have been the one that was once occupied by Karl Marx, who also worked in the Reading Room, or Virginia Woolf or Bernard Shaw.

I also explored Fleet Street, where my friend Bernard McElwaine introduced me at the London Press Club and in newspapermen's pubs like El Vino. Some of the journalists I met there struck me as being almost as eccentric as Corker, Shumble and Pigge, reporters in *Scoop*, Evelyn Waugh's hilarious Fleet Street novel. Waugh could have found more material for his satire in my first meeting with Bernard McElwaine, which took place in the bar of the Hotel Scribe in Paris during my first visit to that city. I was sitting next to two men who were obviously newspapermen and who were arguing about just where they were. "Believe me, John," one of them was saying, "we're in Paris. It was last night we were in Brussels."

What could be more impressive to a fledgling young journalist like myself who aspired to world travel? I introduced myself, and over the years Bernard and his wife, Molly, became my good friends. Bernard was from Saint John, New Brunswick, and was now top feature writer for the London *Sunday Pictorial*, which in the 1950s was selling about 6,000,000 copies every Sunday and was engaged in a heroic effort to outsell the *News of the World* and thus achieve the biggest circulation of any newspaper anywhere. The two papers tried to outdo each other in lurid sensationalism, with many a detailed story about scoutmasters charged with – as it was delicately phrased – "interfering with the clothing" of young scouts. One such story, involving a priest, carried one of the *Sunday Pictorial*'s most admired headlines: "FATHER INGRAM, GO UNFROCK YOURSELF."

"We have five lawyers who read every word before it goes into the paper," Bernard told me, "and still this week we have eleven libel suits. So we must be doing something right." Bernard was forever off to Hollywood, Rome or Tahiti to do stories about movie stars and celebrities. He always had the inside dope, as in his report that Lana Turner's fidgeting on the set of a South Seas movie was caused by ants in her grass skirt. He engineered a great scoop at the Venice Film Festival one day when a young producer called Kevin McGlory approached him in the bar and said, "Bernard, is that Leonard Moseley over there?"

"Yes," said Bernard, "that's Leonard."

"Well just watch this," said Kevin. "I'm going to give him the biggest beating he's ever had." Moseley was the film critic for the London *Daily Express* and he'd just panned Kevin's last movie.

"Look, Kevin," said Bernard, "will you do me a favour? Please wait just five minutes until you start in on poor Leonard."

"I'm very angry," said Kevin, "but for you, Bernard, I'll restrain myself for five minutes. But only five."

Whereupon Bernard bought him a drink and put through an urgent phone call to his photographer. When the photographer arrived Bernard released the angry producer and the *Sunday Pictorial* had another exclusive photostory as the bar, full of movie stars, was quickly turned into a shambles.

At the more sprightly Fleet Street papers, writers not only reported news, but also concocted it. While I was in London,

Bernard had a hand in one of the day's most sensational yarns: the virgin birth. The *Pic*, as his paper was called – and he was "Mac of the Pic" – had found an article in an obscure scientific journal speculating on the possibility of human parthenogenesis, i.e., a woman becoming pregnant all on her own, without intercourse or artificial insemination. Could such a freakish self-fertilization of the egg possibly happen, perhaps once in many million births? After giving this notion the full treatment, the *Pic* said it would like to hear from any mothers who were still virgins. The paper was soon swamped with letters from unmarried girls and women who said that nobody believed them, but they'd given birth to babies even though they'd never ever had sexual intercourse. The paper spent a great deal of money investigating each claim and finally came up with one woman whose story was impressive. Medical experts were hired and extensive tests were done that conclusively proved (according to the *Pic*) that this virgin had given birth without any male intervention. Needless to say, the paper got a lot of mileage out of this, and Bernard was willing to give me all the background material if I wanted to do a story for Canada. I offered it to *Weekend*, but they turned it down for religious reasons. Readers in Fort William would never accept the possibility that there might have been a second virgin birth – and maybe, down the years, several of them.

∼

Brian had long since abandoned the Catholic faith of his upbringing, but he had an abiding, almost obsessive, interest in religion and the Church, as evidenced in his first two novels and others to come. I had much less interest in such matters, but in those days he often lured me into conversations about religion. His reading of Adele Wiseman's novel *The Sacrifice*, winner of the 1956 Governor General's Award, provoked a brief theological exchange between us:

Dear Londoner,

I am reading my free copy of The Sacrifice – it is well written,
although the jacket says there is not one grain of cynicism in
it – such noble people. I must talk to you one day about the
one strange thing all Jewish novels seem to have in common –
there is a tremendous emphasis on the rituals the people follow
and on getting ahead, educating sons, observing the laws, etc. –
but never any reasons for these laws – no philosophy – no
theistic argument – like telling how a machine works without
explaining why it works. Do the writers believe we all know the
Jewish view of the afterlife – or do they not know themselves?
Anyway, this is a Big book, weighs a ton – but so far it is a lot
better than most local products, kosher and non kosher.

                              Bishop Moore

Your Holiness,

You have noticed that most Jewish novels are more interested
in sociology than religion, more Sinclair Lewis than Graham
Greene. And yes, one thing Jewish writers don't make very
clear is the Jewish attitude to the afterlife, while Catholics
seem to be almost exclusively concerned with this, as you make
clear in your Tamarack article. My ignorance of Jewish theology
is formidable, but it seems to me that the idea is that the good
life is its own reward, the good life lived according to God's
rules. And every aspect of life is covered by these rules. I don't
know why, but Jewish sages seem able to discuss the donkey in
great detail without harping on the essential carrot held out
before it. There seems to be very little Hell talk. Perhaps there
wasn't any need to invent a Devil with the Inquisitor or the
Cossacks always around the corner, a perfectly effective way to
scare the kids. I think a lot of Jews feel that you get caned right
on the spot, rather than having to wait until after school. Thus
I think the conversation centres around a) what the caning

was like; and b) how to avoid the next one – instead of the
Catholic talk about what mood the Headmaster will be in after
4 p.m., whether it will be six or twelve strokes and – most
important – if there is any politicking we can do before the
final bell rings to put Him in a better temper. Maybe that's
why – with notable exceptions – Catholics produce such great
dreamers and Jews such great materialists. By the way, you say
no reason is given for the laws Jews follow (or are supposed to
follow). But there is a reason. God issued those laws and that's
reason enough, Buster.

> Blessings on you and yours, my son,
> Rabbi Weintraub

Dear Rabbi,
I found your theological explanation interesting, but I don't
think it's caning now or after school which is the big point –
although it is certainly a point – but rather the tragedy and
irony of the proud chosen elite, doomed to banishment
and hatred – and it is something of this that I lack in Jewish
novels, a sense of their own failings, their harsh pride, their
own flaws – there is too much Adele Wisemanism – "we are
noble, honest, persecuted, poor." Why do we stay as we are?
Why do we consider ourselves an elite? Why do we in the
20th century still believe in this God that continually screws
us? Why are we right and the goyim wrong? These are the
questions other religions, for all their failings, try to answer.

> Leviticus

Dear Leviticus,
If you feel that no Jewish novels deal with their people's quote
own failings, their harsh pride, their own flaws unquote may I

refer you to the most recent novel of a young writer called Mordecai Richler? This might change your mind. Available in better bookstores, hard cover, at $3.25.

John the Baptist

~

In June 1957 we set out on our last visit to the Continent. With our Ford Zephyr we took the ferry from Harwich to Esbjerg and then drove across Denmark to another ferry that took us to Sweden. In Stockholm, Bernice was to visit the university and meet people in her field. On June 22 we dropped in at the Canadian Embassy in Stockholm to find out the results of the federal election back home and we discovered the diplomats there in a state of shock, preparing to take the portrait of Uncle Louis St. Laurent off the wall. The goofy-looking John Diefenbaker, he of the quivering jowls, would be our new prime minister, having squeaked in with his Conservative party. Whatever disaster Dief the Chief would visit on Canada would at least be leavened with comedy. But still, the change in government was worrisome, and I wrote to Brian, nervously, to ask him whether he thought that the Conservatives, with their traditional aversion to the arts, would soon abolish the NFB and use its buildings to store surplus western wheat.

Before leaving Sweden we spent a few days with Arne Sucksdorff, the acclaimed documentary director, at his summer house in the country. His famous feature *The Great Adventure* had shocked some viewers with its shots of wild animals copulating with each other and devouring each other, and in our conversations, much as I tried to embellish my experiences in making our mild Canadian documentaries, I could not come close to matching his tales of dealing with tigers in India.

From Sweden we drove south to Denmark again and rented an apartment for a month in a town near Copenhagen. Here I finally got down to resume work on my novel. Meanwhile, Mordecai had left London to take his ease at his old haunts on the Côte d'Azur.

Tourrette-sur-Loup

June 19/57

Dear Weintraubs,
In case you'd like to know I'm off in half an hour to Juan les Pins for a swim, then with Reuben & Co. to Cannes for a langouste dinner, and from there to the Crazy Horse Saloon for a night of le striptease. This, however, is not the reason for this letter.

I'm writing to announce that we've 90% decided to return to Canada this September . . . I want you to be one of the first to know because unless I sell something between now and Sept. I will be trying to touch you for a loan of $500. . . . (I have a long-term plan for you. Beginning with loans of $25 – remember? – I hope, by always paying you back, to work up to one big bite of $10,000 within the next five years, and then run off somewhere.) Anyway, it's not definite yet that I'll need the $500, so don't panic. But, and this is the point, if I need it come Sept., can you spare it?

What's your news? Are you back on your novel? When are you returning to Canada? We intend to live in Toronto, by the way, not in M ** t *** l.

News from here is small and depressing. Bob Weaver, I understand, thinks Choice [his new novel, *A Choice of Enemies*] is a stinker. Viking thumbs down, after most careful thought, etc., etc. Bk now with old friend Purdy.

What, seriously, do you thk my prospects are of getting some work from film board when I return? Let's say two scripties a year, or something. Will you be back to introduce me around? "Say there, I'd like you to meet Mort, an old friend.

He owes me 500 fish and I was wondering if there was any work for him. . . ."

Awaiting your report on Sweden. See you this autumn, I hope.

Yrs,

M.

Back home, the Canada Council had been established earlier that year and now there would be fellowships for writers, so they wouldn't have to scrabble quite so hard to find funds for a night of striptease at the Crazy Horse Saloon. I wrote to Mordecai from Copenhagen about this new benevolent government agency, and urged him to make his application as soon as possible. And yes, I'd have that $500 for him, if he would give me lots of notice. Also, I brought him up-to-date on the progress of my novel: "I am astonished and sickened to find out just how BAD this alleged book of mine is. Extremely depressing. Never quite realized it. But I will plug along a bit more."

Brian too was now sojourning on the Riviera, as was Mavis. Those two had always been cool toward each other, but I was glad to get a letter from Brian indicating that relations had improved. "We had dinner at Menton last week," he wrote, "and, sir, the Gallant house is the MOST! Bee-utiful! Makes all others look poor. Mrs. Gallant very charming, much changed, all old-world hospitality. . . ."

So there they were, three writers from Montreal, all on the Riviera for the summer, although at different locations. Diana Athill, editor for all three of them at André Deutsch, their London publisher, was also in the vicinity, hovering around and visiting each of them in turn. That year, 1957, Deutsch was bringing out books by both Brian and Mordecai; in 1956, this house had published Mavis's first book, *The Other Paris*, a collection of short stories, most of which had originally appeared in the *New Yorker*.

"Miss Gallant writes with sureness, grace and understanding," the *New York Times* said in its review of *The Other Paris*.

"Without exception, these are superior stories." Writing in the *San Francisco Chronicle*, William Hogan said: "Mavis Gallant . . . is one of the best young women writers in the U.S. [sic] I say women writers not disparagingly, but mean to bracket her with Eudora Welty, Flannery O'Connor, Jean Stafford and other talents who happen to be women."

Writing in *The Observer*, in London, Muriel Spark said of the stories that "all of them are beautifully written." Also in England, *Time and Tide* said: "Miss Gallant's style is witty and incisive, and it is amazing how much observation and how many undercurrents she manages to crowd into such small canvasses."

For Mordecai, *A Choice of Enemies*, his third novel, finally evoked the respect he deserved in his native Montreal. Walter O'Hearn, in the *Montreal Star*, who had skewered his first two books, now wrote: "This is a novel requiring no condescension, no patronage, no patience with a young writer. For the first time I realize Mordecai Richler's possibilities and they are impressive. . . . 'Choice of Enemies' not only has something to say but describes a part of society never described before. This is the Canadian-American expatriate colony in London. They are a curious crew, with as few roots in their adopted land as the Left Bank Americans in Paris . . . and their world is one of pubs and publisher's agents, of film studios and parties. But they are interesting."

"A Choice of Enemies is not only excellent, it is outstanding," the Montreal *Gazette*'s reviewer said. "There are characters which are so alive, so compelling, so strong that the reader is quite unable to put the book down. The fascination does not always hold, but the fact that Richler can exert it puts him in the first rank of novelists." Most reviewers found faults here and there in the novel, but almost all emphasized its strengths. "Mr. Richler observes life with the eye of an inquisitor," the *Toronto Star* said. "Its twistings and sharp details are lifted from the daily parade and burned into paper for all to see. And more, he goes beyond this reporting. His insights of those matters below the surface do not often falter. He writes with a sincerity and compulsion that give this novel very real power."

Writing about *The Feast of Lupercal* in the *New York Herald Tribune*, Sylvia Stallings said: "Mr. Moore's second novel is as good as his first, or better. It is always a pleasure to be able to report this, and particularly so in the case of a writer who plainly has further satisfactions in store for his readers." Claude Bissell, writing in the *University of Toronto Quarterly*, disagreed, finding *Judith Hearne* a more impressive book. Still, he said, *The Feast of Lupercal* was "the best novel written in Canada during the year under review."

The *Globe and Mail* also found the second novel even better than the first. "Now it is clear," its review said, "that Brian Moore is no one-book author but a new giant of Irish literature, a worthy successor to O'Casey, O'Flaherty and O'Faolain. . . . Once more Moore sets his story in his native Belfast and once again he takes as his main character a narrow, unloved virgin. But this time the virgin is male, 37-year-old schoolmaster Diarmuid Devine, B.A. . . . the tragi-comedy of Devine's impotence in the face of temptation is portrayed with a fabulous realism allied to a delicacy of phraseology that bears the marks of genius. . . ."

Also off the press in 1957 was the last of Brian's seven paperback thrillers, the books he wrote to pay the bills while he took time to write his serious novels and his play. From now on he would be able to earn a good living without having to produce these potboilers, which he held in such contempt. This last one, selling for twenty-five cents and bearing the pseudonym Michael Bryan, was entitled *Murder in Majorca*. The front cover, showing the usual sexy lady in distress, bore the blurb: "An island in the sun – where tourists live cheap, and sometimes die that way."

A more inviting picture of a tourist spot on the Mediterranean shore came to me in Copenhagen, in a letter from Jackie Moore:

Welcome Hotel
Villefranche-sur-Mer

July 23

My dear William,
It's time you forget this Scandinavian nonsense and get down
here where it's really happening. Greta Garbo, Lord
Beaverbrook and Jean Cocteau have just sauntered past.
Cocteau kissed the Beaver on both cheeks. Then the Beaver
and Garbo boarded his yacht, which bears a proud New
Brunswick label as home port.

   Also staying chez Welcome: Moviemaker Marcel Carné,
scriptwriter Spaak (brother to the writer of Grande Illusion).
The way the boys are carrying on, making frames with their
hands, plus the presence of a third man carrying what looks
like a script, suggests that on tourne à Villefranche – and pretty
damn soon.

   In our square last night, La Strada Circus performed. There
is also a funny man on a bicycle, plus top hat and cigar, who
plays a fiddle while he trick-rides in front of our quay-side café.
One night a flame-eater set up shop as we were about to have
coffee. A Spanish lady who plays the guitar often comes to call.

   Diana [Athill], who has returned most reluctantly to
Tourrette, where the boys play poker all day, will be back here
on the 25th. She will take Sean's room when he leaves. Hard-
to-impress Sean [Brian's brother], who is here for four days, has
entered enthusiastically into the Villefranche name game. Box
score to date: Jean Cocteau, a regular; M. et Mme. Niarchos et
leur yacht "Creole"; Elsa Maxwell; Grace Kelly; Duke and
Duchess of Windsor; Admiral Brown, head of U.S. Sixth Fleet;
Henry Morganthau, Jr., of the Morganthau Plan; unknown
French count with unknown starlet in toreador pants; Lord
Dudley of the Guinness family; two English character actors,
faces well-known but names not; Lady Sylvia Ashley (ex-Mrs.

Clark Gable); Mr. and Mrs. Charlie Chaplin and family; Alec Waugh expected; Graham Sutherland here but not yet seen. What are you waiting for?

My only problem is one of diet. Hard to keep it off here. Thus three Moores laze away, getting bigger and bigger. I think B. has given you all the bookie news. What are your plans? Let us know. Love,

Jackie

Obviously it was time to head south. A final chore in Copenhagen was to buy a few of the notorious Danish nudist magazines that Brian had requested, for research purposes. Then on down to Hamburg, Frankfurt, Garmisch, Trento, Florence, Genoa and points in between, a hop of eighteen hundred miles in the Ford Zephyr to get to the terrace of the Hotel Welcome, to gaze out at the yachts and sip pastis with friends. It was the beginning of our farewell to Europe. We had already bought our tickets for the ss *Homeric*, from Southampton to Montreal.

II

Almost as soon as we got back to Montreal the gloom started creeping in. I'd experienced bouts of depression ever since I was ten years old, and now I feared that another one was on the way. I was having trouble concentrating on my work, my marriage was not a particularly happy one, and the novel I was working on was unmitigated trash. I did my best to conceal my distress from friends and at the NFB, where I had some assignments, but Mordecai wanted to know why I hadn't written for so long and so, after a few months, I confided in him. And immediately there was a letter in response:

5 Winchester Road
London N.W. 3

Dec. 14/57

Dear Bill:
I hope you are in somewhat better spirits now and that you will write again soon. Christ knows, the more I thk of it the less you have to be depressed abt (not that that's any help to you). But you have very quickly established yourself as a damned good and wanted man at the NFB. If it means anything to you I still thk that the Saskatchewan Traveller film was a fine job, something any one of us wd be proud of, and I can't understand

why you seem to be doubting yrself so deeply as a writer. You are certainly one of my most valued and intelligent friends and it grieves me to thk of you sitting there looking out the window all day, and possibly not sleeping at night. I feel a bit uneasy abt writing this letter because at times like this, it seems to me, everything you write or say is the wrong thing. But, as far as I can make out, you've got a good wife, talent, intelligence, good and loyal friends and very little to complain abt.

I remember your saying to me that you felt you had wasted the last year or two. Well, I have always objected to that particular concept of time, and – offhand – it wd seem to me that two years in London, France, Africa, Sweden, etc. should strike you in retrospect as more enjoyable than wasted. Maybe you feel bad abt your novel, but I never heard of anyone – Ted Allan aside – who didn't feel punk abt his novel after the first and even final draft.

Last night we went to visit Stanley and drank vodka with him until one a.m. He's most depressed, drinking a good deal. He and Florence hardly see each other (the baby looks fine). Ted Allan was here one night and is supporting four people and three analysts. He's not working and is in bad shape.

Please let me know what bookies you'd like for Xmas. Will send you New Statesman, Spectator subs anyway. Please write soon, old chap, if only a short note.

Mordecai

In Montreal, we found an apartment near Côte des Neiges on Ridgewood, a street with a feeling of impermanence about it. It looked to me like the abode of people who were on their way up in life – or on their way down. And I felt I was on the way down. The sovereign remedy for depression was, of course, alcohol, but as I increased my daily dosage I realized that like most medications it had its side effects.

Apt. 6
3280 Ridgewood Avenue
Montreal

Jan. 15, 1958

Dear Mordecai,

Hell, it's almost a month since I got your letter. Please forgive me. I will forego all the usual explanations, excuses. Thanks for your kind, encouraging words re my depression. Really appreciate this.

Dire hangover this morning. Had a few sundowners (gin and tonic) with Father Moore on Lansdowne yesterday afternoon, and as you know sundown comes quite early in Montreal this time of year. Then I left the Moores to their dinner and went downtown, Bernice being occupied with some McGill meeting. I repaired to the Press Club to chat with sundry old hacks, the most dissolute of whom asked how you were. Much Scotch. Throbbing, hung-over head this morning and thus no work unless perhaps this afternoon.

Did Brian tell you he was one of three speakers at a meeting at the Jewish Public Library last night on Canadian lit? The others, a Yiddish poet and a French novelist. Must have been hilarious. I was a good sport and didn't go, as he didn't want spectators. Brian has finished the umpteenth rewrite of his play and I've read it. It's bloody good. Certainly hope he has luck with it. Could make him rich.

What are you doing? TV playwrighting? Bking? Most anxious to hear. Please write. Don't delay because I delayed.

Bill

Much as one rejoices in the success of friends, like Brian's presumed future on Broadway, it does nothing to lessen one's feelings of failure, self-loathing, etc., etc. Actually, one of the principal roots of my gloom was envy of the triumphs of Brian

and Mordecai, as compared with my own puny accomplish-
ments. I must learn to live with this, I kept telling myself. But
now, watching the editing of an NFB film entitled *First Novel*
only confirmed my sense of futility, even though Mordecai would
have to share the blame with me. We had collaborated on the
script in London and the credits would bear both our names.

In this little drama we follow the fortunes of a fictitious young
writer called Harry Merton as he sends off his manuscript and
suffers three rejections before having the book accepted by a
publisher. At first he's elated – and then dismayed to learn that
his advance against royalties will be only $200. "Two hundred
dollars doesn't seem like much for two years' work," he says to
the publisher. But the publisher points out that in Canada a first-
rate, serious novel sometimes sells only a couple of hundred
copies. "A thousand is excellent and anything over that is
superb." The publisher will probably lose money on Harry's book,
but says that it's a good book and ought to be published. "Maybe
your next one will be more saleable," he says.

But Harry isn't in it for the money, and after some agonizing
as to whether or not he has a real talent he decides, with his
wife's encouragement, to quit his job as a newspaper reporter and
become a freelancer, trying to spend as much time as possible on
a second novel. Selma, his wife, will support both of them, in a
frugal life, and we see neighbours gossiping about this poor
woman who goes to work every morning while her able-bodied
lout of a husband relaxes at home all day. In the film we follow
the disappointments of publication and the agonies of waiting
for reviews, which are mixed. In the end, we leave Harry trying
to decide whether he should continue as a novelist or go back to
a regular job. I found the film, when it was finished, to be pedes-
trian, with the acting and direction mediocre, to say nothing of
the script. But when it appeared on television, Brian told me he
found it good, and even realistic. But I felt he was humouring
me, knowing my state of low spirits. I was more inclined to agree
with the *Montreal Star*'s reviewer, who found the young hero to
be "sulky and self-pitying."

But perhaps there was one good bit of dialogue in the script, at the very beginning, when Harry and Selma take the manuscript, just completed, to the post office to send it off to a publisher by registered mail. HARRY: "What if it gets lost in the mail?" SELMA: "You've got four carbon copies at home." HARRY: "Yes, but what if the house burns down?" This, Mordecai and I felt, would be recognized by every writer as absolutely true to life.

~

London, March 1

Dear Bill:

Mighty good to hear from you after so many moons.

Ted Kotcheff – he's new in these parts – is going to produce my first TV play in April, or so he and ABC-TV say, tho I'm still waiting for my contract and getting mighty impatient. CBC wants revisions on the same one for Canada. Play #2 is out in Canada and here, and I'm all but finished #3. After that there's still some other stuff to be cleaned up before I can get back to my novel end of April. If all my commercial work works out – and it's still too early to tell – I'll be free for a year at least.

A funny thing abt that Maclean's piece (glad you liked it): Putnam's, the new president there, wrote me abt it and asked me, Jesus, to write him a funny novel. "I had no idea," he writes, "that you had a sense of humour." Wd I be interested, etc. Wrote back saying my new one was under option to Little, Brown. Sorry.

Nathan Cohen has butchered me in Tamarack Review, as you may have seen ("Richler heroines have small breasts") and – by God – only in Canada wd somebody attempt such a long [13 pages] and definitive piece on a young punk who has published a mere 3 bks. Makes me feel like I'm dead, or something. Anyway the best and only answer I have to that is my short story coming in the next issue of that very same magazine. It's called "Mortimer Griffin, Shalinsky, and How They Solved the Jewish Problem," and I hope you'll like it.

I was twenty-seven a few wks back, so I'm catching up.

M.

3280 Ridgewood, Mtl.

March 29

Dear Mordecai,

Did you know you're famous in Newfoundland? My mother was telling me she was talking to a man from there who was in Montreal looking for a place to live before moving here. She asked him what part of the city he was considering. "Anywhere except Snowdon," he said. "That's where those black-market Jews live who walk on Decarie Boulevard on Saturday afternoons." He read it in a book way back yonder in Newfoundland. That's fame for you, boy. Tell Nathan Cohen to shove *that* up his Tamarack.

What am I doing? I'm earning a living, rewriting some awful scripts the Film Board bought. They're based on that CBC Radio series "Jake and the Kid" – did you ever hear it? Prairie dramas, real cornpone stuff, podner. Rustic wit, as light and airy as lead. The Board wants to make a TV series out of it. I've been at it for several weeks, and now the original author, W. O. Mitchell, has arrived in town and I work with him, after a fashion. A nice enough fellow, and I hate to hear him yelp in anguish whenever I try to trim some fat off one of his hayseed orations, explaining that movies are a brisk, visual medium. It's really a crazy, mixed-up business, with too many cooks for this turgid broth, including your pal Frank Lalor from CBC Toronto, in an editorial capacity. Mitchell and Lalor have both taken

short-term apartments on Ridgewood, right next door.
Mitchell has brought wife and child in from Alberta, plus small
dog. Dog so far is only party not busy revising somebody's script
revisions. We have merry script conferences up at the Film
Board, but Mitchell will not attend these as he gets too
emotional. So Lalor goes up to speak for him, like a lawyer. I
am getting very expert on knifing and back-stabbing at script
conferences, which I now realize is by far the most important
part of a script-writer's training. As I said, it's a living.

Feeling homesick for London these days. Are you still
coming to Toronto in Sept.?

Farmer Bill

~

It was in that year, 1958, that I developed a habit even more
expensive than alcohol: psychoanalysis. It was widely believed,
back then, even by intelligent people, that Daddy Freud's
formula could allow a person to find out what was *really* bother-
ing him – deep down in his unconscious – and this would help
him cope with things like writer's block, fatigue, women, self-
loathing and booze. So four times a week I would drag myself
down to the office of a highly recommended, stone-faced old
geezer and lie down on his couch. For fifty minutes I would
ramble on, complaining, describing my dreams or often saying
nothing, and he certainly didn't say much. Lying down, I would be
staring up at the ceiling, unable to see whether he, sitting behind
me, was awake or asleep. For this, at the end of each month, I
would present him with an enormous cheque.

None of us, in those days, suspected that by the year 2001
only a few diehard mystics would still believe in Freud's mumbo-
jumbo; for people with their wits about them, it would command
as little respect as the phrenology of the nineteenth century. But
Freudian dogma does, of course, always make for stimulating
intellectual parlour games – that ego, id and superego stuff, plus

the spicy suspicion of sex underneath everything – but as I and many others were to learn, it had no discernible therapeutic effect whatever. Still, I persisted with old Stone Face (am I being hostile, Doctor?) for several years, mainly because I felt rotten so much of the time and kept hoping for that big "breakthrough" – something that never came. After all, what else was there, in those years before anti-depressant medications? Before trying analysis, I'd even tried a few jolts of electroshock, in a hospital, to lift me out of my gloom, but to no avail. Actually I continued to feel lousy until it finally occurred to me   some years later – to stop drinking and avoid starting the day with a black, throbbing hangover. I felt much better after that, and grew phenomenally wealthy by no longer having to support Dr. Granite-jaw, the Press Club and several liquor stores.

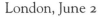

London, June 2

Dear Bill:

I was very glad to get yr note this morning abt SHALINSKY. I'm glad you liked the story so much – I had hoped you would.

The news from here is plentiful and mostly excellent:

1. I'm off to the South of France again on Saturday. Cathy has been there for two wks. We have taken an enormous villa on the sea with the Manns. It's in Roquebrune, some twenty minutes' walk from Monte (and more important, I guess, only a little farther to the Italian border and safety. Two pedalos, disguised with palm leaves, will be in constant readiness at the beach. Laden with gin, pate and slingshots we can – if necessary – make a run for Genoa).

2. I wrote to the Canada Council to say thanks for the fellowship, the two grand, but what abt. my travelling expenses? To my amazement a letter came this week saying that the director had approved an additional grant of $500

for travelling. Nice, what? We will call our speedboat Miss Canada Council.

3. My first TV play, PAID IN FULL, went off rather well here. Very good review in the Times, smashing review in the Daily Mirror, big blast against in the Daily Mail. Provinces 10 to 1 strongly in favour. Ratings, tops, and a phonecall of congratulations for Richler-Kotcheff from Howard Thomas, director of ABC-TV. They will do more by Mort next season.

4. I have rewritten the screenplay of ROOM AT THE TOP. 500 quid for three weeks' work is nice, but better still is that Jack [Jack Clayton, the director] is so pleased with what I've done to the script. Am very financially solid now, embarrassingly so, and I can dilly and dally with my novel for months and months, which was the general idea.

Robert Weaver writes that Peter Scott – remember him? – has written a big pro-Richler anti-Cohen article for the summer Tamarack.

What are your news? Are you still on Jake and Kid? What abt yr novel?

M.

In the winter 1958 issue of *Tamarack Review*, the literary quarterly, Nathan Cohen, drama critic and broadcaster, had written a long and scathing critique of Mordecai's three novels. "Most of the men and women who pass through his pages," Cohen wrote, "are so small, so worthless, so obviously (according to him) undeserving of compassion that they are not worth caring about." The heroes in these books, he said, are "selfish, oblivious of human dignity, cold, insensitive, conscienceless, wantonly destructive of personal relations. They have no nobility of spirit. Indeed they are worse than the people around them since they presume to know better and insist on their superiority."

In the summer issue of *Tamarack*, Peter Scott, the poet, took Cohen to task for these assertions. Cohen's piece, Scott said in a long article, raised not only the problem of the Canadian artist but also that of the Canadian reviewer. "Mr. Cohen's convictions have made him mistake his facts," Scott wrote, quoting scenes in the books where the heroes are far from being "cold, insensitive, conscienceless." Methodically, and sometimes sarcastically, Scott listed fallacies in Cohen's reasoning.

Cohen's article quoted Mordecai as saying that his compulsion was to say what he felt about values and "about people living in a time . . . when there is no agreement on values." Comparing Mordecai with other Canadian writers like Robertson Davies and Morley Callaghan, Cohen said Mordecai was alone in asserting that he dealt with "the larger issues of our age." But, Cohen said, Mordecai was not really in touch with his time. Noting Mordecai's depiction of Jewish family life, Cohen said it was out-of-date and unreal, and his preoccupation with the "the Marxist mirage" and the Spanish Civil War was not "an issue of current validity."

The controversy continued on the radio program *Anthology*, where Robert Fulford argued against these assertions of Cohen's. Mordecai's concerns, as reflected in his novels, Fulford said, were very much those of other important young writers of the era. And, as the author of *A Choice of Enemies*, Mordecai had made a choice for himself, siding against "those people who would see mankind as a series of groups, capable of being manipulated in one direction or another. He is against those who would send us through life shouting and reacting, in stereotyped ways, to stereotyped figures and ideas. Perhaps most important, he is against those who would oppose, by political or personal means, the autonomy of the individual. In the 1950s, this is not so easy a choice as it might seem to some of us."

Speaking about youthful skepticism about power, authority, organization and leaders, Fulford said that "this position is an important one and actually deals, however shakily, with some of the central facts of our time. . . . I think we should all be glad that this position is represented so absorbingly, so variously, in the work of at least one Canadian writer."

All this argument, in print and on the radio, made it clear that only four years after the publication of his first book, Mordecai had already become the most controversial of Canadian authors.

~

Villa Beatrice
Rue Louis Laurens
Roquebrune (A.M.)

July 25, 1958

Dear Bill.

I've not answered yr letter for so long because the news I've got is largely depressing and painfully personal too. Coming to the point, Cathy and I have separated and will be getting a divorce one of these autumn days, I guess. Cathy is all right – don't worry abt her. She's living in Villefranche and I see her from time to time. She's got a job there, at a children's camp for Americans, and the idea of her keeping busy is a good one. I'm taking care of her financially, of course.

I don't see that there's any need or point to go into details. There was no real incident, so to speak. Probably it's simply that we've both been unhappy for a long time. . . . God knows she's a fine girl, and I wish her well (I hope this doesn't sound fatuous), but we could no longer make it honestly together.

I'm alone here at the villa now and working very hard indeed on my new novel. Its tentative title is THE APPRENTICESHIP OF DUDDY KRAVITZ and I hope it turns out well. I expect to be done with the first draft come Sept. 1 and then I must take a couple of months off to earn some money. I'll be going back to London in Sept. I'll be here until Aug. 25, anyway, and then I may take it into my head to fly down to Malaga for a few wks, where Ted Kotcheff has a villa. Probably, tho, I'll return to

5 Winchester Road. Cathy intends to stay put in Villefranche for some time.

Wish I would hear from Brian one of these days. I guess I'm in the mood where I want warm letters from my friends.

Best to Bernice, Brian, Jackie.

M.

3280 Ridgewood

Montreal, July 31

Dear Mordecai,

Your letter arrived just this minute and I can't tell you how damned sorry I am to hear your news. Beyond that, and really feeling it, I don't know what to say. Everything that comes to mind seems so platitudinous. "Hope it's all for the best for both of you," etc. Although it's seldom for the best for both. Still, better than indefinite misery for both.

But Christ, why this obvious philosophizing? From your letter it seems that this has been building up for a long time now. I know that it can't be rash, and that you've given it plenty of thought. For my own part, it makes me sad when I think of all the bloody good times I've had with both of you, here in Montreal and then on Church Street and Winchester Road. I guess you're both pretty lonesome, but you both seem to have the ability to make friends, so that should mitigate it a bit.

It's a good thing, as you say, that Cathy has a job to keep her busy. And to hear that you're still hard at work, with plans for many months ahead. Has Cathy any long-range plans? Will she stay in Europe? You say you're coming back to Montreal by spring. Does that mean that Toronto is out? Would much prefer to have you here, of course.

The tentative title you mention for your book suggests that you are now in the comic novel field. Rotter. That's my racket, see, although I don't know when I'll ever get off my ass and get on with this so-called book of mine. If yours is as funny as SHALINSKY it should be good indeed.

Write. I'll be more prompt answering in future.

Bill

5c Kensington Church Street
London S.W. 8

Aug. 29/58

Dear Bill:

I'm back in London and working on some radio, TV, etc., that has been commissioned. I did – miraculously, I thk – complete a first draft of my novel before leaving Roquebrune, but I'm afraid to look at it yet, and will leave it in the cooler for a while. It's not a comic novel, tho – I hope – there are "comic" sections in it and it is a lot funnier than anything I've ever attempted before. Am very worried abt it, anyway.

Cathy – when last heard from – had taken a ship from Nice to Gibraltar, and I hope she will visit Ted Kotcheff in Malaga, but she hasn't shown up there and she refuses to keep me informed on her movements. I hope she'll return to London eventually, but meanwhile she wants none of it.

For the last couple of weeks I've been staying with Reuben and Elaine and tomorrow I move into 5c Kensington Church St. for three-four weeks. Then Ted Kotch will move into Winchester Road with me for a bit – we may look for a suitable bachelor flat afterwards. Ted will be doing another play of mine this season and I seem to be OK financially, better than ever before, actually, tho I have precociously graduated into the alimony class.

Ted Allan has finally got to China. He writes it's wonderful, fabulous, etc., etc., and one regrets that he's made this leftist booster's trip 30 years too late. He'll be back next wk with – I'm sure – glowing reports on Mao.

Florence and Stanley are getting a divorce, I thk. Mike and Sheila have had a baby boy. Doris [Lessing] is vacationing in Franco's Spain. Derek Gardner is away. So is Diana.

Write again soon.

M.

~

Brian and Jackie were back in Montreal now after a vacation in the Hamptons, on Long Island, and had good stories to tell about the abundant social life there, about endless parties with New York writers and painters, about meeting people like Phillip Roth and Neil Simon. Their days down there, on the beach, got them started thinking about pulling up stakes and moving to New York, a good place for a writer to live. But for me the prospect of their leaving town was dismaying; I had come to count on their support in these days of personal gloom and doom; besides the Moores and the Cherneys there were no other friends I really wanted to see.

After work, around five o'clock, I was often at the Moores, having a drink with Brian, a drink we invented and called the Gin-Master – half gin and half Cinzano. Besides hashing over current projects, we enjoyed re-examining some of the scandals and intrigues of our old newspaper days at the *Gazette*. In that newsroom there had been a great cast of eccentrics for us to recall, men and women lame but still game as they laboured under the heel of H. J. Larkin, managing editor. One of our old colleagues who particularly fascinated us was Karl Gerhard, the reporter who covered labour unions and their strikes.

Brian and I were sure that Gerhard was Larkin's principal spy in the newsroom, and that it was he who had reported me for the misdemeanour that got me fired back in 1950. Gerhard's background made him well suited to espionage. He had been a journalist of some sort in Germany and had emigrated to Canada *circa* 1930. Around the office we believed that he had been interned as a Nazi agent during the war, but right after the war the *Gazette* welcomed him onto its staff. Some details about Gerhard's past came to light in a bit of research I did many years later. Before the war he travelled widely in Canada, giving lectures on how Hitler was greatly misunderstood. He also set up branches of the Deutsche Bund, a Nazi organization for Canadians of German origin. The RCMP had kept a file on him since 1934 and, in 1938, during a spy scare, questions were asked about him in the House of Commons. But after the war, none of this bothered the *Gazette*. Karl Gerhard was made labour reporter because, after all, nobody knew more about the ways of Communists than an old Nazi.

At the time, many of us at the paper augmented our meagre salaries with moonlighting and sidelines, and Gerhard was no exception. During the turmoil in Palestine, as might be expected, he would sit at his *Gazette* desk writing press releases denouncing Zionism on behalf of the Arab League of Canada. And at the same moment, because there was always a tragi-comic aspect to life in that newsroom, Charlie Lazarus would be sitting at the very next desk tapping out press releases denouncing the Arabs on behalf of the Zionist Organization of Canada.

Karl Gerhard, Charlie Lazarus, Tracy Ludington, Myer Negru, Joe Thomson, Larry Conroy, Tiger Gilliece – all the old *Gazette* foot soldiers. As Brian and I sat, sipping our Gin-Masters up there on Lansdowne Avenue, these men and a dozen others lurched through our reminiscences. But if Brian were to move to New York, who would there be to relive those days with me?

∿

5 Winchester Road
London NW 3

Nov. 8

Dear Bill

Am writing to ask a favour.

My tely play, BENNY, based on that old short story BENNY, THE WAR IN EUROPE AND MYERSON'S DAUGHTER (you may remember it) is going to be done here on Jan. 4. And the set designer, Tim O'Brien, just abt the best here, has asked me if I could get him some Montreal photos. I know you're damned busy, but I'm anxious for this play to come off well, and could you take an hour and maybe two off, drive down to St. Urbain Street, and take some photos for us? (I could ask my old man or my brother – but they'd get it all wrong, I know.)

What we need roughly (you can visualize the rest) are:

1. Some shots of outside staircases.
2. Outside shots of a cigar & soda store. Inside, too, if possible, and details of window displays.
3. Ditto a garage.

And anything else you can thk of.

Area I had in mind is St. Urbain corner Fairmount, Laurier Street from St. Urbain to Jeanne Mance, anything ard there.

Elsewhere: I hunged in my novel [*Duddy Kravitz*] a few days ago and, bejesus, the reactions are dandy. "I laughed out loud. Remarkable, head and shoulders above anything you've done before" – Joyce W. [his agent]. "Clearly the best thg you've ever done" – Diana Athill. And other fulsome remarks. Still feel most uneasy, however, because this is the "quickest" novel I've ever done, also the longest, 130,000 words. Creepy.

Carl Foreman producing Stanley and MacDougal's latest flick, a quickie with Peter Sellers. Wolf Mankowitz producing an Art Buchwald musical coming season. Doris Lessing has replaced Ken Tynan on Observer. Temporarily. Tynan gone to

New Yorker. His wife, Elaine Dundy, was offered 30 Gs for her
bookie by Walter Wanger.

Hope you can take those pix.

M.

3280 Ridgewood

Dec. 9

Dear Mordecai –

Keep wondering if you ever got the pictures I sent you. I took
about two dozen and sent them off to you pronto, airmail. It's
about a month ago now.

Just read your graveyard piece in The Montrealer. Very
amusing. Good.

Have just read Canada Made Me, Norman Levine's new
book, which will certainly cause some panics around this
smiling, beautiful country. Louis Melzack at the Classic tried to
talk me out of buying it, saying it was too revolting, disgusting,
untrue and unfair. I told him that was no way for a bookseller
to talk and he sold it to me most reluctantly. As you know, it's a
kind of travel book, coast-to-coast, with sketches of people
Norman met on the way. The writing is really excellent – fine
descriptive passages – but he certainly did find a lot of sordid
stuff, bleak towns, vapid people. No wonder Melzack would
like to see the book burned; for people like him, if you can't say
something nice about Canada don't say it. So be warned,
young fellow.

Norman certainly does pan some very easily identifiable
people, without mentioning their names. People in Saskatoon
will know who he's talking about when he tells what a woman
told him about her abortion. By the way, he mentions staying
at your mother's house ("Mrs. R.") in Montreal and is not very
flattering in his description of her. I must say he's very frank

about his own problem – poverty – and gives details about his frequent efforts to borrow money. In one very good scene, a rich friend says no, neither borrower nor lender be, but he buys Norman a new suit of clothes instead. Norman is happy. He needs a suit. It's a depressing book, but really good. And watch for his great, sickening tour of a slaughterhouse in Winnipeg. Have you got his address? I'd like to drop him a note.

Did you get the pix? Not much new here. Write.

B.

5 Winchester Road
London NW 3

Dec. 14/58

Dear Bill:

Thank you for those photos, which were just what the stage designer ordered. Thanks a lot.

Have not read Norman's book yet – will get it soon. Haven't got his address, but you can write him c/o Putnam, and by God he needs cheering up and wd like to have even the shortest note from you. He called last week to say he was being evicted on Jan. 7, so help me. I keep avoiding him, I'm afraid, but, man, I have my own P.P.s (personal problems).

Good old Sam Lawrence [editor at Little, Brown] writes to Joyce W.: "I have just read Mordecai Richler's novel and I wanted to give you and the author my immediate reaction. I was struck by the power and force of this novel, and to my mind it is by far the most exciting and vigorous novel Mordecai has done to date. I am truly impressed and enthusiastic about this book and hope that my associates on the board will share my feeling. As I said before, this is merely a preliminary report, and I shall do everything possible to expedite a final decision. . . ."

Well, the thg for me to remember is that last time the associates on the board did NOT share Sambo's feelings, so . . .

Am most anxious for you and Brian to read my MS (and enumerate misspellings, factual errors, other slips) and will ship one off as soon as available. Have planted THREE errors on purpose. CAN YOU SPOT THEM and win the free auto-graphed copy?

Have not done much work this month. Am really beat, man. This has been a fantastic work (not to speak of P.P.s) year. . . . Abt the P.P. part you know. Abt the work, man, I wrote a novel, rewrote a film, adapted a TV play, wrote two original TV plays, several stories, articles, and two radio plays. I AM TIRED. I DESERVE A REST, what?

Am in a waiting and party-going period. Brian tells me you thk I'm happy, or I sound happy, or something, and what if I am, man?

Ted Kotcheff and I pride ourselves in keeping the best-stocked bar in Swiss Cottage. When folks ask for Scotch we are inclined to say, "Which brand do you prefer?" We had a big party here Sat night, and by gum you wouldn't recognize the old No. 5 Winch Rd. There's a nifty partition up in the hall, shutting the flat off, a char comes daily, and two men are putting in a john, my very own john.

Rumour is circulating (or did I tell you earlier?) that Ted Kotch and I are . . . well, buggers. Am doing my best to encourage this rumour.

Have bought a tux (a long time ago, many years ago, he lived on the Left Bank and wore blue jeans). Needed it for the TV Ball. Am now wearing it to work. A swell outfit, sir.

Write, please, and tell old man Moore to write too.

Best,
Mordecai

12

The title of the film was *Black and White in South Africa* and no National Film Board production had ever caused as much agitation in high places. The film's narration, which I wrote, detailed the injustice and brutality of South Africa's apartheid system, something most Canadians knew little about. After seeing the film, the racist government of South Africa protested loudly, and the timid time-servers in Ottawa, in charge of Canada's foreign policy, wet their pants in alarm. The fact that the film was named by the *New York Times* as one of the ten best documentaries of 1958 did nothing to discourage efforts by the Department of External Affairs to have it suppressed.

The film was one of a series about the Commonwealth of Nations, formerly the British Empire. There were thirteen films in the series, made for television and the classroom, and I wrote eleven of them. Some of the films showed how independence and self-government was coming to former British colonies, but in South Africa the all-white regime was imposing ever-increasing repression on the country's native peoples. Fewer than three million whites were keeping eight million blacks in abject poverty and exploiting them as cheap labour. Affronted by segregation, without civil rights and forced to live in squalor, blacks were becoming increasingly bitter. But their protests were ruthlessly suppressed and South Africa, our film said, had become a police state. A new law decreed that criticism of government legislation was punishable by flogging.

Yielding to South African pressure, Ottawa persuaded the
NFB to withdraw the film from international distribution, despite
its popularity in the United States and elsewhere. But when
there were rumours that it might also be withdrawn in Canada, I
secretly phoned Hazen Argue, member of parliament and head
of the CCF Party, and told him about it. Argue's questions to
External Affairs, conveyed to Prime Minister Diefenbaker, led
to Ottawa's backing off for fear of a public outcry if it became
known that the film was being suppressed.

Writing about the affair years later, Gary Evans, a historian of
the NFB, said, "The Film Board had been one of the first public
voices in Canada against apartheid, and *Black and White in South
Africa* had helped mould public opinion, as students, professors
and other concerned citizens saw and discussed the film in hundreds of community, religious and public-affairs groups. . . . Most
would agree that on the issue of South Africa Diefenbaker
caught up with public opinion and then led it. . . . When all the
dust had settled, [the film] was probably one of the ancillary
factors that tilted Canada to take the lead in driving South
Africa from the Commonwealth in 1961."

For me, having a small part in this affray was invigorating, a
spark of light amid my recurring glooms, a feeling that something positive had been achieved, in contrast to the futility of
the psychoanalyst's couch.

∿

5 Winchester Road
London NW 3

Jan. 23/59

Dear Bill:
A couple of days from now I'll be sending you airmail
(registered) a copy of the DUDDY [*The Apprenticeship of Duddy*

Kravitz] ms. I'm anxious, of course, for you and Brian to read it and tell me what you think. But I want you to go through it with an eye to factual errors (not a strong point with me).

Jack Clayton says all the film data is accurate, but what about the "made-up" prices for the Bar Mitzvah films – what do you think? (Note: A lot of these queries will seem senseless until you've read the ms.) Don't worry about land values and prices quoted, they are made up, but I'm checking these with a lawyer and notary. Also Atlantic [his American publisher] has already warned me about epileptics being 4-F. They have also sent me a sheet correcting errors in Reform synagogue service. The rest is up to you, old chap.

Atlantic has asked for a minimum of revisions, almost nothing, and I don't even have to do that much. Ditto Deutsch. But I must check legal details, errors, etc. and have ms. ready to go by Feb. 20 if I'm to make autumn publication. So once the ms. arrives could you read it muy pronto and advise me here?

Another thg. (This is confidential, though. Keep it between Brian and yourself). But McClelland and Stewart have seen my ms. and have offered to take a minimum first order of 2,500 copies if I can get free of Collins [Deutsch's Canadian distributor]. Collins – I don't like them anyway – will only take a first order of 1,500. So I am going to see what can be done. Jack McClelland is most anxious to get the bookie.

On the debit side, I seem to have a slipped disc. Damned painful. Have bought myself a splendid cane. Was going to get a sword cane (Wilkinson blade) but charge is 12 quid. Had a great time in the cane shop, tho.

M.

3280 Ridgewood Avenue
Montreal

February 6, 1959

Dear Mordecai,
I've finished DUDDY and let me say right away that I think it's
very, very good. It's certainly your best to date and I'd say
prospects are good for a large sale and great critical reception.
You've got a much more memorable central character than in
your previous books and that, I think, is the main thing. There
is much better construction without loss of vitality. It certainly
moves forward and has great drive.

At the same time, I wouldn't be on ole pal if I didn't register
my reservations (God, that sounds pompous, doesn't it?). But I
remember your telling me in the fall that you were worried
that it had gone so quickly and perhaps you didn't do enough
revisory work. I think parts of it do show signs of haste, and I
wished to hell they didn't. The thing is that while Duddy is
great, some of the lesser characters don't come off nearly so
well, and I think this lessens the effect of a "big" book like
this, where the focus is fairly wide. I couldn't dig Uncle Benjy
or figure out exactly what was going on there. With Yvette,
too, I felt that credibility was weakened by haste. I couldn't
a see wrong-side-of-the-tracks chambermaid pulling off
complicated real-estate deals. I'm not saying this is impossible –
nothing is, in fiction – but when you're selling as unusual
proposition as that you've got to go out of your way to make
it believable. . . .

But – most of it was really terrific. The Bar Mitzvah
movie was out of this world, old chap. Also the cadet
parade. The going home from school, with the stop at the
Christian Mission. The Cuckoo Caplan and other hotel
bits. I haven't got the book in front of me, but these things
stay in mind.

(AMAZED to see that YOUR Reform rabbi talks about Jewish sports. So does mine, damn it, in my bkie – Sport in the Old Testament. Guess there's a limit to gags available, eh?)

Nothing much new here. Bourgeois poker on Saturday night, honest toil otherwise. Again, I almost killed myself laughing at that movie scene and some of the other funny stuff.

B.

With this letter I enclosed a list of nineteen factual errors, or what seemed to be errors, in the Duddy Kravitz manuscript. There was no "four o'clock train to Toronto," I told Mordecai. It left at 3:30 standard time or 4:30 daylight saving time. It was Adrien, not Adrian Arcand, and the Liberal party was not in power in Quebec in 1948. Also, I told the author, there were signs in his dialogue that it was time he left England and came back to Canada: no Canadian, for instance, ever spoke of "an" hotel.

"Thanks for yr notes," Mordecai wrote to me. "They were useful, helpful and applied in most cases. Sometimes not, tho, i.e., at Baron Byng High School we did call the men teachers 'masters.' The question always was, 'Who's your class master this year?' . . . If your Reform rabbi speaks on sports I will write letters to the editor saying wherefrom you got it. Tough shit, old man."

I had passed the *Duddy* manuscript on to Brian, who read it and sent his reactions to Mordecai. And now Brian gave me the letter he received from Mordecai, responding to Brian's critique:

London, Feb. 16

Dear Brian,
I'm glad, very pleased in fact, that you dug Duddy so much. Some of yr criticisms I agree with, some I object to. That springs partially (and naturally) from a difference of approach to the novel (not so different, however, as essentially I consider

myself a moralist) and something else: Duddy is essentially the first vol. of an intended trilogy. The next one, tentatively titled DUDLEY KANE'S FIRST MARRIAGE, I hope is only a few years off. But the final volume, as I thk of it, will be impossible for me to sit down to for another ten or fifteen years, anyway. DUDDY, too, is the springboard for a whole clutch of novels, big and small, about St. Urbain Street alumni. There's one coming about Hersh, who appears briefly, and a short one in notes abt Uncle Benjy.

Briefly, I'm staking out a claim to Montreal Jew-ville in the tradition of H. de Balzac and Big Bill Faulkner. And that, Sir, is why I must come home for a year anyway, and keep doing that every third year.

Why I must come home is tied up with some of yr criticisms, i.e., Calder is a writer's bluff – I don't know nearly enough abt guys like that – and I must find out more, plenty more, if they are to appear in my books. I also agree that Yvette doesn't quite come off. This kind of thg I hope to remedy, too, but I also fear a congenital weakness in the creation of women characters. (Our different temperaments, talents, etc., aside, I could never have written Judith Hearne – or Jessie Hershhorn, if you like.)

However I thk, and others all agree here, that John Peter Dyer is a dandy bit of characterization. What do you thk? Abt Vergie there are split opinions. As for me, I like him better, had more fun writing abt him, than anybody bar Duddy.

There was, naturally, the MacPherson story to begin with, but the moral idea behind Duddy was to get inside, and show how sympathetic in many ways, the go-getter, the guy nobody has time for – remember the scene with Uncle Benjy – really is. That's why I was so happy when Kazin [the American critic] said, ". . . but he has also avoided the obvious device of making his protagonist contemptible." This was crucial to me, and that Kazin – and I thk you and Bill too – got it has delighted me. The intention is moral, but not social-moral, i.e., assimilation, etc., as you ask for. Oh, this is all so difficult in a letter. We can talk abt it sometime.

Anyway, I've just finished going through the ms., tightening, and I've cut some 5-6000 words. As the book now runs to some 125-130,000, it's all to the good, I thk.

Again, I'm happy that you like the bk, and I hope to hell you will soon be writing yourself out of yr bk. God, you are really putting in a sweat. A sweat, man.

Best to Jackie. Tell Bill I will write shortly.

M.

∾

I finished the second draft of my novel in March and nervously handed it to Brian for his appraisal. He decided to give me his critique in writing, and when I started to read it I was delighted. It was not in Brian's character to bubble over with praise, so I took his muted approval in his first paragraph as an enthusiastic endorsement. "After finishing the book," he wrote, "I think it's well worth your while to give it some more time. Maybe it will need more than a month's work. But in the end you have a good central character, a good romantic situation and quite a number of funny situations. The plot seems to me to be well worked out, with minor flaws which are mostly your desire to over-explain something which you feel to be implausible."

"Minor flaws . . ." It was music to my ears. Having heard how scathing Brian could be in criticizing the books of other writers, I took these measured remarks as encomium indeed. But then, as I read on, the clouds gathered. "When I finished reading the second half," he said, "I had the impression that I had been presented with several forms – farce, fantasy, realism, satire – and that the author had not fused these elements successfully. Or rather that no one can handle these techniques well enough to make such a fusion successful. Even Waugh doesn't try to mix all of these elements as you do. And you try for a Waugh ending. But Waugh you ain't. . . ."

I was starting to bleed now. Brian of course knew of my admiration for Evelyn Waugh as the greatest of all comic writers, and his gratuitous comparing of me and The Master was, I felt, brutal. But there was worse to come. "I found the second half much more confused than the first," he wrote. "Again everything seemed overdone, but this time it was not so much a question of repetitiveness (it was repetitive too) as much as a question of being unfunny. The local jokes and author jibes at local customs were, to me, not much above the local humorist level and very often below it because they were simply the author saying this province is full of bad guys, etc. At various points in your discourse you tee off on Duplessis, McConnell types, etc. You merely say these guys are crooks. Is this news or funny or what?"

There was much more – notes that he'd scrawled in his notebook as he'd read along. "Father Tumulty unfunny . . . Mrs. K. wouldn't say, 'I've got your number' . . . Libel here? . . . "gnarled with rage"? . . . too documentary . . ." There were three pages of this stuff, with many comments on plot and character, and then his final summing up:

"I think with minor excisions and a few chapters rewritten, first chapter and last two or three, you could have a Canadian funny book. To make it an international funny book I think you would have to write a complete new draft with a lot of agonizing reappraisals of whether or not fearless facts about local crooks (which is journalism) is fiction. I say no."

I had been savaged. My dear old friend Moore had administered a caning of the kind he had suffered at the hands of the priests at that dreadful school in Belfast. For several days I licked my wounds and wondered whether I shouldn't consign my manuscript to the fireplace. Finally I went up to Lansdowne Avenue to confront my tormentor and see if I couldn't squeeze just an ounce or two of approval out of him.

Supplying me with a few Gin-Masters, Brian told me he had been purposely harsh, to bring me to my senses – before I even took leave of them. He knew my propensity for making a long, loud and obstinate defence of any position I held, no matter how wrong it was. He wanted to get through to me, and a sledgehammer seemed the appropriate tool. He reminded me how pleased he had been when I'd first told him I was writing a novel, how much he wanted me to become a member of the authors' club. He wanted me to write a book. A good book. And the only way to write a book was through work, work, work. In view of the fact that I was a lazy slug, trying to solve my problems by lying down on a head-shrinker's couch, he had to arouse me to revise, revise, revise. So go home and start rewriting. There is – repeat is – a potential book there.

I did go home and forced myself to read his notes again. And they started making sense to me – a lot of sense. Slowly I started rewriting. And if *Why Rock the Boat?*, as the book was eventually titled, managed to find a publisher – the first publisher it was sent to, in fact – it couldn't have happened without my swallowing Brian Moore's harsh medicine.

～

In London, Mordecai had rewritten the script for *Room at the Top*, directed by his friend Jack Clayton, and the film had won the British Film Academy's award as the best film from any source. Later, in Hollywood, it won an Oscar for the actress Simone Signoret and another for Neil Paterson, the writer of the original – and very faulty – screenplay. Unfortunately Mordecai got no screen credit for his rewrite work, but, as he told me, this turned out to be no problem at all.

5 Winchester Road
London NW 3

April 30

Well, Weintraub, the word is out. SOMEBODY didn't get a credit, by George, but up & down Wardour Street they are

saying, "That bum Paterson couldn't have written
'Room' (biz term for 'Room at the Top'). So, dammit,
chaps, who was the script doctor and where is he?"
Well, the word has leaked and my eversharp scalpel
has been called in to serve once more. This time the
patient is a thriller by two tricky Frenchies – the chaps
who wrote Les Diaboliques and Vertigo – and the
anxious producer is one Sid Box. This time, too, my
surgical fees have gone up. Long and short of it is
I've been offered £1,500 for six weeks to rewrite this
scriptie, for John Mills. If any further surgery is required
I will be paid £250 weekly as long as my blade is
needed. Well, this coolie has put his stuck stage
play aside, as for £250 there are damned few abortions
I won't perform (don't tell Nathan Cohen). I will
get sole credit, it seems.

On the other side of the ledger, Variety has panned
my TV play BENNY. It missed by a mile, they say. But
rumour has it that Box wants me for a big James Mason
epic when this medium budget scriptie is done, but this
boy is writing no more flicks this summer. Summer is
book-time, God damn it.

You wouldn't recognize 5 Winchester Road, what with
a new toilet, a fridge coming Tuesday, a car ditto, and a
telly later in the week. Ah, the hi-life. Ah-ha, the
doorbell. It's that sweet feller from Fortnum & Mason.
Swan steak. Again. If thgs break as well as they
indicate, next year I will give a grant to the
Canada Council.

> Best,
> Dean of the Script Doctors

National Film Board
P.O. Box 6100, Montreal 3

June 6, 1959

Dear Mordecai,

My news is that Bernice and I have finally parted. It's been
coming for a hell of a long time – these things always do, don't
they? – and it became very obvious to me last Saturday that
the time had come. Since then, for the past week, I've been
sleeping on Alex and Gloria Cherney's sofa. I know it's for the
best and Bernice agrees with me. I will spare you the details of
what a wrench it was to pack the bag, say good-bye, etc. You
must know all about that stuff, as who doesn't these lousy days.
But actually, at the moment, I can only say that I have a great
sense of relief. You get sort of emotionally exhausted and any
clear-cut decision lifts a huge weight. There have been tentative
partings between us before, but this one I know is for keeps.

I know it'll be better for me and I hope it'll be better for
her, too. In our quiet little way we've been doing each other
considerable harm, I think.

I hate all the details that must now ensue – division of
property, custody of the cat, living arrangements, etc. Damn.
But the thing that bothers me most is that I have friends to
turn to and I don't think Bernice has. She's a lonely person. I
wish I could have changed that. Needless to say I go through
a fair amount of guilt, remorse and so on. But I really don't
feel much like talking about it in a letter. It's pretty bloody
complicated.

As for the practical future, I think but am not sure that
Bernice will occupy the apartment all summer. Then, beginning
of September, she will leave for her trip to Europe (a week's
conference, three weeks' holiday). Then I might move back
into the apartment. When she comes back she will look for digs
nearer McGill.

BUT it occurs to me that if you come back to Montreal in September, you might like to share the place with me. It's bloody comfortable, big, and has two bedrooms. What do you think? On the other hand, I feel as a result of your last letter that Wardour Street will keep offering you millions and we will never see you again on these shores, except for a flying weekend visit on the way to the Coast. Ho hum. Seriously, though, if you've staked out St. Urbain Street as your Yoknapatawpha County, you better hurry back, eh? You said so yourself. So why go the way of all flesh? I am feeling lonesome, miss your company, and we could have some high jinks around here in the fall and winter. SO COME HOME and tell them to shove their quids up their Elstree rectums.

Bill

5 Winchester Road

June 10

Dear Bill,
Your news is sad but not altogether surprising – hope you don't find that irritating, but I'm afraid it's only the marriages that last which I find surprising these days. You sound lonely and troubled, and no wonder! Man, I know the remorse and guilt bit & how it all hits at very late hours. Well, I'm sorry. Because this means you've both been through the longest six or eight months and I'm sure you're weary. If you're going through with a divorce you've also got a pretty lousy year ahead with sharpie lawyers and phony evidence and strained meetings – like you say, division of property, etc.

Well, it's harder on the women, for somehow (and no matter what) the friends seem to go with the men. But I certainly think it'll be easier on Bernice than it was/is for Cathy. She's got, well, a 'career,' and she's younger too. But if this marriage has only made you both miserable then there's really no point – in fact it's only more cruel to carry on with it.

Brian and Jackie are about the only couple I know of who seem to have a happy marriage. A solid one. I've never seen them go at each other – score mean points jokingly as I've seen you-Bernice, Cathy-me and others go at it again and again – and do each other, as you say, considerable harm. Still, I do not believe all marriages are doomed. And speaking for myself, I want and intend to have children.

The idea of the two of us sharing your flat sounds like fun, but is impossible. I'll tell you why and also why I've delayed my trip home again and again. It's not Wardour Street that's keeping me here and I DO intend to make St. Urbain my Yokanpppp . . . County. It's Florence Mann that's keeping me here. I'm waiting for her divorce to come through so that we can return to Canada together. I don't know whether this surprises you – whether you've heard rumours from returning travellers – but, anyway, that's the way things are. We are in love. And we are going to get married when we can. All this is highly confidential – not to go past Brian & Jackie – tho it's probably obvious to many people here as Florence and I are together every night and have been seen together almost everywhere. . . . But nothing must be said until Florence gets her divorce – the first decree should be in on June 28 and the final decree three months later.

Anyway, we intend to return to Canada a couple of months or so after the final decree comes thru. Cathy, who knows about most of this (I spoke to her), will be here in October for our court hearing – then I'll have to wait until three months pass before we get our final decree. . . .

Just one thing for the record. My marriage was finished before I got involved with Florence – she's no 'home-breaker,' as they say – in fact both our marriages were done. I just don't want you or the Moores to start off with any prejudices against Florence as naturally we want to be seeing much of you once we're in America.

I guess that's enough about my own affairs and I only go into it now to explain why my trip's been delayed again and again and why I can't share a flat with you. Don't know what your vacation plans are for this summer, but if the mood hits you late one night why not fly over here? I've now got a car and we cd go for a trip. If yre short of money and want to come over I can lend it to you, you know. Think abt it.

Well, write soon because I think and worry about you and hope to see you soon. And meanwhile take care and God bless –

                              M.

Mordecai was wrong in his prediction that our divorce proceedings would be an ordeal. As we resided in Catholic Quebec, where there were no divorce courts, all we had to do was have an Act of Parliament passed in Ottawa dissolving the marriage. This was the simplest of matters, a well-oiled procedure of conspiracy and perjury.

It started with a visit to my apartment by a private detective, hired by our lawyer, who would testify that he had found me living with a Miss Jane Stevens, and that I had committed adultery with her. This, of course, was total fiction, but it was what had to be said before the Senate divorce committee. Bernice also had to go to Ottawa, where she testified that there was no hope of reconciliation. Bored and disbelieving, the senators did their part in this familiar charade and before long I received an impressive document from Ottawa advising me and the world at large that "Her Majesty, by and with the advice and consent of the Senate and House of Commons of Canada, enacts as follows: The said marriage is hereby dissolved, and shall be henceforth null and void for all intents and purposes." Other provinces had divorce courts, and Quebec would have them too, in the future, when the church relaxed its grip, but here, in 1961, was another reminder that Quebec was – and always would be – distinctly different.

Brian and Jackie were also destined to divorce, although no one would have suspected it at the time. This saddened me, as it was I who had introduced them to each other a decade earlier. But they parted in 1964, and Brian and Jean Denney were married three years later, finding happiness together until his death in 1999. Mordecai and Florence were married in 1960, and theirs too was to be a happy and enduring union. In 1967, Magda Landau and I were married, and this wonderful woman would bring me stability and joy. But until 1967, I would revert to being a bachelor.

~

Amagansett, N.Y.

August 26, 1959

Dear Mordecai,

Summer seems to be almost over and here I am winding it up with ten days' rest Chez Moore in the never-never land of the Hamptons. I've been in and out of New York since the end of June, at the newsreel libraries selecting footage for my new project. Not unpleasant, staying at the Algonquin amid the ghosts of the Great, all expenses paid, and lots to do after work. Saw various plays including the new Tennessee Wms which was lousy. Saw the Soviet Exhibition and was so impressed that I think I will move to Birobidjan.

Spent weekends here in Amagansett. Great beach, great weather, much socializing. Interesting people, 50 per cent of whom are in analysis – writers, painters plus rich civilians. The Moores are in the very thick of things, their main problem being which invitations to turn down. Each house we visit is greater than the last. The other night we were at the abode of a Dirty Old Man with a YMCA-sized swimming pool in his backyard. He protested vigorously when the ladies insisted on wearing bathing suits, saying this was against house rules. Then was caught peeking in window as they were changing.

One drunken party was at the home of people so rich they have an estate with grounds "just like in the movies." (How's that for good description?) At this party many dropable names from Broadway, etc. During the proceedings I fell into disgrace by being caught by the host stealing a bottle of his champagne. I had asked a young (not so young) lady to come swimming with me, down at the midnight beach, perhaps skinny-dipping, and she said we would have to have a bottle of wine. Caught. Embarrassing. Oh.

Met Philip Roth here and while he seems to be a very nice chap, and I like his work, I can't say that I take to him. Brian's Judith Hearne play has a new lease on life, with José Quintero picking up the option for a year. You may have heard of him, one of the top directors these days. Moores plan to stay out here into September and then get an apartment in New York. So I guess it's good-bye Montreal for them, especially as he's got that $5,000 Guggenheim now.

You must try to get down to Amagansett next summer. Duddy would be happy here, as all the talk is about land acquisition and building houses. It is hoped that by sensible zoning this part of Long Island will be able to keep out undesirable elements, like writers with low Nielsen ratings, etc. Write me at Ridgewood, eh, as Bernice will be vacating and I'll be moving back in.

Bill

Amagansett, Sept. 15

Dear Bill,
Like man, well, we've got ourselves a pad in the Village. Like on West 15th Street and the number is 150 and our unlisted

phone number is CHelsea 2-3279 and we'll be making the scene there as of Sept. 28. Crazy? Well it's $225 a month, furnished, four rooms, dishwasher, teevee and all that jazz. It's top apt in four-apt converted house and Jackie got it yesterday.

As for the scene out here, it's changed, man. Trelevan is back for the last two weeks of the month and others come out weekends but the parties are over, daddy. . . . Even Josh Greenfeld has sloped back to the city and only Roth remains among the scriveners, writing busily day and night, full of projects and self-esteem, while Old Moore languishes, his typewriter hooded, his muse silent. From your Amanda I hear nothing, darling.

José Quintero darling is casting "Motel" and won't be able to go to work with me on play until Oct. 1. End of page. How are things?

Brian

3280 Ridgewood Avenue
Montreal

October 18

Dear Mordecai,
Enclosed please find Duddy reviews from yesterday's Gazette, Friday's Newsweek, plus ad from today's Sunday Times, part of a full-page Little, Brown ad. No review in today's Sunday Times or Herald-Trib. I watched the daily Times all week, but nothing there. But, as you know, there's lotsa books coming out this time of year. I was surprised, however, that the Montreal Star had nothing yesterday. Guess Siskind hasn't finished sharpening his axe.

The book has arrived from Boston and thanks. Not my favourite jacket, if you want to know. But a lovely book, a lovely book.

Bernice and I have now gone through the revolting business of splitting possessions. She got Simpson the Cat, whom I miss very much. It's very quiet in the apartment without the little bugger jumping around. Workwise, I plug on with the tedious details of producing this film series. I should be finished at the end of January and then plan to take six weeks off and finish my novel once and for all. Then I'll show it to you.

By the way, a number of people at the NFB told me they enjoyed your Duddy stuff in Maclean's. Did I tell you I've read Brian's new book? Damn good.

When are you coming over? Write.

Bill

"This is a great book and when Mr. Richler has rubbed off the rough edges of his prose he is probably going to be the best writer in Canada," the Toronto *Telegram* said in its review of *The Apprenticeship of Duddy Kravitz*. "I don't think there is a false line," the reviewer continued, "a blurred image or a contrived motivation in the whole book. Duddy Kravitz IS . . ."

"Mr. Richler comes out of this exercise as the first of Canada's Angry Young Men," the *Montreal Star* observed in praising the novel, while the Montreal *Gazette* said, "Mr. Richler – who is still in his twenties – is becoming something of a legend in his own time." In the *New York Times*, the headline over its review was, "MONTREAL METEOR."

Many of the reviewers attempted to summarize the book, but the best of them was probably Richard Lister, writing in the London *Evening Standard*: "Duddy," Lister wrote, "was a mother-less boy who had an amiable, boasting taxi driver as his father and a clever, better-loved elder brother. He was ugly, shifty, felt small, disregarded, unimportant, and he fought back with an indomitable will to achieve at any cost.

"Duddy, as his rich uncle on his death bed prophesies, becomes a 'pusherke – a little Jew-boy on the make.' And yet Mr. Richler manages to wake in us an intense interest in, and even a sympathy for, his thoroughly nasty, foul-mouthed, ruthless, swindling little hero.

"'A man without land is nobody,' his respected old grandfather told him as a child, and he never forgot it. He was working as a waiter in a summer camp when he discovered a lake which could be a gold mine if it were properly developed, and though barely eighteen he set about buying up all the land surrounding it.

"Getting the money, as each lot comes onto the market, becomes his ruling passion. He wears himself out doing three jobs at once. He goes without food and sleep, lives on drink and benzedrine, goes bankrupt, hardens his heart, is loyal only to his family, loses his girl, betrays his friends, tries blackmail and forgery. But he gets his land.

"And the odd thing is that we are as delighted as he is at the achievement, and crush down, as he does, the memories of what it has cost in terms of other people's unhappiness and the hardening and warping of his character. And we leave him at the end standing on his own land with his family, triumphant but completely revealed."

In his assessment of the year 1959's Canadian fiction, Robert Fulford, writing in the *Toronto Star*, said that *The Apprenticeship of Duddy Kravitz* was the novel he most enjoyed, and that it was his candidate for the Governor General's Award. But once again in 1959 the judges for the award passed over the best novel for a forgettable one, Hugh MacLennan's *The Watch That Ends the Night*, with its characters constructed out of sturdy Canadian plywood. After saying that this book's characters were dull, its atmosphere bland and its story commonplace, Fulford said that its most disturbing aspect was its "intellectual poverty." By contrast, he said, Mordecai's book "gave us what no other Canadian novel of the year gave us: a genuinely memorable character."

Mavis Gallant's first novel, *Green Water, Green Sky*, was also published that year. "Handled in her suave, New Yorkerish style," Robert Fulford wrote, "it was easily the most expertly written of

1959 Canadian novels." The *New York Herald Tribune* said the book was "delicately controlled, clearly written, the pathetic but sinister story of a destructive mutual love. . . . This is sophisticated writing that probes the human heart."

"In this subtle, disturbing, beautifully-written novel," the *Saturday Review* said, "Mavis Gallant writes of the disaster that results from a relationship founded on the mutual need and antagonism of a woman and her daughter, where love turns inward and festers, bringing about inevitably the disintegration of both characters. . . . Miss Gallant has an astonishing talent for evoking a time and a place by the use of a single sharp detail. . . . Shrewdness of insight, exactness of imagery, and illuminating wit make it a novel that will be of interest to readers of serious fiction."

∾

New York Hospital
Medical Floor

Sunday

Well, Sir,
Bob Costello went to Libya this week and came back today (7-day trip). Mort (see enclosed) went to Le Sex-Appeal. I went to the Wall and will not be back, they say.

As Cyril Connolly once put it, "The lights are going out and it is closing time in the playgrounds of the West." My high-priced physician looks down on me sadly (suggesting a liver test after the tale I tell him), shakes his high-priced finger and says a few sad words. Another pint of blood is ordered and the patient sinks back in a steady coma of phenobarbital, feeling at long last like a small boy who has been allowed to stay out until midnight but who is suddenly called in by the adults and sent to bed for keeps.

In other words, after 38 years the party is over: No longer in Homeric endurance shall we [drunkenly] drive Volkswagens at dawn or run through the magnums of the great years at New Year's Eve. As my great compatriot Brendan Behan might have put it, "I Am 38 And I Do Not Want To Die!" So it's X-rays tomorrow, another week in the jug here and then a new sober Moore, unbearable prig, anti-social finger pointer, a perfect example of mens insana in corpore sano.

No news other than Total Universal Disarmament seems fit to put beside the above. As yet I do not know the extent of my injuries, required penance, future plans. Why not come down for the weekend?

Brian

3280 Ridgewood Ave.

Thursday

Dire Sire,
What a nasty piece of news is this! Obviously you are having your full share of the miseries this semester. Get well quick, say I.

As Jackie probably told you, it was pure telepathy that I got telephonitis and called you the other night. Sean called me later. I had no idea.

I'd love to come down for a weekend but financially things are tight. Any luxuries, like $175 for a few car repairs, disrupt things very badly.

A few fairly severe Film Boardic parties here, but certainly nothing to compare with your Rabelaisian evenings. A Hispanic evening last Saturday at Sani and Bella Idelsons' abode in which Sani announced that he had become the first Jewish novice in Opus Dei, a new Spanish lay order which accepts only college graduates.

Man, I wish I had more news, more yuks, more cheer. Work, couch, Peter Dawson Scotch (the cheapest available) – that's all. The simple life and fairly depressing. No Amandas in sight to brighten things. Please write me very soon like and tell me what gives in your innards.

Get well.

Bill

150 West 15th, N.Y.C.

November 16

Dear Humbert Humbert,
No drink has passed my lips since that fatal All Hallows'
Eve. . . . I rise, work perfunctorily for a few morning hours, have an hour and a half nap. Then out for a walk and then home, prepare wife's gin and tonic, sip a tomato juice, read a little and to bed by eight to look at TV and read some more. Asleep by eleven.

Back for an X-ray in three weeks. Saw doc the other day and was told I had a very large ulcer there. Was given a book on ulcers, calculated to produce another one. My trouble is all psychological, this book says.

Quote: Among our patients with duodenal ulcers we have found that all of them had a lack of security in childhood. In some this was a result of broken homes, due to the death of a parent or divorce; in many cases it was due to poverty with worry over food and clothing; and often both parents worked, leaving the children on their own. In some it was due to being different from those around them, due to being foreign or of a different race or religion. In these situations they felt unloved or inferior to other people and insecure. You

will probably recognize many of these things in yourself . . .
Unquote.

Does this fit me? I do NOT recognize myself.

Yrs,
Unloved.

3280 Ridgewood Avenue
Montreal

November 20

Dear Unloved,
Your wretched ulcer is indeed sobering news, and leave us pray
that time, gentle treatment and lots of milk will subdue it.
Meanwhile let me tell you a cautionary tale that will prove
that we are all better off without the Demon Rum.

This tale begins at 5 p.m. in the offices of Canada's National
Film Board. Another day is coming to an end and the great
documentary machine is grinding to a halt. Coats and hats are
being put on when Rita says, "Bill, you old fool, how about
giving me and Nellie a lift downtown?"

Rita is the new Unit C secretary. She is tall, blonde and
bursting out of her skin-tight dress. She is 18 years old. She is
in a chronic state of hysterical laughter, walks with undue
undulation, fills the air with suggestive remarks, and calls her
elders "you old fool." Since her arrival, our whole national
filmic purpose, which is defined by Act of Parliament, has
slowed down perceptibly.

And so I head out to the parking lot with Rita and her
buddy Nellie. Nellie is 20 and it is impossible to look on
her without thoughts of extreme carnality. We climb into my
sturdy British Ford Zephyr and Nellie says, apropos of nothing,
"I hate these slobs who ask you out and don't even have a

late-model car." I interpret this as meaning that she thinks my Zephyr is adequately late-model.

The drive downtownwards is filled with girlish laughter, although the driver is suffering extreme anxiety. "Ever since I joined Unit C, I can't stop laughing," says Rita. "I think I'm going mental. My mother says quite a few in our family are mental."

"Your father's mental, isn't he?" says Nellie.

"He was all right when he was an alcoholic," says Rita. "But he got religion and he gave up the drink and now all he does is sit and look out the window. What an old fool."

"Well, girls," the driver says nervously, "we are now at Ridgewood, which is where I live. Yonder bus will take you downtown, where I hope you will have a good but prudent time tonight."

"You got anything to drink in your apartment?" asks Rita. The reply, naturally, is affirmative, and Rita cries, "Let's live it up!"

The size and opulence of the apartment fills them with admiration. "How about giving me a key?" says Rita. "When I get home at four in the morning my slob of a father locks me out. I'd be better off here than sitting on the goddam doorstep."

"Are you going to make mad, passionate love to us?" says Nellie. This remark contributes immensely to the host's anxiety. As he pours the drinks he wonders exactly what the Criminal Code says about having girls of 18 in apartments.

"Am I ever impressed by people who actually have liquor on hand," says Rita. "I mean, you don't have to go out and buy it."

"Are you Jewish, Bill?" says Nellie.

"Yes, I am."

"I always like to go out with Jewish boys," says Nellie. "They have lots of money and a good education. My father hates Jews. I brought a Jewish boy home once and when I introduced him my father didn't even look up from his paper. I could of clobbered him."

"These people are crazy," says Rita. "They think Jewish boys all have beards and wear a beanie. You don't wear a beanie, do you, Bill?"

"No."

"Let's live it up!" cries Rita, pouring herself a staggeringly large drink. "I'm going to get loaded again tonight. Everybody thinks Michael and me are having an affair, but we're just getting loaded all the time."

"When did you start drinking, Rita?" I ask.

"When I was twelve. I was big for my age. Don't you think I'm big, darling?"

"You are very big indeed."

"Do you think I'm sexy?"

"Yes, dear, you certainly are."

Well, chaps, I have seldom seen such boozing as followed. These girls have an incredible capacity, perhaps wooden legs. Me, I am guzzling the hooch to still my raging anxiety and to dispel the picture of that father, gazing out of his window.

"We were supposed to meet Monique downtown," says Nellie.

"Phone her up," say I. "Tell her to come over. Tell her to pick up a bottle. I'll pay for it."

Monique arrives. "I never bought a bottle before," she says. "I thought maybe I look too young." But Monique looks, and is, 18, and evidently that is all right with the Quebec Liquor Commission. However the thoughts I am having concern federal offences, not provincial, and I drink heavily to drive them from my mind. Monique drinks too. She may never have bought a bottle, but she certainly knows what to do with one.

"Let's live it up!" cries Rita. "You want a breast or a leg, darling?" She is on the phone, ordering chicken from St. Hubert Bar-B-Q. Nellie is in the kitchen, where she has discovered some lamb chops. As I show her where to find the frying pan and other items, there is, in this small kitchen, considerable physical contact between us. I think of her father and get the hell out of that kitchen. Was it Nellie's father or Rita's father who is always looking out the window? At this point I can't quite remember. Maybe both fathers.

In the living room, the record player is now going and Monique and Rita are dancing together. I cut in and dance with each in turn. Nellie, who is farthest gone in drink, comes out of the kitchen and wants to be danced with. I oblige, and we dance very slowly, with a hold of such contiguousness as would get us thrown out of any ballroom in the country.

St. Hubert Bar-B-Q arrives, lamb chops are ready, and we eat, washing it down with dollops of Scotch.

"Now I would like to ask you girls a question," say I. "Just what policy do you follow in the matter of intimate relations with the opposite sex?"

"I'm a virgin," says Rita, "and I'm going to stay that way until I get married. I'll clobber any slob who tries to put his filthy hands on me. I'm big. I can hit hard."

"How about you, Monique?"

"Me too. I never have either."

"Well," says Nellie, "I did it once and have no regrets. He has left town. I would do it again, with the right person."

"You're crazy," says Rita.

"Would you like to dance, Nellie?" say I. We dance, very slow and close again, creating palpable arousal in myself.

"Aha," says Nellie, unavoidably aware of my condition. She looks at me, grinning.

"It's getting late," I say. "Why don't Rita and Monique go home?" I have momentarily forgotten the muscular father.

"Are you out of your mind?" says Rita. "I'm staying right here."

"This is boring," says Monique, and she leaves.

Nellie goes into my workroom and passes out on the sofa.

"Boy, do I ever love getting loaded," says Rita. "Nellie and I always look after each other when we're loaded. We're buddies."

Only thing is that Rita seems fairly sober. The host is certainly loaded, though. It is now eleven o'clock and Rita is regaling me with long accounts of drinking parties and of clobbering men who have put hands on her.

We go into the workroom and wake up Nellie. "I want to stay here tonight," says Nellie.

"No you don't," says Rita.

It is established that Nellie will stay at Rita's that night. I drive them home.

"Good night, girls."

"Kissie, kissie," says Rita. I kiss them both good night. The two buddies stagger through a doorway and I wonder if that father is still gazing out the widow, if he can see my licence number in the dark.

I drive back to my lonely pad and sniff the perfumy air.

The moral of this story is that the next day I had one hell of a hangover and a large number of disturbing thoughts. You are lucky to have that big ulcer, sir, and be off the booze and not let things like this happen to you. I am sure that barbiturate addiction will lead to much more satisfying, Coleridgian fantasies than the reality of my disturbing soiree.

Last night Gloria and Alex had one of their dinner parties and outdid themselves in the cookery. It was reassuring to be with older folks again.

Nice to speak to you on the phone and hear you sounding cheery. Hope you continue to mend fast.

Yr. Obt. Servt.
Errol Flynn manqué

13

"I would commend to your attention a new book called The Irish Genius," Brian wrote to me in January 1960. "The cover is one you will find of interest. You need this for your collection, so get it." I soon found a copy of the book, a collection of short stories, and noted the cover. It listed names of seven contributors, among them James Joyce, William Butler Yeats, Sean O'Faolain – and Brian Moore. Brian was certainly coming up in the world, hobnobbing not only with the shades of Yeats and Joyce, but also with the famous in New York.

150 West 15th, New York

January 5, 1960

Well, sir,
Attended a New Year's Eve party with Carl Reiner, Gwen Verdon, Barbara Bel Geddes, Eli Wallach and others too numerous to mention. Roger Straus of Farrar Straus was drunk and told me he loved Lupercal. Anyone who tells me this is O.K. He says Charles Jackson (The Lost Weekend) loved it and pressed it on him. C. Jackson is O.K.

After the party, at which I drank real drinks sparingly, a large black chauffeured limousine drove B. B. Geddes, Wink [her husband], Jackie and me home. But B. B. G. said party had only gone on until three and what was wrong with New Year's?

So we went to the African Room to hear Chief Bey beat the drums. Chief is big with B. B. G. and after the show shut at 6:00 a.m., Chief changed into his street clothes and we went over to the B. B. G. pad to admire their conversation pieces which included a Pissarro, a Picasso and a bottle of Bollinger Brut. We came home at 8 a.m. Happy New Year.

Good things have been happening, darlings. Judith Hearne, Editions Plon, introduced by Gabriel Marcel. Also from the French capital, a fine, fast thriller called Flamenco Pour Un Requiem, par Michael Bryan.

Sunday we went to the Lower East Side and walked among the street stalls. Have you ever been there? It is just like dear old Warsawa. Then walked across Williamsburg Bridge and into Brooklyn and Mike asked why we didn't need passports to go into this new country.

How is yr sex life?

Brian

Via Biferno 3
Rome

Jan. 29. 60

Dear Bill:

Got yrs this morning and here's the pitch: We intend to jet-it to Montreal on March 15, arriving at 5:30 a.m. We'd leave Rome in the morning for Paris, lunch at Laperouse with Ted Kotcheff, who'd fly in from London for the meal, have some cognacs at the Flore, and then fly to Montreal that night. Yes, sir, the last of the big spenders.

Putting up that notice at the Film Board is a dandy idea – what we want is a six-month sublet. . . . We may be homeless for the first four-five days while we apt-hunt, so can you put us up at your flat for those first few days? Let me know. Daniel can sleep on a couch, as long as there's a bed for us. Yes, we'll stay in the city, but we'd like to cut out for Long Island-New York in June. Be swell if you cd go Stateside at the same time.

I've already written to Moore about our plans. I have also written Jackie OUR NEWS. Our union is going to be blessed with an ISSUE. We are expecting said issue to come Aug. 1. I wrote to Jackie asking her to tell me what she knew and cd recommend by way of doctors, hospitals, etc. I'd also like to know more abt maids. Alex says $100 monthly, living-in. BUT . . . are such girls plentiful/good/and do they help with the kid (Daniel is three)?

Meanwhile, I'm working on my Shalinsky-Griffin novel. Yes, it will be swell to see you. We can get our cars pepped up and race together on the new Laurentian Highway.

M.

3280 Ridgewood Avenue
Montreal

Feb. 9

Dear Mordecai,
Congratulations, Daddy-o! That's great news. And call him Bill, eh?

Your travel plans most impressive. Please bring me a container of Boeuf en Daube from Laperouse. Please advise me of the inevitable changes in plan. Yes, I will probably be able to drag myself out of bed for the plane on the 16th at 5:30 a.m. Oy vay. Everyone tells me live-in maids, who look after children, are easy to find.

Delighted that you would like to stay with me. You can have my bedroom, with double bed. Daniel can sleep on the chesterfield and I can sleep on the couch in my workroom. I'll be working at home at that time, but can close the door. If you want to work, there's the dining room.

Everybody speaks well of DUDDY. Some too well. One of the most boring women possible cornered me at a New Year's egg-nog party and insisted on running through the plot with me. "Who was your favourite character?" she wanted to know.

This is the first time my new cat, Archie, has seen me typing and he watches, astonished. Then he runs around the room like crazy. But my heart still belongs to old Simpson, who now lives downtown.

Daddy-o, I'm going mad with work. Last minute rush, advanced deadlines, the bastards. Please keep me informed about your plans.

B.

At the NFB I had now become a freelance producer as well as a writer, and the advanced deadline being inflicted on me was for *Between Two Wars*, a series CBC-TV now wanted for April. Actually, the making of these three documentaries had been giving me more satisfaction than anything I had done for a long time, and now all that was lacking was enough time to do the final polishing more thoroughly. But in the end it all worked out and, it seemed, quite well. "The whole production had wit, style and good editorial judgement," the *Montreal Star's* television reviewer said.

Between Two Wars, which would be much used in schools, was a social and political history of Canada from 1918 to 1939, a period of particular interest to me as these were the decades of my birth and childhood. Researching the political past was easy, but I couldn't find any useful books about Canada's social history, so I had to spend long hours leafing through old newspapers and magazines to get the feel of the era. As for the visual material, I spent much time going through the dusty archives of the newsreel companies in New York, looking for Canadian items. There I found some treasures like visits to Canada by people such as the

Prince of Wales, Mary Pickford and the glamorous Queen Marie of Romania. I found the Human Fly climbing up the front of Montreal's City Hall, tin lizzies on bad roads, bathing beauty contests, Prime Minister R. B. Bennett sounding foolish, Canadian soldiers on their way to fight the Bolsheviks in the Russian Revolution and a big Imperial Airways flying boat inaugurating air mail service across the Atlantic.

In the 1920s and 1930s, long before television, movie houses showed newsreels before the feature film, and one thing I was anxiously looking for in the newsreel libraries was the footage a Pathé cameraman had shot in the late summer of 1929, when my father, reluctantly, jumped off the deck of that ship and into the waters of the Montreal harbour to demonstrate the Ever-Warm Safety Suit. But, alas, I never found that footage.

~

February 2

A Lazy Day:
Scene, New York.
   Outline of action: Author at typewriter 9 a.m. after successful battle with Immigration Dept. Back to Work Now is the slogan. Writes one para. Has coffee. Rewrites para three times. Phone rings. Josh Greenfeld wants to know if I would like to go to Actors' Studio to see actors' classes presided over by Lee Strasberg. Struggle of conscience and quick decision. 10:30 a.m.: Leave house. 11 a.m.: enter Actors.' Sit among Lee S., Franchot Tone, Shelley Winters, Rita Gam, Lee Grant, others, to watch Viveca Lindfors (world's most beautiful woman) act out a scene in bra and panties. Play is Brouhaha, London smash written by her husband, but Who Cares? N.G. play, V.G. body. Lee Strasberg speaks. Tape recorder switched on to record his immortal words.

Author leaves with Playwright Greenfeld and Fellow Scrivener Herbert (Man Who Was Not With It) Gold and eat lunch in actors' cafeteria. Herb tells me Norman [Mailer] called him a fairy in print. Herb is mad. He is divorced and has two kids. He is Not A Fairy. Herb gives me his phone number and we part.

Josh and I go to Josh's pad, then phone the missus and we all repair to Cafe Figaro for more discussion, Spanish coffee, bearded neighbours. Time 3:00 p.m. Walk desultorily through Village killing time until drink time. Drinks at five. Dinner at seven. Wife to see Enfants de Paradis. Author sits at typewriter at last and writes letter to Film Board friend. Tomorrow We Will Work. Or Will We Have Time?

Yours,
Gadge

Brian was now meeting all the right people in the New York theatre world and had become a member of the Playwrights' Unit of the Actors Studio. He was rewriting his play once again, this time working with his new director, José Quintero, a man who was not easy to work with. Quintero was forever cancelling meetings and needed two hours every day for his psychoanalyst and two hours after that to ponder what had transpired on the couch.

But despite all his unremitting hard work, Brian's *Judith Hearne* play was destined to come to naught. In a letter that he signed "Arthur Miller manqué," Brian told me about a scene from his script that had been staged at the Actors Studio. "Luckily I was in hospital." he wrote, "but Jackie went. Performance, direction and scene were lousy, she says. After the scene, playwrights including Buddy Schulberg and Billy Inge, and writers Norman Mailer and Rona Jaffe (God knows why) all criticized. I received a report of their criticisms from Mrs. Elia Kazan, who tells me scene is not good and that on the evidence I am a better narrative writer than a playwright."

There was more rewriting to follow, but eventually the project was abandoned by both writer and director. The playscript of the unproduced *Judith Hearne*, in its several versions, would eventually be consigned to the archives, among the voluminous Brian Moore papers.

~

3280 Ridgewood Avenue

July 26

Dear Brian,

The usual profuse apologies for being such a bad correspondent. But there just hasn't been much to report and I've been in one of my gloomy periods.

I think I've finally finished all the revisions on my book. Mort, still in Montreal residence on Dornal Avenue, said he thought the version I showed him was publishable without revisions, but he suggested a few. Some I did, and I thought of a few more on my own. It is now 75-80,000 words – more than a third shorter than what I showed you more than a year ago. I have both pruned and slashed. Local jokes, Duplessis jokes, are out. I am heartily sick of the whole trivial thing by now and can hardly bear to give it that one last reading before giving it to the typist. But will do so. Then typing. Then Mort will send it off to Jack McClelland. Mort has dreamed me up a bit on this thing, saying it's the sort of junk Maclean's might condense and serialize and that British producers are looking for a little comedy set in Canada. I don't dream-up easily these days, but I need some dough. . . .

It may astonish you, but not a drop of booze in any form has crossed my lips since Bastille Day, 12 days ago. I had a physical check-up and M.D. suggested a few tests at the hosp., and then said there is a wee bit of liver damage. Not much, just the beginning. He says that at this rate I might be in trouble in about five years. Suggested I try abstinence for a bit and am doing so. Then another test. I shudder when I think of how much I must have poured into myself over the years. Particularly last few months. I am undertaking short abstinence as much out of curiosity as for health. A new experiment. I find I miss the stuff much less than I thought I would. Watch Mort and others guzzle without envy. Perhaps by and by I will take a moderate social drink now and then. Who knows? What a bore I'm going to be.

I have hopes of spending second and third weeks of August in N.Y., on biz. Then, perhaps, a week in Amagansett. Could you stand a dry Wntrb, if still dry then?

Bill

Amagansett, N.Y.

July 28

Dear Liver:

Your letter to hand this morning stopped all thoughts of work (easily stopped in this climate) and set me to thinking about *my* liver. That's life. My grandfather died of cirrhosis of the liver at age 44 and I have always been given to understand that even a wee bit of liver damage is not something to be tampered with. Yet in a very real sense the news that you had stopped drinking made me feel very happy and induced agnostic prayers that the same power that enabled you to stop smoking for so many years would work again. As my confessor used to say, "I urge and entreat you not to resume these filthy habits, my child."

I have been invited to no great parties this season. Life would be quiet if not for the unending stream of visitors, many of whom have to be accommodated here because there are no rooms free at any of the local inns. All very work disrupting. At the moment my feelings are low vis-à-vis work. Advance copies of Ginger [his new novel, *The Luck of Ginger Coffey*] have gone out to various sources and have been greeted by silence, and friends who read it still say, "Judith Hearne" – my millstone. None of my short stories have sold and no money is coming in except for Jackie's Weekend earnings. In addition I move on slowly with new book, wondering if it will ever find a public as it is *very* unlike my other stuff.

One bright note: Went shark-fishing on monster boat with Wink Lewis, Bob Costello and David Shaw last week. Went out 8 miles off Montauk Point with Capt. Frank Mundus of the Cricket II. Drew sharks by pouring cupfuls of blood over side. Many sharks. I caught 3, one of them a 100-pounder. David Shaw fought for an hour with a 254-pounder and boated it. Arrived à la Hemingway at dock to roped-off crowd of spectators, tourists, etc., taking our pictures with their box cameras. Blue sharks we got.

Half hour shot again. Back to work. Keep dry and don't catch cold.

Yours,
Shark Papa

When *The Luck of Ginger Coffey* finally appeared, a month after Brian's letter, some reviewers compared it unfavourably with *Judith Hearne*, but all praised the writing and some insisted it was the best of the three books he had published to date. Margaret Laurence, writing in the *Vancouver Sun*, was among those who preferred Brian's first book, but this new one, she said, was still a very fine novel. "Ginger presents to the reader no truth in the abstract, but only the utterly convincing truth of his own existence," Laurence wrote. "He is. He will not be ignored. And because he is so truly Ginger Coffey, he is also Everyman. Author Moore can perform that rarest of all writing feats – he can create life on the printed page."

One reviewer who put *Ginger Coffey* first among Brian's novels was Jack Ludwig, who, writing in the *Tamarack Review*, said that it was "quite possibly the best novel Canada has had – a more expansive, more penetrating *Juno and the Paycock*, a book related to the Bloom of Joyce's *Ulysses*, the Gabriel Conroy of his story 'The Dead.' Ginger Coffey is – may Ireland forgive me for intruding Yiddish! – a *shlimazl*, a man of poor luck; like Joyce's Bloom he carries no objective signs of the heroic, only the inner touch – good will. Ginger Coffey belongs to the modern classification of *unheroic hero*, an ordinary character for an extraordinary destiny, an end to loneliness, some form of holy communion in this most secular of worlds."

Unlike Brian's two previous novels, this book was not set in Ireland but in Canada, in a wintry Montreal. Ginger Coffey, aged thirty-nine, is an immigrant from Ireland, a man with unlimited ambition and limited abilities. He has counted on Canada to turn his life around, to find him a job much better than the mediocre ones he had in Ireland. But he stumbles and fails at everything he tries, including a poorly paid job as a proofreader at a newspaper. His illusions are stubborn, but they die eventually, especially after his long-suffering wife takes up with another man. But in the end, the novel's great strength lies in the way it convinces us that Ginger can give up his self-delusion, accept his limitations and reconcile himself to a humdrum life of mediocrity. He finally finds comfort in this reality, and it is a victory.

The novel offered great descriptions of Montreal, especially the shabby side of the city, and some of its memorable characters, as a laudatory review in the *New York Times* put it, were "Dickensian in their grotesqueness and vitality." *Time*, straining as always for the vivid trope, rhapsodized. "Words drop on Novelist Moore's pages," it wrote, "with the errant grace and purity of snowflakes, and occasionally an epigrammatic hailstone comes rattling down on the author's adopted homeland, e.g., 'Money is the Canadian way to immortality.' 'Canada is a bore.' But in the end, Ginger Coffey refutes both charges." After reading this, I could always irritate Brian by asking, "How are the hailstones today? Any of them epigrammatic?"

The Luck of Ginger Coffey was destined to win the Governor General's Award for fiction for 1960. In December, Brian flew to Toronto for newspaper, radio and television interviews, and to attend a party at the home of Jack McClelland. Here he met Mordecai, who had moved to Toronto in November after summer and fall in Montreal. And at the party Brian heard something of great interest to me:

New York

Wednesday

Dear Author:
While up in Horrid Toronto Sunday night for a two-day show biz stint I ascertained the following gossipel truth:

A Mr. Ratcliff, a former Houghton Mifflin editor who has recently joined McClelland Stewart, was the first reader of your manuscript. He told me, unsolicited, that he thought it one of the funniest things he had read in ages and had recommended it enthusiastically. He said he was going to reread it critically now. At this point McClelland J. G. broke in to say he also thought the book great, well written, funny, etc., but trailed at the end. He had sent it to Little, Brown [a possible American co-publisher] in hopes and was waiting their answer. Both said how economical and fine the writing was.

All this means, in hard fact, that the book is funnier and better than your Montreal friends led you to believe and that it will, I am sure, find a U.S. publisher.

Mordecai is having his cognac warmed by waiters these days before being served it by waiters in the best restaurants. He says he is broke. No wonder.

Brian

3280 Ridgewood
Montreal

December 28, 1960

Well, sir,
I am flying high. I am in, but not quite in, and neurotically
worrying. As Jack McClelland says, "There is no doubt" about
Little, Brown, but . . .

Saw him in Toronto at Mort's Boxing Day party and liked
him very much. More hockey-player looking than publisher,
but very nice. We had a long chat. Gist: he had just been to
Boston and all reports from LB readers are very favourable and
they want to do it (but it hasn't been before the BOARD).
McCl wants to do it. BUT all reports have some "minor"
reservations, mostly concerning end of bk. His editor, Ratcliff,
whom you met, will digest all reports and send me a super
report ("Though we don't want to tell you how to write the
book"). I will think about all this and then Ratcliff will come
to Montreal and reason with me. Then, if we agree, a contract
will be forthcoming.

McClelland would like me to have the completed ms. by
end of February, and he will publish in the fall. I'm sure I can
manage this, but what worries me is just what they will want
done with the ending. McClelland stresses that it is "plot"
rather than writing that is in question. For me, the plot is the
only thing I'm satisfied with (I recall your saying, after reading
the first garbaged-up version, that the plotting was good).
It's the writing that gives me a pain, but I think I've done
almost all I can, though I want to try some more polishing,
shortening. But McClelland hints he would like to see the
boy get the girl at the end. Which, to me, destroys all
the previous logic. I don't think comic books need happy
endings. They just have to end logically, and I think mine
does. It's not that I feel this is inviolable art, but I'm trying
for a certain kind of irony in the resolution of the story and

wouldn't want to replace it with something crappy that I can't believe.

All the literati were at Mort's party: Fulford, Weaver, Dobbs, Ross McLean, and elder statesman Callaghan, sadly ukasing.

Splendid Xmas dinner. Mort is lucky, Florence is a wonderful cook. I reciprocated with dinner at the place where the waiters, as you know, warm the cognac. Mort, depressed because it was me who was squandering on the cognac and not him, called for the plug-in telephone and made two long and hideously expensive calls to London, just to say hello. This threw me into a state of nerves, to the extent that I had to have my cognac rewarmed. "I haven't phoned in six weeks," said Mort, who claims to be broke and not to have worked in a month. "We must start economizing in the New Year," said Florence. "Take that goddam phone away," I said to the waiter. "I enjoy these things," said Mort. "You don't know what it's like to once have been poor."

What's with thee? Write.

Bill

14

Taku Hotel
Whitehorse, Yukon

April 15, 1961

Dear Brian,
Whitehorse is a metropolis compared to Dawson City, where I
was last week for my Film Board chore. They even have
television in Whitehorse now, cable TV, with about 300
subscribers. They show mostly kinescopes of boxing and
wrestling, but their most popular program is when they simply
point their camera out the studio window for an hour or two,
to show who's out and about on the main street. Everybody at
home wants to see this, especially on Monday morning when
the Mounties are marching their prisoners over to the court-
house. Everybody wants to see who was arrested for disorderly
drunkenness on Saturday night.

This Taku Hotel is a palace compared with the Occidental
Hotel in Dawson City, where I resided last week. I arrived
there at night and checked in at the bar, the Occidental
having no front desk. I was given my key and sent up the creaky
stairs to my room, but first had to pass through the second-floor
lounge. Here there were five burly men sitting around a table,
drinking hot buttered rum and playing poker. The room, as is
common in the frozen north, was very overheated, and the

sweating poker players had all stripped down to their long johns. In the haze of cigar smoke, these gents, in their woolly underwear, made for a fine northern vignette.

A few days later, relaxing at the bar, I chat with Ole Christenson, hotel proprietor. "Ole," I say, "any airplanes around here going anywhere interesting?" Ole nips out onto the wooden sidewalk (Dawson City, population 500) and comes back with Ron Connolly, who happens to have a load for Old Crow. "Sure," says Ron, and the next day I am aloft. The plane is full of lumber and I am sitting behind pilot Gord Barch and co-pilot Dawn Connolly, pretty wife of Ron. It seems to me that Gord clasps Dawn's hand a bit too amorously as they haul together at some lever that must be hauled to straighten the plane out. This, plus their consulting a pamphlet entitled, roughly, "How to land a DC-3 on skis," makes me somewhat nervous, and I clutch my Rolleiflex tightly.

When I tell people here in Whitehorse that I've been to Old Crow I am somewhat of a hero. Everybody says two things: "Most isolated place in Canada" and "Only good Indians in Canada." Well, it is indeed very far north and Gord and Dawn clasp hands again and give the plane a little dip in my honour as we cross the Arctic Circle. We land on the frozen river and the Indians [as Aboriginals were then called] come running to unload the lumber. Also on hand is the Rev. Hamilton, the forlorn little Anglican minister, who invites me to lunch in his untidy little rectory. Here his wife, Gladys, serves up some caribou steaks, which would never go over at Moishe's. I decide to case this town and stay overnight, as Gord and Dawn are coming in again tomorrow with more lumber.

Well, there are 200 Indians and eight whites in Old Crow. The whites include two Catholic missionaries, Oblates, here to convert the Indians, all Anglicans, to the True Christian Faith. As things are getting a bit boring at Anglican H.Q. after lunch, I make profuse apologies and hurry down the street to the other store. Here I am welcomed by Father Bouillard, who says

his partner, Father Mouchet, is in Fairbanks, Alaska, coaching
the University of Alaska ski team.

"How long have you been in Old Crow?" I ask Father
Bouillard. "Ten years," he says. "Have you made many
converts?" I ask. "No, we have not yet made any." "Don't you
get discouraged?" "Why should we be discouraged?" he says.
"What is ten years in the history of the Church?"

Chief Charlie Abel Chitza now arrives to meet the man from
Outside. He is Chief of the Vanta Kuchen and a most imposing
chap. He agrees to give me a ride on his dogsled and we go
screaming across the lake. A great ride, although in my
Montreal store clothes I almost freeze my balls off, it being
15 below [Fahrenheit]. The next day, after sleeping in the
schoolhouse, I abandon the whites and spend the morning with
Chief Charlie. He takes me to visit many Indian cabins (it's a
segregated town, the eight whites living in the West End), and I
buy a large black bearskin from his brother-in-law. By and by
the DC-3 arrives and this time it's Gord and Ron (where's
Dawn?). Chief Charlie says come back in the summer and he'll
take me down the Porcupine River in his canoe, into Alaska.

And so Dawson City again. I borrow the bank manager's
Volkswagen and drive off to Bonanza Creek, to see exactly
where George Washington Carmack found the Klondike
mother lode in 1896. With me are Black Mike Winage and
Harry Leman, a native of your Belfast. We get stuck in the
snow and Black Mike and Harry leap out of the car, tear down
trees, push and pry. After two hours we are out of the snow. I
am almost dead, but Black Mike, aged 92, is not even breathing
hard, and neither is Harry, who is 90. Both were here during
the Gold Rush of '98, panning for gold, but they didn't go
home afterwards, like most of the others did. Now they do odd
jobs around town, to supplement their old-age pensions.

"In nineteen-o-two I bought a girl seventy-five dollars'
worth of champagne for just one dance," says Harry, as we drive
off to Discovery Creek. "I was worth four hundred thousand

dollars once," says Black Mike. "Let's stop at Marie's for a beer," says Harry, and when I agree to this they are convulsed with laughter. Marie's burned down fifty years ago. A weird thing.

So out of the past and down here to modern Whitehorse. Phone call from Nick Balla, at the NFB in Montreal. "While you're up there," he says, "why don't you go over to the Nahanni and see if there's a film there for us." I vaguely remember reading a magazine article about the legend of the Nahanni, a river in the Northwest Territories that runs through a place called Headless Valley. It's there that they found the skeletons – decapitated – of men who were looking for the fabulous lost gold mine. There's talk of hairy, nine-foot-tall mountain men, far up the river. Few people ever visit this remote wilderness and Indians won't go there because it's too spooky.

The Nahanni is 350 miles east of here and so I'm up at 4:00 a.m. this morning and take off with Lloyd Romfo, bush pilot, in his little Cessna, which I have hired for $395. We get almost as far as the Pelly Mountains and I am fair crapping myself as we can't see the mountains for fog and snow. Waiting to hit that ole mountain. So Lloyd turns round and says we'll have to try again tomorrow. Which we will.

Will I hear from you before you leave for Ireland? I hope to be back in Montreal in a week or ten days. Perhaps you'll write.

Bill

The weather was fine the next day and after a few hours of flying Lloyd Romfo steered the Cessna through some mountain passes until we found the South Nahanni River, a wide swath of snow-covered ice, smooth and serene, with no hint of the wild rapids under the ice. "Look down," Lloyd said, banking the plane so I could get a good view of Virginia Falls, twice the height of Niagara. They were quiet now, frozen into a jagged sculpture of ice, but it was easy to imagine how turbulent these waters would become when unleashed by warm weather.

Flying south, following the river, we passed through a deep canyon whose walls rose straight up from the shore. High in the canyon walls, level with our wing tips, were large, dark caves. "That's where the wild mountain men live," Lloyd said. "With their White Goddess?" I asked, remembering the magazine article. "She's in there too," said Lloyd.

Finally we reached our destination, Nahanni Butte, a tiny settlement at the mouth of the river, where it flowed into the Liard River. Lloyd put the plane down gently, on its skis. We got out, stretched our legs and trudged across to the shore. A man who had heard the plane came out of his log house to greet us.

"For the love of Mike, it's Lloyd Romfo," the man said. "What the hell are you doing here? Are you lost?"

"No, we're just looking at the river," said Lloyd.

Gus Kraus was a tall, sturdy man of about sixty. He'd lived in the Nahanni country for half his life, as a trapper and prospector. Now retired from these activities, he was the unofficial mayor of Nahanni Butte, the only settlement on the river, down here at its "civilized" end. There were about forty Indians and ten whites in the community. If anybody knew about the Nahanni, it would be Gus.

He took us up to his house, where his charming Indian wife, Mary, gave us tea and chocolate cake. I asked him about the legends.

"It's all baloney," Gus said.

"Mountain men, covered in hair? Giants?"

"Baloney."

That part of it was all the invention of Sunday supplement writers a thousand miles away, Gus said, but there was something strange that did happen on the Nahanni way back in 1908. That was when a search party found the skeletons of Frank and Willie McLeod. Near the skeletons was a note saying the McLeods had found gold, lots of it. But the gold was gone, and so were the skulls of the skeletons. Hence the name Headless Valley. Every so often, after 1908, a few prospectors would fight their way up the turbulent Nahanni to look for the McLeod bonanza. Nobody ever found it, but at least a dozen of the seekers either disappeared or were found dead, some in mysterious circumstances.

These days, Gus Kraus told me, there was only one man who was still convinced there was gold up there, and who kept looking for it, summer after summer. His name was Albert Faille, pronounced Fay-lee, and he lived in Fort Simpson, a hundred miles away. After we said goodbye and thanks to Gus and Mary, Lloyd flew me to the village of Fort Simpson and we found Albert, living alone in his little cabin on the shore of the Mackenzie River.

Yes, said Albert, he'd be going up the Nahanni again this summer in his small boat and yes, the NFB could rent a boat and follow him, if we wanted to. "As long as you don't slow me down," he said. "I've got to get up there, do my looking around and get out before the river freezes up."

He assured me he knew where the lost McLeod mine was, far up past the falls, in a country where the mountains still had no names. He had tried before, every summer for seven years, but each time he had failed to get that far. Once his boat had capsized in the rapids, and he had almost drowned. Another time the cold weather had come early and the river had frozen. Unable to get home, he had built a cabin and had spent the winter in it. He managed to shoot a few small animals, but his food supplies were inadequate for the long winter and one day he bit into a piece of homemade bread and saw blood on it. He knew he had scurvy. His teeth started to ache fearfully and he pulled four of them out with a pair of pliers. But this year he'd be more careful, and he'd get out well before freeze-up.

I listened to all this incredulously. Albert Faille was now seventy-three years old; his hands trembled when he lit his pipe and when he walked an old back injury made him bend almost double. "But when I put a pack on my back it straightens me up," he said.

For this year's trip, he'd be leaving at the end of June. He'd be going down the Liard River and up the Nahanni, travelling in his eighteen-foot flat-bottomed river boat with an outboard motor. His destination was a place called Roaring Hell Creek, about 450 miles from where we were now.

"We'll be coming with you, Albert," I said. "Are you sure that's okay?"

"I'll be glad of the company," said Albert. "As long as you don't slow me down."

~

3280 Ridgewood
Montreal

June 4

Dear Mordecai,
I presume you are now well settled in, back in dear olde London towne. Lucky bugger. You realize, I trust, that you left some stuff behind in this apartment after you stayed here. To wit: Daniel's truck (plastic), his building bricks, bag with Florence's wool and knitting in it, Florence's straw hat, Noah's baby seat for auto, unidentified three-section padded object which must have to do with baby, rack for drying laundry, one white shirt. Shall I put all this in a box and ship it to you? But I don't think I could get the drying rack in. Too big. Please instruct on shipping. By ship or by expensive air?

Film Board is sending me on a mad trip (their idea, not mine) to Northwest Territories for three-four days, to hire boats, personnel, arrange radio communication, etc., for cameraman who is going up later to shoot my Old Man and the River idea. Poor cameraman will be up there for two months, very isolated, and I have to arrange for things like food. I will be flying up later to join him and Albert on the river, but only for a week or so.

Here, all is pressing in. Met Herman Gollob, editor of Little, Brown, Boston, at Leonard Cohen-Irving Layton party. Herman blithely told me that the incomparable funnybook, Why Rock the Boat?, by William Weintraub, will be coming out in the United States of America (how about that?) on August 21. Jack McClelland had given me the impression that it was coming out in Canada in October, but at the party Jack was too busy guzzling and pinching asses to discuss this anomaly. August 21 seems to me to be a bad time, but I guess they know what they're doing.

BUT proofs have arrived and I have been given all of two days to deal with them. Have entered protest about this.

What else is new? Irv Layton's new poem is how he could lay Jackie Kennedy, but he won't because the President has enough troubles as it is. He will read this at a poetry session in Pittsburgh next week and he has sent Jackie an invitation. What's the use of trying to write humour when the real clowns steal the show? Nona Macdonald came to the party with me and Irving invited her to bed with promises of unknown ecstasies. What an asshole he is, this versifying buffoon.

Love to Florence, Daniel, Noah. Write.

Bill

Oughterard
Co. Galway, Ireland

Sunday, June 11

Dear Sir,
We write you from our hundred acres, with the little woman outside on the stone patio in the sunshine overlooking the lake and the islands. Quiet in our stone (whitewashed) study we look out on the formal gardens which come before the vegetable gardens and the two boathouses where reposes our

trusty Evinrude motorboat and the twin garages where – normally – our grey-and-red Morris convertible stands.

It stands not now because our Man, Jim Kelly, had a little accident with it the other night, running us head on into a car driven by a policeman (who was in the wrong). When the broken glass cleared both drivers rushed to greet each other, crying, "Is anybody hurted?" and when it was found that there was no loss of life and limb the great local phrase came into play: "It could have been worse, ah yes, it could have been worse. Weren't we lucky now that we had the accident and that nobody was hurted."

The main purpose of this letter is not to describe the locale here but to tell you that the postman came on his bike yesterday with a long missive from Willis Kingsley Wing [his New York agent], which said, in part, "I will be glad to hear from or talk to William Weintraub and hope we may be able to work together. Your estimate of him and his possibilities weighs very heavily with me." I had told him you were reasonable, had a future, etc.

We have just arrived here and are expecting our first visitors next week – family first. My Man (part of our "couple") says, to everything I say, "Ah, you're verry right, sir." Isn't it nice to have a Man like that? No need for an analyst when you have a Man.

Do write. And write or call on Willis Wing, who is now, it would seem, your Man.

Brian

3280 Ridgewood

June 20

Dear Brian,
A joy to receive your letter. And thanks for the Wing intro. I have hopes of starting another book in the fall,

and maybe he'd be able to extort a better advance for
that one.

Mort writes from London to say that he is rewriting
somebody's screenplay at 350 quid per week for four weeks.
And he has got that Guggenheim. He has rented a maisonette.
Asked for your address, which I supplied.

I can report that the political situation at Nahanni Butte,
Northwest Territories, has deteriorated since I was there in
April (missionary trouble), though all is well at Fort Simpson.
At Fort Liard the wounds have healed since last winter's
unfortunate occurrence between the Mountie and the
schoolteacher.

This is only a brief report based on my insane three-day visit
to these points, where I hired men and boats for the forthcoming
Film Board expedition. I also did important research. The
cameraman, Don Wilder, asked me to find out whether he
should bring a revolver, in case of grizzly bears. Definitely bring
a revolver, said Corporal Johnston, RCMP, Fort Simpson.
Definitely do not bring a revolver, said Frank Bailey, game
warden, Fort Simpson. If you panic and fire, you have to hit the
grizzly just right; if you just wound him, you only make him
more angry. Just look the bear in the eye and back away slowly,
rather than start a fight. In the north, I have learned, no two
experts ever agree on anything. Much like your literary world.

At Nahanni Butte my friend Gus Kraus tells me that the
Evangelical Pentecostal Mission, from New Jersey, there to
convert the 40 Indians away from their Roman Catholicism, is
making a fortune. After each of Rev. Howard's articles in the
New Jersey Pentecostal News (or whatever), in which he tells
how un-saved the poor Indians are, the mail pours in and Gus
swears he has seen the Rev. opening the envelopes, sorting the
5s, 10s and 20s into piles and saying, "God provides." It all goes
into the Rev.'s pocket, of course. The Hudson's Bay man at
Fort Liard told me that last summer, when the Rev.'s
refrigeration plant broke down, Rev.'s private plane flew twice
weekly to Fort Simpson to buy ice so his kid would not have to

go without ice cream. Pentecostals and the like are all over the north, having been kicked out of China by the Communists. They build themselves nice, big houses here and raise nice families.

Father Dupont, Oblate, shakes his head at all this. A pleasant young guy, he gave me letters to post to his parents in Paris. He asked me if I was Protestant. "Non, mon père," I said, "je suis juif." "Mais c'est presque la même chose, n'est-ce pas?" he said. To you Papists, us heathens are all the same, n'est-ce pas?

I really like the north and look forward to going back in early August. I will fly in to Roaring Hell Creek or Rabbitkettle Lake or wherever Albert and Don Wilder have reached (we will have been in touch by radio). Don will have finished his shooting and he will fly home. I will come back down the Nahanni with Albert in his boat and get his life story from him for the film narration – and maybe a magazine piece. Trip down the river will take a week, with camping on the shore at night. Albert is not a big talker, and is reticent about his past, so I will need the time – and diplomacy.

Will let you know if Albert found the lost gold mine and if I have managed to buy shares in it. Meanwhile have fun in the Emerald Isle and write me as soon as you get to London, with your address there.

Trapper Bill

❧

Our film *Nahanni*, made from the thousands of feet of celluloid shot on the river by Don Wilder, was destined to make old Albert Faille immortal. At film festivals it won seven Canadian and international awards. In England, schoolchildren wrote poems about Albert's journey. In Montreal, a group of young musicians formed the Albert Faille Blues Band; in Toronto a couple named their newly born daughter Nahanni; in New York, a professor of psychiatry screened the film for his students as an example of obsession; in Minnesota, a group of outdoorsmen formed the Albert Faille Wilderness League. Pierre Trudeau saw the film and went on a canoe trip up the river; a few years later the shores of the Nahanni, which before our film had seldom been visited, were made into a national park, and now many people come.

The film was a simple affair. It showed Albert leaving his little cabin in Fort Simpson, loading his boat, launching it into the Mackenzie River and setting off in his quest for gold. "Some say there's no gold there," the film's narration says, "but Faille is sure there is – the McLeod mine, the lost mine. Four hundred miles to go. Eight weeks. Perhaps seven, if the river's good."

The film shows Albert making camp for the night, on the shore, and cooking his bannock on his campfire. In the morning he sets off again. "Three days on the Liard River, and then the Nahanni," the narration says. "A sudden rise of mountains from the plain. Nahanni Butte, the Headless Mountains, the Funeral Range. Tombstones for the men who died, looking for the gold."

Now we follow Albert's progress up the Nahanni for the first 150 miles, through three high canyons, fighting his boat through whitewater rapids and riffles. Here, on one previous trip, he was swamped and almost drowned. The camera work throughout is outstanding, with Don Wilder and the two boatmen I'd hired following Albert in their forty-foot boat. And there were magnificent high-angle shots, made by Don after clambering up mountains.

Now the falls, and the narration says: "Virginia Falls – twice as high as Niagara. Few men have seen them, for few men ever come this far up the Nahanni. But Faille's destination lies far beyond this roaring barrier. Now the ordeal, the portage. Everything will have to be carried up, around the falls – the food, the gasoline, the motor. And lumber, to build another boat on top. Everything will have to be carried a mile and a quarter uphill. It will take at least a week."

In the film, we see Albert doing all this, although in reality he made only a few portage trips for the camera, with the airplane we hired taking most of his burden from below the falls up to the top. But if the NFB hadn't been there, he would certainly have done it himself, at the age of seventy-three, as he had done in the past. And we do see him building the little boat that will take him another two hundred miles, at least, up the river.

Albert's new boat moves smoothly up quiet waters until it comes to a very rough patch. The motor won't get the boat through this, and so we see Albert, waist deep in water, struggling to haul the boat forward with a rope. And the narration says: "Faille has been on the river for almost seven weeks. Now he has only forty miles to go, but the Nahanni is no longer the way he remembers it. The ice of spring has brought down tons of rock and silt, and has laid it on the river bed. The channel is gone. What was once deep, smooth water is now a foaming peril.

"Only forty miles to go, but too far to walk, too rough. Not enough time before winter. But maybe a new channel will be cut by next year. Eight times he has tried, eight times he has failed. But he will try again. 'I'll be dead or drowned before I quit,' says Albert Faille."

On August 15, I flew to the Nahanni from Watson Lake, Yukon, to join Albert and Don at their camp on the river. Only a few days before, Don had filmed Albert's defeat, vainly trying to pull his boat through those unexpected rapids. Now I could see the disappointment in Albert's pale blue eyes. His back seemed more stooped than ever.

Don, his work finished, flew out in the plane that had brought me in, leaving me alone with Albert. The next day we set out down the river, in his little boat, and during the next week that boat took me through the most magnificent country I had ever seen. The Nahanni was always changing character: sometimes it was as placid as a quiet lake, and then it would foam into rapids that tossed the boat wildly about. We glided past the looming mass of Sunblood Mountain, left the splendour of Virginia Falls behind us, made our way through towering canyons.

It was exhilarating to travel through totally uninhabited country, never seeing another soul. We'd travel most of the day, stopping for lunch and again in the late afternoon to make camp.

Now and then we'd look up and see an eagle wheeling high over-head, perhaps looking for a lamb in a herd of mountain sheep. Now and then a caribou would run back into the forest, frightened by the sound of our boat. Each evening we would sit around the campfire and talk, and Albert would reveal a bit more of himself. Slowly I pieced together a picture of a strange and lonely life.

He told me he had been born in Pennsylvania in 1888. He was brought up by foster parents and knew nothing of his real parents. Life on the foster parents' farm was hard, and he grew to hate their cruelty. At the age of eight he ran away from home and since then had spent most of his life alone. The eight-year-old boy wandered across the countryside, sleeping in barns and factory boiler rooms, sometimes travelling with hoboes, some-times earning a few cents doing chores on farms. "Nowadays they'd pick you up and put you in school," Albert said, "but in those days a kid could be on his own."

He learned how to ride freight trains and by the age of ten he was in Minnesota, learning how to trap animals and sell their skins. For most of the years to come, trapping was to be his main livelihood. By 1924 he was married, but trapping in Minnesota had become unprofitable, so he headed up to Canada, to the Northwest Territories. His first winter there, on Beaver River, yielded a good catch of lynx, marten, mink, fox and beaver. He sent for his wife, Marion, and went to Edmonton to meet her, but despite his enthusiasm for the Beaver River country she refused to come and live with him in the wilderness. Albert had an ago-nizing choice to make, and he chose the north. Marion went back to Minnesota and he never saw her again, although he sent her money regularly until she died.

Eventually life on the traplines became too gruelling and Albert decided to become a prospector and look for the leg-endary gold of the Nahanni. He told me about his early searches while we were camped in Headless Valley, where the skeletons of the McLeod brothers – without the skulls – had been found. The McLeods had not been murdered, Albert assured me, despite what the legend said. They'd probably starved to death and bears had carried off their heads. All the other prospectors who had perished on the Nahanni – Jorgenson, Hall, Mulholland, Eppler, Holmberg and others – had all died of natural causes, Albert insisted. There'd been no legendary mountain giants to murder them. By natural causes, he said, he meant drowning, freezing, burning, landslides, grizzly bears, starvation.

In 1932, Albert had found the bones of his friend Phil Powers in the ashes of a cabin that had burned down. In 1949, the body of a man called Shebbach was found in his cabin; his diary showed that he had been without food for forty-three days. Just before he died he wrote DEAD MAN HERE on a piece of wood, nailed it to his cabin door and went inside to die.

How had Albert managed to survive? After all, he had travelled the Nahanni more than any of the others. "Well, some of them had bad luck," he told me, "and some were careless. I've always been careful. And besides, my number hasn't come up."

I asked Albert why he wanted to find gold. If he struck it rich, would he have a fling in some big city, like Toronto or New York? After all, he hadn't been Outside since his trip to Edmonton, thirty-five years before. But no, he didn't want that. "Maybe I want to start a gold rush," he said. "Get a lot of people to come here. They'd say, 'It's the Nahanni Gold Rush. Albert Faille started it.'"

I said goodbye to Albert at Nahanni Butte. I headed home from there and he continued on to Fort Simpson, to spend the winter, alone as always, in his little cabin. He was to make two more summer trips up the river, but then his health deteriorated and he could travel no more. Albert Faille never found his gold, and there has never been a gold rush on the Nahanni. He died twelve years after our trip together. In 1990, when his admirers in Minnesota learned that the wooden cross that marked his grave had fallen over, they raised money to commemorate him with a handsome granite tombstone.

~

11 Parkhill Road
London, NW 3

Sept. 13, 1961

Dear Bill:

Well, best of luck to you with the bk, man. Fulford writes that
it has arrived on his desk, very handsome jacket, but he has not
read it yet. Weaver writes that the pres. of Canadian Book
Club, Peter Martin, thinks it's hilarious indeed, and will opt for
it as a winter bk choice. This, old man, cd mean 4-500 copies.
500 copies at 3.50 makes abt $175 for you.

Brian and I, old pros of Hampstead, make rude jokes daily
abt Weintraub's first fruit. Ah, we've been thru it many times,
son. A painful process.

Over here am still struggling with my non-fiction bk, and it
is a struggle. And am being courted by producers Betty Box-
Ralph Thomas. Took me to din-dins at the Mirabelle (very
posh show biz) and asked me to do an original script. Said I'd
thk abt and eat with them again. Am stalling, waiting for
return of Ivan of Foxwell from Tahiti, as he said he wanted me
for his next, possibly, and he's a gentleman, he is.

Brian and I are taking over lit. Spectator. He's doing a
"front" on Exile's Return next wk and next month I'm doing
a front on Mailer, Normie. Am going to Israel end of Jan. for
Maclean's and am booking a house in Amagansett come April.

Am mentioning your book to numerous producers here. Cd
you afford to airmail me two extra copies? You never had an agent
like me, you know. Invest, invest. Should only set you back a fin.

Florence is well and is having an easy time of it. Baby due
end of Oct. Noah walks. Daniel starts school Thursday, with
appropriate cap and scarf.

See you at Xmas, we hope. Best to Alex and Gloria, Sani
and Bella. Write.

M.

31 Wellington Square
London S.W. 3

September 25

Dire Sire,

The telephone rings and it is a somewhat dazed Mort reading from your splendid reviews, one after another good – and the bad ones are just personal spite – "I have known Mr. W. for many years" – a great line that. Need I tell you that we are delighted? And that, hearing of all your radio and TV appearances, we all feel that you will outdistance all of us.

Now I must apologize for not writing all summer. I wrote no one. I was feeling very low and am still low although not so low. I tell you this in confidence, as you, an expert on feeling low, used to tell me, *in confidence*. Anyway, you know how I felt and how, at such times, there is no urge to write. Write I did, but only for pelf. Holiday [magazine] took my piece on Belfast O.K. and this week I make my debut in England with a lead review in the Spectator, flagellating the British and asking if anti-Americanism has become the anti-Semitism of the British and French intellectuals.

As for my long novel, I have put it aside and am contemplating writing a short funny book. Watch out! On the fillum front, we are waiting for John Huston to sign. He was to sign it in six weeks – it is now almost two months. Silence from N.Y. and nails bitten raw in London. If this final deal blows up as all the others have I shall retire to a Zen monastery.

I am happy to report that while we are enjoying London and digging the Brit scene, the little woman has decided that N.Y. and not here is the place where we shall lay our heads forever. So it will be back there in April, deo volente.

London, I find, is no cheaper than N.Y. I do not mean rents, but food, liquor, etc., and certainly restaurants. There is nothing between the good and the awful. Of course the Bard [Mordecai] does not know these things any more. Money is something he

uses in the manner of Gulbenkian. However we are
enjoying seeing him here and he, as usual, has been
kindness personified.

I predict your book will go over big here. I mean this.
Your B.O.M. [*Book-of-the Month Club News*] review is a good
portent, I feel. I mean for the U.S. And if the book sells
anything like 3,000 in Canada you are made with Little,
Brown for life. Fellowships open up, but can you afford
to live on one?

I have just been thinking that you have one advantage over
the rest of us writers. You have already got carbon copies of the
Letters of W. W. (all of them).

Love from all of us. Michael [now seven years old], when
told the news, took a personal pride in the matter and
announced to us that "Bill is my friend." That's fame!

Brian

~

"Book report: Why aren't they laughing in Montreal?" This was
the heading over Peter Gzowski's column in *Maclean's* in which
he pointed out that *Why Rock the Boat?* was getting very good
reviews elsewhere in Canada but not in my hometown, Montreal.
The *Ottawa Citizen* said it was "tremendously funny," but the
Montreal Star's review, by Alan Randal, sneered at the book and
said it "has its funny moments, but they are few." Commenting on
the book's satirical approach, Walter O'Hearn, writing in the
Gazette, said that "it attacks conditions which never existed or
which disappeared years ago."

Gzowski's column noted that both Montreal papers had
mustered big guns to attack the book, both Randal and O'Hearn
being managing editors. The book, of course, was about a
Montreal newspaper, a fictional one called the *Daily Witness*.
The reporters who worked there "were proud of the massive
boredom their paper was able to achieve." It was, perhaps, the

country's worst paper. Great stories that might be offensive to advertisers were routinely suppressed. But our hero, the naive Harry Barnes, nineteen-year-old cub reporter, thought the *Witness* was a fine place to work. In trouble from the start, poor Harry was desperate not to lose his job – and equally desperate to lose his loathsome virginity.

I was delighted by Randal's and O'Hearn's attacks, as they helped boost sales of the book, thanks to Peter Gzowski's column about the affair, and discussions on the radio. In the *Toronto Star*, Robert Fulford wrote not only an approving review, but also, a week later, another full column about the book, this one on the Randal-O'Hearn strictures. These two might say the book had nothing to do with reality, but, Fulford said, "allowing for the usual comic novelist's exaggeration, [it] fits everything I've ever heard about Montreal newspapers."

While I much appreciated Walter O'Hearn's diatribe, one thing in it wounded me. I should have written a good satirical novel, he said, but "why, then, has he come up instead with The Office Boy's Revenge?" There was a certain amount of truth in the revenge part of that, but, dammit, Walter knew very well that when I was fired by the *Gazette*, eleven years earlier, I was a reporter, not an office boy.

3280 Ridgewood
Montreal

October 3, 1961

Dear Brian,
A real joy to hear from you at long last. Sorry to hear that you have been feeling low (which I will surely keep confidential). To an old low-man like me, this does explain your long silence. Was it the Ould Sod that did it? Ah, the answer is never that easy. Still, glad to hear that you are pulling out of it, as you indicate.

Thankee for your encouraging prediction that the book will
find a London publisher. You might like to know that the
American reviews are now starting to come in. The Wichita,
Kansas, Evening Eagle and Beacon says it is "hilariously
slap-happy," which I suppose is good. "Zany Without Question,"
sez the Pittsburgh Press. The New York Times says I am "a
really first-rate farceur" and the Los Angeles Times says the
book is "full of easy chuckles." Not sure I like that. Do they
mean easy for the reader or easy for the writer? I worked hard
on some of those chuckles.

Radio and television here continue. Was invited to CFCF TV
to be interviewed by Jimmy Tapp (I know you want all the
details). Well, producer says to Jimmy, "We're going to open
with harbour noises and you're rocking on that see-saw. Then
you say, 'Why Rock the Boat?' has nothing to do with rocking
and nothing to do with boats.' Then you get off the see-saw and
call Weintraub over and you both sit on the stools." "Do I have
to do that?" says Jimmy. "Yes, it's a great gimmick," says the
producer. And thus it was done. Jimmy's opening words to me
were, "Bill, I've read this book and you know, it's more fun
than anything I know of except kissin'." (Once again this made
me lament the fact that I chose my present hard life instead of
that great new medium, television.)

Have just been listening to CJAD where taped interview with
Miss Doris Clark was aired. My mother phones to say she hopes
I never again require a job with a Montreal newspaper. No, I say
bravely, all that is behind me. You see, Doris asked me what I
really thought of the local bladders and I said you couldn't
expect much from journals which were just side-interests of
sugar barons and printing-plant magnates, guys who weren't
interested in anything except not offending their industrialist
pals in the deep leather chairs of the Mount Royal Club. At the
end of the interview, Doris hastened to tell her listeners, "The
opinions just voiced are not those of this station. . . ."

Thought of you and our old mutual Gazette days the other
eve when I went to a free-load for the press at the Lasalle

Hotel. Remember that pleasant checked-tablecloth dining room where we used to have dinner? Well, omnia mutantur, nos et mutamur in illis, as Miss Prew used to tell us in Grade Ten. That cozy room in the old Lasalle has been turned into a wretched Gay Nineties bistro with a honky-tonk piano player, and this was the grand opening. Drinks were served to us by nubiles in tiny black skirts and Gay Nineties black mesh stockings. These were National Theatre School girls, making some pin money. Onwards with the Canadian arts.

All our old pals were there, sloshing it down – Doyle, Stanley, Fitz, Frankie Lowe, etc. Many asked about you. It was a lively scene, but I was sad, thinking only of the days when this travesty of a bistro was an honest restaurant where we ate so well. Montreal is going to hell in a handbasket. All the good, old, oaken woodwork is being replaced by trendy tinsel. Remember that old German (Swiss?) waiter who used to bring us, in that room, those braised short ribs of beef? Remember the sauce, the tangy aroma? Was it rosemary? Sage? Remember the night when I reached over with my fork, uninvited, to sample a piece of Harold Whitehead's blueberry pie, but before I could get it old Harold rapped me hard on the knuckles with his fork?

Ah, those were the days, a decade ago, when we were young. Or are we still young? I'm not sure. Please advise.

Write.

Bill

Acknowledgements

Before their deaths, Brian Moore and Mordecai Richler gave me permission to quote from letters they wrote to me over the years and which I'd been hoarding in my files. I am immensely grateful for this. My thanks also to Mavis Gallant to quote from her letters, which I've also kept. I've abridged some of these letters for this book, as they were often two or three pages long.

For helping me solve some research problems, I thank Joseph Blumer, Denis Sampson and William Johnson. I am also very grateful to Apollonia Steele and Marlys Chevrefils of the Special Collections Division, University of Calgary, for supplying me with copies of book reviews from the Brian Moore papers and the Mordecai Richler papers.